EUROPEAN UNION LAW
UPDATING SUPPLEMENT

Since its publication in 2006 European Union Law quickly established itself as one of the leading textbooks on the market. When it was first published, it offered a lucid account of the law of the European Union still reeling from the 'failure' of the Constitutional Treaty. With the ever changing European landscape a detailed postscript to the first edition is very timely. This supplement provides updating material to the main text, arranged to follow the current chapter structure. Its unique narrative approach which mirrors the main text's design and organisation allows students to link updating material with ease. Examining the road to the Lisbon Treaty and the recasting of the borders of the European Union, it offers the most current survey of the law of the Union.

PROFESSOR DAMIAN CHALMERS is Professor of European Law at the London School of Economics and Political Sciences.

GIORGIO MONTI is senior lecturer in law at the London School of Economics and Political Sciences.

EUROPEAN UNION LAW

TEXT AND MATERIALS

Updating Supplement

DAMIAN CHALMERS
GIORGIO MONTI

CAMBRIDGE
UNIVERSITY PRESS

CAMBRIDGE UNIVERSITY PRESS

Cambridge, New York, Melbourne, Madrid, Cape Town, Singapore, São Paulo, Delhi

Cambridge University Press
The Edinburgh Building, Cambridge CB2 8RU, UK

Published in the United States of America by Cambridge University Press, New York

www.cambridge.org
Information on this title: www.cambridge.org/9780521070133

Damian Chalmers and Giorgio Monti © 2008

First published 2008
Reprinted 2009

Printed in the United Kingdom at the University Press, Cambridge

A catalogue record for this publication is available from the British Library

Library of Congress Cataloguing in Publication data
European Union law : text and materials / Damian Chalmers . . . [et al.].
p.   cm.
ISBN-13: 978-0-521-82041-7 (hardback)
ISBN-10: 0-521-82041-3 (hardback)
ISBN-13: 978-0-521-52741-5 (pbk.)
ISBN-10: 0-521-52741-4 (pbk.)
1. Law – European Union countries.   2. European Union.   I. Chalmers, Damian.   II. Title.
KJE947.E878   2006
341.242′2 – dc22   2006002818

ISBN-13 978-0-521-07013-3 paperback

CONTENTS

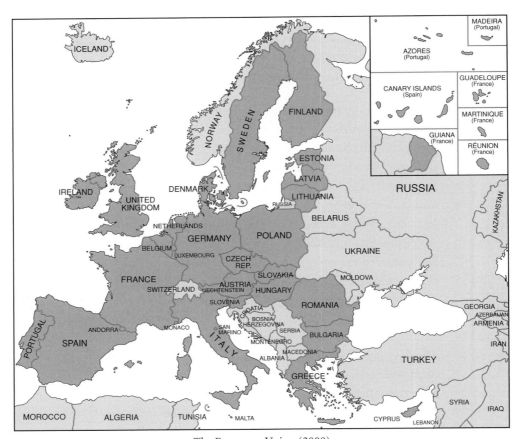

The European Union (2008)

PREFACE

European Union law has moved on fast since the publication of the main text. The most prominent development is the Lisbon Treaty signed on 12 December 2007. The rejection of the Treaty by the Irish referendum on 12 June 2008 throws considerable question marks over its ratification. All the other Member States, bar the Czech Republic who is awaiting a judgment on the Treaty's constitutionality by its constitutional court, are proceeding with ratification, and the Irish have been asked to present a way forward when the Heads of Government meet in October 2008. It seems inconceivable that the Treaty will enter into force on 1 January 2009. There is still considerable political momentum behind it, however. Whatever the Treaty's fate, it is likely to remain legally significant both as a critique of the current arrangements and as a possible source of amendments to these arrangements, which may be provided by it or other means.

Lisbon is, however, only part of the story. There have been important legislative developments, most notably Directive 2006/123/EC on services in the internal market, which revolutionise other chapters of the book. The Union judiciary has been particularly active. It gave 692 judgments in 2007 – a record – and inevitably this has had implications for the development of its jurisprudence. We therefore found significant changes to most areas of the textbook, and the only chapters not addressed in these updates are chapters 18 and 19 on Financial restrictions and Trade restrictions and public goods.

None of us liked updates which could only be read whilst constantly cross-referring to the main text. We thought it important that each chapter in this update have a narrative suggesting a purpose to and explanation of what took place and allowing recent developments to be placed against the broader legal context. Therefore each chapter can be read without constantly cross-referring to the main text.

We have used the new consolidated numbering of the treaties proposed by the Lisbon Treaty where a new provision has been introduced by that Treaty. For pre-existing provisions we have used current numbering but have provided a reference to their new identification, should Lisbon enter into force. We have used the acronyms LTEU and LTFEU to refer to the Treaty on European Union and the Treaty on the Functioning of the European Union following Lisbon. Whilst TEU and TFEU will undoubtedly be used if the Lisbon Treaty comes into force, we have decided on the

'L' as a prefix in this interim period to avoid confusion with the existing Treaty on European Union.

The Treaty of Lisbon is published in the Official Journal ([2007] OJ C 306/1) and Consolidated versions are available on line at http://europa.eu/lisbon_treaty/full_text/index_en.htm

Finally, as ever, we would like to thank Sinéad Moloney and Nadine El-Enany. It has been a pleasure to work with them, and these updates would not have happened without either of them.

DC
GM
4 May 2008

TABLE OF CASES

European Court of Justice: Cases in case number order

European Court of Justice: Cases in alphabetical order by party or common title

EC Commission, competition decisions

EC Commission, merger decisions

National Courts

EU legislation and policy documents

Commission Communications

Commission Decisions

Commission Notices/Guidelines

COSAC

Council Framework Decisions

European integration and moving beyond the Constitutional Treaty

1. Introduction

The European Union has been dominated by two processes since 2005: responding to the failure of the Constitutional Treaty and recasting the borders of the European Union. On the face of it, the two seem quite discrete. The former has been a process of introspective, internal institutional reform which has led, after some soul-searching, to the signing of the Reform Treaty, or Treaty of Lisbon, on 13 December 2007. The latter process, culminating most strongly in the accession of Bulgaria and Romania to the European Union on 1 January 2007, seems more focused on enlargement and external expansion. However, there is a meeting point between the two. Both the Treaty of Lisbon and the terms and conditions of membership offered to those now joining the Union suggest a third theme, which is the increased differentiation and contingency of membership rights of the Union. The idea of a Union in which all Member States and citizens enjoy equal rights across its territory is looking ever more far-fetched, and this may well be the theme which increasingly dominates the Union of the next five years.

2. From reconstituting to reforming the European Union

(i)   The road to Lisbon

At the end of June 2005, ratification of the Constitutional Treaty had reached an impasse. On the one hand, a significant majority of Member States, eighteen, had ratified the Treaty, with two, Spain and Luxembourg, having held successful referenda. On the other hand, two Member States, France and the Netherlands, had held referenda in which their populations had voted against the Constitutional Treaty. Of the remaining seven Member States, six (Czech Republic, Denmark, Ireland, Poland, Portugal and the United Kingdom), were scheduled to hold their own referenda. Of those six States, there was a significant chance of a 'No' vote in all bar Portugal.

The Union was faced not with a single recalcitrant State, such as Denmark and Ireland with previous amending Treaties. It was instead confronted with a deep divide. Crudely, two-thirds of Member States wished to press ahead with the Constitutional Treaty, whilst one-third did not. Analysis of the situation suggested the split to be even more problematic. The one-third wary about continuing the ratification process carried four of the seven largest Member States: France, Poland, the Netherlands and the United Kingdom. It also comprised States exclusively from North and Central Europe.

Further complications became apparent when analysing the reasons for the 'No' vote in the Netherlands and France. Despite voters being reasonably well-informed about the details of the Constitutional Treaty, the reasons for their vote had little to do, in most cases, with its legal details. Opponents were protesting against globalisation, the consequences of the 2004 enlargement, fears about Turkish membership of the Union, and in the Netherlands there was anger amongst voters at the perceived power of the large Member States in the Union.[1] Populations in both States still had largely positive impressions of the Union.[2] If advocates of the Constitutional Treaty could point to little sustained opposition to particular provisions, opponents could argue that there was so little enthusiasm for it that voters used it as an opportunity to address other issues.

A period of reflection was called for by the European Council. In October 2005, as a response, the Commission prepared Plan D:[3] a programme for debate about the future of the Union which was to take place within each Member State and, at a pan-Union level, between EU Institutions citizens, civil society, social partners, national

---

1 Flash Eurobarometer 171 and 172 – European Constitution: post-referendum survey in France and in The Netherlands.
2 The Commission pointed to 88 per cent of the French and 82 per cent of the Dutch still having positive perceptions of the Union in the period after the referendum. EC Commission, *The Period of Reflection and Plan D*, COM (2006) 212, 2.
3 EC Commission, The Commission's contribution to the period of reflection and beyond: Plan D for Democracy, Dialogue and Debate, COM (2005) 494.

Parliaments and political parties. While the Commission claimed that 'D' stood for 'Democracy, Dialogue and Debate', it could very well be said to stand for 'Doing Nothing'. The remainder of 2005 and the whole of 2006 were marked by institutional inertia.

It was the Finnish and German governments who used their Presidencies to re-launch the reform process. In the latter half of 2006, the Finnish government prepared the ground for progress made during the German Presidency by engaging in a series of consultations on how to achieve institutional reform, assessing the results and then providing the German government with a strategy for reaching agreement. Alongside this, a series of prominent politicians, acting under the umbrella of the organisation named the Action Committee for European Democracy, began to publish articles in the press indicating that the time for listening was over and that the time for action had begun.[4] In March 2007, at the 50th anniversary of the Treaty of Rome, the German government obtained a commitment from the other Member States to place 'the European Union on a renewed common basis before the European Parliament elections in 2009'.[5] In other words, they had committed to a deadline for ratifying a new treaty. This was so politically sensitive it was agreed that only the heads of the three European Institutions, and not the individual Member States, would sign the new treaty.[6]

The German government's strategy for reaching an agreement was to close the gap between the Member States in a highly structured manner. There was a proce-dural and substantive dimension to this. Procedurally, the strategy was a two-fold process in which 'political agreement' on the central points of disagreement would be reached in closed, confidential negotiations between ministries, named 'sherpas'. Only when political agreement was reached on the main points would the second stage, an Intergovernmental Conference (IGC), be opened. Its tasks, however, would be limited by the mandate of the political agreement, and so restricted to translating the political agreement into legal detail and resolving any ambiguities. States wishing to introduce new points or reopen old debates would run the risk of being accused of having breached the existing political agreement, and therefore of having acted in bad faith. The process was thus to be a relatively confined affair subject to few external risks or interventions.

In terms of substance, the strategy involved the use of the Constitutional Treaty as a starting point, along with the question of what had to be offered to make the Treaty acceptable to those national governments constituting the recalcitrant third.

---

4 The website is www.iue.it/RSCAS/research/ACED/MissionStatement.shtml The site also contains press arti-cles by its members.

5 EU Council, *Declaration on the occasion of the fiftieth anniversary of the signature of the Treaty of Rome*, (Brussels, 25 March 2007), paragraph 3.

6 On this and the secrecy surrounding negotiations leading up to the June agreement, see House of Commons, Research Paper, EU Reform: A New Treaty or an Old Constitution, (2007, Research Paper 07/64) 10–14.

Ultimately, for these States, the Treaty was not a question of reform, but a series of individual concessions.

The Heads of Government met between 21 and 23 June 2007 to conclude the first stage of the process. The outcome was a sixteen-page mandate that was to provide the basis for an IGC that the Heads of Government indicated was to be completed by December 2007 and was to be confined to the terms of the mandate. It also indicated that the new Treaty was to follow the text of the Constitutional Treaty unless otherwise specified by the mandate. The subsequent IGC was, consequently, highly limited. By 19 October a text had been agreed informally between the Member States. On 13 December 2007, the new text, the Treaty of Lisbon, was formally signed. A new record for ratification was made, with Hungary being the first State to ratify the Treaty a mere four days later.

The conclusion of the Treaty was a significant coup. It involved amendments to all of the articles in the TEU and to 216 provisions in the EC Treaty.[7] There were, moreover, significant differences that had to be bridged between the twenty-seven Member States, each with their own distinct agenda and constituencies. Yet this negotiating triumph came at a cost. In particular, it created a double bind; if the Treaty of Lisbon differed significantly from the Constitutional Treaty, its nature of reform was more closed and more accelerated than any other to date. There was a lack of transparency and an exclusion of national parliaments that not only remained to be justified, but could yet bounce back to the haunt the process at the ratification stage.[8] The other half of the double bind concerns the possible response that the reform process is justified on the basis that the Treaty of Lisbon is not substantially different from the Constitutional Treaty. Yet that would open negotiators to charges of arrogance and hypocrisy – arrogance for ignoring the referenda results in France and the Netherlands, and hypocrisy for having claimed to 'listen' throughout the Plan D process, when this was plainly not the case.

(ii)   The Treaty of Lisbon

Crudely, we can say that there are four possible outcomes of EU treaty reform. First, the process can reform the symbols and iconography – elements such as the preamble or statements about the mission or nature of the Union. On the face of it, this will not change what the Union actually *does* on a daily basis, but is nonetheless significant in terms of the way in which people identify the Union and the associations they make with it. Second, it can reform what the Union does. This relates to the powers and competencies of the Union. Third, reform can affect *how* the Union does what it does. This is concerned with institutional change and the question of how the Union

7 Statewatch, www.statewatch.org/news/2007/oct/eu-refrom-treaty-tec-external-relations-3-5.pdf
8 It is unsurprising therefore that such a high proportion of EU citizens wish for a referendum. On this see G. de Búrca, 'The European Constitution Project after the Referenda' (2006) 13 *Constellations* 205.

exercises its powers, rather than what its powers are. Fourth, the Union can engage in legal reorganisation as part of its treaty reform process. This is the exercise of drafting, codifying and tidying up the texts. Whilst being highly legalistic, this task is nevertheless important in determining the language of the Treaty provisions, and the relationship between them, which will be subject to subsequent interpretation and adjudication.[9]

(a)   From Constitution back to Treaty

The Treaty of Lisbon, in the words of the mandate to the IGC, seeks to abandon the 'constitutional concept'.[10] This abandonment has a number of dimensions.

At the most general level, the Treaty of Lisbon was to be seen as simply another reforming treaty in the tradition of Maastricht, Amsterdam and Nice, and not as any attempt whatsoever to constitutionalise the Treaties. The phrase 'Constitutional Treaty' was therefore dropped. The abandonment of the constitutional concept has also played itself out in particular substantive provisions. The most ephemeral symbols of European constitutionalism, the European Union flag, anthem, motto and holiday, have been removed. More significantly, it could be argued that at a symbolic level, the Constitutional Treaty had all the signs of the establishment of an autonomous European constitutional democracy: there was a primacy clause, a Bill of Rights in the form of the European Union Charter of Fundamental Rights, and Union regulations and directives were to become known as 'laws' or 'framework laws'. The Union was to have its own legal personality and Foreign Minister. Provisions were put in place concerning the measure of representative and participatory democracy to be used by the Union. Whilst the exact working out of these provisions resulted in more curtailed powers than those enjoyed by most liberal democratic states, they did convey the imagery of statehood.

Almost all these provisions were removed by the Treaty of Lisbon. The provision establishing the primacy of Union law over national law and the detailed enumeration of the Union Charter of Fundamental Rights were removed from the substantive text of the Treaty. A Declaration was instead attached setting out the primacy of Union law and a provision added requiring the Union to respect the rights, freedoms and principles in the Charter.[11] Union legislative measures were to return to their traditional designation as regulations and directives, and the Foreign Minister was to be known as the High Representative. To be sure, sixteen Member States signed a Declaration stating that the symbols of the Union – the flag, the anthem, the motto, the provision on the euro as the European Union currency, and the holiday – would remain

---

9 A good initial analysis of the Lisbon Treaty is provided by P. Craig, 'The Treaty of Lisbon: Process, architecture and substance' (2008) 33 *ELR* 137.
10 Council of the European Union, IGC 2007 Mandate (Brussels, 26 June 2007), paragraph 1.
11 Article 6 LTEU.

as 'symbols to express the sense of community of the people in the European Union and their allegiance to it'.[12] Yet the fact that this was hidden away as a remote Declaration signed by a bare majority of States indicated constitutionalism's fall from grace. Nevertheless, some provisions were retained. The provisions on legal personality and on representative and participatory democracy were left intact. If the constitutional conceit was abandoned by Lisbon, there was, therefore, an indication that some of the concerns that had led to it, namely the democratic quality of the Union and the idea that it should have a more autonomous presence, were to prevail and to continue to be addressed.

(b)   Two Treaties of equal value: the Treaty on European Union and the Treaty on the Functioning of the European Union

The Treaty of Lisbon has not resulted in a single new Treaty text, but instead, has created two new treaties. One, confusingly, is named the Treaty on European Union (LTEU). As well as replicating the existing TEU, broadly, it can be said to perform eight functions. First, it sets out the mission and values of the European Union – respect for the rule of law, the principle of limited powers, respect for national identities and upholding democracy and fundamental rights. Second, it sets out the demo-cratic principles of the Union and provides for the active contribution of national parliaments to the functioning of the European Union. Third, there is provision for a neighbourhood policy, whereby the Union is to develop a special relationship with neighbouring countries. Fourth, it sets out the composition and functions of the EU Institutions. Fifth, there are detailed provisions on the Union's external action in the LTEU, in particular both its common foreign and security policy and its com-mon security and defence policy. Sixth, procedures are set out for amendment of the two Treaties. The seventh function is that it provides for the legal personality of the Union. Finally, there are provisions governing asymmetric integration. These include the circumstances in which a Member State may leave or be expelled from the Union and when States may engage in enhanced cooperation, the procedure whereby some Member States may develop Union legislation amongst themselves where there is not sufficient will for that legislation to be adopted by all Member States.

The second treaty is the Treaty on the Functioning of the European Union (LTFEU). This sets out the explicit competencies of the Union and, with the exception of external action, the detailed procedures to be used in each policy field. In legislative style, it is similar therefore to the existing EC Treaty. There is, however, one significant adaptation taken from the Constitutional Treaty. The competencies and their nature are catalogued at the beginning of the LTFEU:

---

12 Declaration 52 on the symbols of the European Union.

Article 3(1) LTFEU The Union shall have exclusive competence in the following areas:

(a) customs union;
(b) the establishing of the competition rules necessary for the functioning of the internal market;
(c) monetary policy for the Member States whose currency is the euro;
(d) the conservation of marine biological resources under the common fisheries policy;
(e) common commercial policy.

2. The Union shall also have exclusive competence for the conclusion of an international agreement when its conclusion is provided for in a legislative act of the Union or is necessary to enable the Union to exercise its internal competence, or insofar as its conclusion may affect common rules or alter their scope.

Article 4(1) LTFEU The Union shall share competence with the Member States where the Treaties confer on it a competence which does not relate to the areas referred to in Articles 3 and 6.

2. Shared competence between the Union and the Member States applies in the following principal areas:

(a) internal market;
(b) social policy, for the aspects defined in this Treaty;
(c) economic, social and territorial cohesion;
(d) agriculture and fisheries, excluding the conservation of marine biological resources;
(e) environment;
(f) consumer protection;
(g) transport;
(h) trans-European networks;
(i) energy;
(j) area of freedom, security and justice;
(k) common safety concerns in public health matters, for the aspects defined in this Treaty.

3. In the areas of research, technological development and space, the Union shall have competence to carry out activities, in particular to define and implement programmes; however, the exercise of that competence shall not result in Member States being prevented from exercising theirs.

4. In the areas of development cooperation and humanitarian aid, the Union shall have competence to carry out activities and conduct a common policy; however, the exercise of that competence shall not result in Member States being prevented from exercising theirs.

Article 5(1) LTFEU The Member States shall coordinate their economic policies within the Union. To this end, the Council shall adopt measures, in particular broad guidelines for these policies. Specific provisions shall apply to those Member States whose currency is the euro.

2. The Union shall take measures to ensure coordination of the employment policies of the Member States, in particular by defining guidelines for these policies.

3. The Union may take initiatives to ensure coordination of Member States' social policies.

6 The Union shall have competence to carry out actions to support, coordinate or supplement the actions of the Member States. The areas of such action shall, at European level, be:

(a) protection and improvement of human health;
(b) industry;

(c) culture;
(d) tourism;
(e) education, vocational training, youth and sport;
(f) civil protection;
(g) administrative cooperation.

The central question bedevilling the two treaties will be the relationship between them. The Treaty of Lisbon states that each treaty is to have 'the same legal value'.[13] It is, however, unclear what this means. Is each to be interpreted in the light of the other? If that is the case, it could lead to the more detailed LTFEU being given an expanded remit as a result of the broader mission of the LTEU. Or does it mean that each curtails the other? In which case, many of the broader provisions of the LTEU will be little more than rhetoric as they will be curtailed by the substance of the LTFEU.

There are also particular concerns about external action. In principle, this is dealt with by the LTEU. But there are many issues – humanitarian aid, sanctions, external trade, international agreements – which are governed by the LTFEU. Insofar as issues intersect these fields and broader foreign and defence policy concerns, there will be controversy over which treaty should govern them.[14]

(c)   A retrenchment of the powers of the Union

The Constitutional Treaty had enumerated a number of new explicit competencies. These were in the field of energy, intellectual property, space, humanitarian aid, sport and civil protection. Whilst discrete legal bases were provided for activities in these fields, the EC already had capacity to carry out activity and had taken measures, in some instances in an extensive manner, in all these fields. This lack of significant extension of Union powers or competencies was subject to two caveats. The first was that all three pillars were brought into a single framework. Whilst provision was made for the Common Foreign and Security policy to continue to be treated discretely, the activities currently governed by the third pillar, policing and judicial cooperation in criminal and civil affairs, were now to be governed by the same procedures as those traditionally applied to EC activities. The second caveat was a corollary of this. The EC Treaty contained a provision, Article 308 EC, which permitted the EC to legislate to realise broad Community objectives if there was no other specific EC legal provision that catered for their realisation. This provision remained in the Constitutional Treaty, and was known as the flexibility provision, but was amended to allow legislation to be adopted where no other *Union* legal base provides for this. Contained in Article 352 LTFEU, it therefore has a potentially far wider remit than was previously the case as it applies not merely to the EC Treaty but to all Union activity.

13 Article 1(2) LTFEU.
14 It could of course be argued that this is not a new problem as the same question occurs when matters straddle the EC Treaty and the second pillar. The point is simply that the new treaties do not address the issue sufficiently.

The Treaty of Lisbon did not alter the new competencies agreed upon in the Constitutional Treaty beyond a new reference explicitly allowing the Union to take measures to combat climate change.[15] It did take a number of measures to rein in the two areas where Union capacity was extended.

In relation to the unification of the first and third pillars, a Protocol provides the United Kingdom and Ireland with the option of choosing whether or not to participate in individual pieces of legislation related to what was formerly the third pillar.[16] If either Member State chooses not to participate, it would not be bound by that legislation. More generally, all Member States sought to draw some of the teeth from the unification of the pillars through the insertion of a new proviso stating that national security remains the sole responsibility of each Member State.[17] Security remains an amorphous concept but clearly has both an internal and external dimension and extends beyond State secrets and law and order to include matters such as energy or economic security as well as the broader public order. With regard to the flexibility provision, it has been amended so that it cannot be used as a legal base for matters relating to common and foreign security,[18] and a Declaration was inserted stipulating that it could not be used to enable de facto amendment of the Treaties.[19]

The Treaty of Lisbon also addressed a more general concern that there remained insufficient safeguards to prevent Union measures being adopted that would unduly encroach on national autonomy. There were two particular types of encroachment against which protection was taken.

The first related to the concern that market liberalising measures might in some way undermine national public services. At the insistence of the French government, a Protocol on Services of General Interest was added which stated that nothing in the Treaties affected the competence of Member States to provide, commission or organise non-economic services of a general interest.

Second, there was also concern about encroachment by EU law on national ethical choices. A further Protocol was therefore added on the Application of the Charter of Fundamental Rights to Poland and the United Kingdom. This Protocol stated that the Charter did not extend the ability of any court to declare Poland or British measures incompatible with EU fundamental rights law. As these States had particular concerns about the development of EU social rights, the Protocol provided that Title IV of the

---

15 Article 191(1) LTFEU.

16 This Protocol has the same shape as that agreed on immigration and asylum at the Treaty of Amsterdam. The new Protocol will therefore integrate the Amsterdam Protocol and be named the Protocol on the position of the United Kingdom and Ireland in respect of the area of freedom, security and justice.

17 Article 4(2) LTEU. Prior to Lisbon, the position was less austere requiring Union law merely to respect the Member States' right to maintain law and order.

18 Article 352(4) LTFEU.

19 Declaration 42 LTFEU on Article 308 of the Treaty on the Functioning of the European Union. The Declaration states that 'this Article cannot be used as a basis for the adoption of provisions whose effect would, in substance, be to amend the Treaties without following the procedure which they provide for that purpose'.

Charter, in which most of these rights were incorporated, was only justiciable in these States insofar as the latter provided for them in national law.

A careful reading of both Protocols suggests that neither of them pre-empts EU law. The Protocol on Services of a General Interest does allow EU law to intervene to regulate the exercise of national competencies, and the Protocol on the Charter is largely concerned with preventing the extension of judicial power in this field, thereby implicitly admitting judges have an existing power to review. They are therefore to be seen as shots across the bows, indicating that Union law must be developed with caution in these fields. The feeling that this is largely about mood music, albeit significant mood music, is reinforced by a unilateral Declaration made by Poland to the Treaty that 'the Charter does not affect in any way the right of Member States to legislate in the sphere of public morality, family law, as well as the protection of human dignity and respect for human physical and moral integrity'. As a Declaration, it has limited formal legal force. As a political statement, it indicates a crisis would be provoked if it were too nakedly transgressed.

(d)   Recasting the institutional setting

Beyond the question of constitutionalisation, the Constitutional Treaty was largely about institutional reform. Its central concern was not to affect what was done but how it was done. Its institutional reforms were adopted largely unscathed in the Treaty of Lisbon.[20]

With regard to law-making, the central theme of the Constitutional Treaty was the increase in Qualified Majority Voting (QMV) and in the powers of the European and national Parliaments. These reforms have been maintained. There is therefore provision for the extension of QMV to about fifty new areas and a provision allowing for legislative procedures based on the unanimity vote in the Council to be altered to QMV without the need for an Intergovernmental Conference has been retained. In terms of the powers of the European Parliament, the co-decision procedure, which grants it a veto, has been applied to thirty-three new areas. In addition, it has been granted significant powers of assent, most notably with regard to Article 352 LTFEU and anti-discrimination, whereby its agreement must be obtained before any legislative proposal can become law. Finally, the supervisory powers granted to it over delegated law-making by the Commission have also been retained. The Treaty of Lisbon also extended the powers granted to national parliaments. They were granted additional time to consider legislative proposals and increased powers to call for a proposal to be reviewed on the ground that it does not comply with the principle of subsidiarity, which provides that Union measures should only be adopted if the objectives of the action cannot be sufficiently achieved by Member States and by reason of their scale or effects can be better realised through Union action.[21]

---

20 These are dealt with in more detail in chapter 3.
21 Protocol No 1 on the Role of National Parliaments in the European Union.

The internal reforms made to the Institutions by the Constitutional Treaty have been maintained. Commission membership is slimmed down to comprise, from 2014, a number corresponding to two thirds of the number of the Member States. The President's power to dismiss individual Commissioners is retained. With regard to the European Parliament, the cap on the number of MEPs in the European Parliament, 732, is retained. The rules on the configuration and organisation of the Council as well as the new voting weight for QMV have been kept intact, with the latter requiring 55 per cent of all Members including the States representing at least 65 per cent of the population to meet the threshold, and at least four States are required if a measure is to be blocked.

The institutional innovations have also been maintained. The European Council, the body comprising the Heads of Government and State, is made a formal EU Institution. The position of a new President of the European Council elected for a once renewable two and a half year period is also preserved. The position of the Union Foreign Minister, who is to be a member of both the Council and the Commission is still in place, although the position is renamed High Representative of the Union. Finally, similar provision is made for the citizens' initiatives whereby the Commission is obliged to consider proposals for legal measures made by petitions of one million citizens who are nationals of a significant number of Member States.

3. W(h)ither European Constitutionalism

In a prescient article in 2003, the distinguished political scientist, Philippe Schmitter observed that the attempt to create a pan-Union democracy might prove challenging for a number of reasons. In particular, nation-states had relied on a number of supports to underpin their democracies. These have included a single set of constitutional rules considered sacrosanct by their publics; a political administrative with the monopoly of legitimate violence over the territory; stable territorial boundaries; a distinctive and exclusive population that identifies with them; an extensive mass of exclusive competencies; and sub-units which have the same legal clout and representation within them.[22] Whilst it can be argued that a number of States do not have all of these, Schmitter's argument is that having none of these makes a pan-Union democracy difficult, if only because it makes the politics and political system so different from national politics. Citizens do not identify with the Union in the same way as they do with their States. The EU simply does not have the clout or hold of a national system over public debate.

These observations seem prescient in the light of the fate of the Constitutional Treaty. It required the suspension of disbelief by Union citizens for it to be treated with the same reverence as national constitutions, and the referenda indicated a

---

22 P. Schmitter, 'Making sense of the EU: Democracy in Europe and Europe's democratization' (2003) 14 *Journal of Democracy* 71, 75–9.

certain unwillingness on their part to engage with Union issues. Yet Schmitter's article made a second point, that although it might be difficult to establish a pan-Union democracy, this does not mean that the democratic quality of Union law-making and administrative processes do not matter.[23] He observed that the Union was sufficiently important in what it did that its functioning affected the quality of democratic life in all the Member States. To protect democracy in the United Kingdom, France, Greece, Poland etc, it was necessary to place democratic controls on the working of the Union.

It is this ethos that has permeated the Lisbon Treaty. There is an important shift in tone. It is not establishing a pan-Union democracy; rather it is concerned to protect democracy in the Union. There is no longer a concern to establish any kind of political community, instead there is a concern to ensure that a Frankenstein is not created which develops large numbers of our laws and administers our lives in an undemocratic way. The Lisbon Treaty is notably, therefore, not a mere tidying up exercise, but seeks to anchor the Union more firmly in an ethos that is centered on four core principles. These are all set out in the opening provisions of the LTEU.

The first is that the Union is founded upon and must respect a set of liberal values that are shared across the Union and form part of a common identity. The Preamble to the LTEU, therefore talks of the Union drawing inspiration:–

> "from the cultural, religious and humanist inheritance of Europe, from which
> have developed the universal values of the inviolable and inalienable rights of
> the human person, freedom, democracy, equality and the rule of law."

The nature and content of these values are set out in the first substantive provision of the LTEU.

> **Article 2 LTEU** The Union is founded on the values of respect for human dignity, freedom, democracy, equality, the rule of law and respect for human rights, including the rights of persons belonging to minorities. These values are common to the Member States in a society in which pluralism, non-discrimination, tolerance, justice, solidarity and equality between women and men prevail.

These values are not rhetorical, nor do they form some general aspirational goal. Instead, they are to be recognised by the Union and must not be violated by it.

> **Article 6(1) LTEU** The Union recognises the rights, freedoms and principles set out in the Charter of Fundamental Rights of the European Union . . . , which shall have the same legal value as the Treaties.
> The provisions of the Charter shall not extend in any way the competences of the Union as defined in the Treaties.
> The rights, freedoms and principles in the Charter shall be interpreted in accordance with the general provisions in Title VII of the Charter governing its interpretation and application

---

23 *Ibid.* 80–2.

and with due regard to the explanations referred to in the Charter, that set out the sources of those provisions.

2. The Union shall accede to the European Convention for the Protection of Human Rights and Fundamental Freedoms. Such accession shall not affect the Union's competences as defined in the Treaties.

3. Fundamental rights, as guaranteed by the European Convention for the Protection of Human Rights and Fundamental Freedoms and as they result from the constitutional traditions common to the Member States, shall constitute general principles of the Union's law.

The second and third principles are reworkings of themes already strongly present in the TEU. The principles are, however, recast in slightly though significantly different language.

The second principle is a presumption that legal and administrative power lies in the first place with the Member States. They stand at the centre of the Union and the Union institutions only have those powers granted to them by the two Treaties. The Union must respect not only their core functions but also, importantly, national identities. The emphasis on the latter is new and particularly evocative, as it suggests that the Union must be particularly deferential to local traditions, identities and cultures and not simply characterised by discrete tasks carried out by national administrations.

Article 4(1) LTEU In accordance with Article 5,[24] competences not conferred upon the Union in the Treaties remain with the Member States.

2. The Union shall respect the equality of Member States before the Treaties as well as their national identities, inherent in their fundamental structures, political and constitutional, inclusive of regional and local self-government. It shall respect their essential State functions, including ensuring the territorial integrity of the State, maintaining law and order and safeguarding national security. In particular, national security remains the sole responsibility of each Member State.

The third principle is one of mutual comity. The Union institutions and Member States must cooperate to realise common objectives, but must do so in 'full mutual respect'; a new notion that suggests both an equality between all of them and a norm that each must not transgress on the prerogatives and powers of the other.

Article 4(3) LTEU Pursuant to the principle of sincere cooperation, the Union and the Member States shall, in full mutual respect, assist each other in carrying out tasks which flow from the Treaties.

The Member States shall take any appropriate measure, general or particular, to ensure fulfilment of the obligations arising out of the Treaties or resulting from the acts of the institutions of the Union.

The Member States shall facilitate the achievement of the Union's tasks and refrain from any measure which could jeopardise the attainment of the Union's objectives.

---

24 Article 5 LTEU sets out the principle of conferred powers for the Union and that it is governed by the principles of subsidiority and proportionality. On the new procedures see pp. 58–61 of the updates.

The fourth principle is set out in a new title on 'Provisions on Democratic Principles'. It requires the Union to respect two forms of democracy: representative democracy and participatory democracy.[25]

> **Article 9 LTEU** In all its activities, the Union shall observe the principle of the equality of its citizens, who shall receive equal attention from its institutions, bodies, offices and agencies. Every national of a Member State shall be a citizen of the Union. Citizenship of the Union shall be additional to national citizenship and shall not replace it.
>
> **Article 10(1) LTEU** The functioning of the Union shall be founded on representative democracy.
>
> 2. Citizens are directly represented at Union level in the European Parliament. Member States are represented in the European Council by their Heads of State or Government and in the Council by their governments, themselves democratically accountable either to their national Parliaments, or to their citizens.
>
> 3. Every citizen shall have the right to participate in the democratic life of the Union. Decisions shall be taken as openly and as closely as possible to the citizen.
>
> 4. Political parties at European level contribute to forming European political awareness and to expressing the will of citizens of the Union.

These principles go to the quality of constitutional democracy that must be observed by the Union. None talk up the idea of the Union as a new or emergent political system or political community. Instead, all are in the form of a series of constraints it must not violate, rather than a number of goals it must realise. Within its terms, this ethos avoids the hubris of the Constitutional Treaty and makes a great deal of sense, and the corollary principles seem uncontroversial. Yet even here, a trick might have been missed. The Union is instructed to respect national democracy and behave in a democratic way, yet there is still the perception that it sits external to and divorced from the Member States. To meet these requirements, it is supposed to drum up its own resources through Union institutions developing new forms of self-restraint and checks on one another. As Bellamy observes, this seems bizarre when most of these lie within the Member States themselves rather than within the Union institutions:–

> the EU should have built upon it and to some degree adapted it to the mechanisms of democratic accountability. Here too there is a need to domesticate EU decision making. As we saw, the apparent dilemma confronting the EU is that citizens want more democratic control, yet do not want to participate in EU wide elections. The obvious solution that parallels what has occurred hitherto in the field of law is for the national parliaments to play a more active part in EU decision making. For EU level decisions do not simply affect a superior level of activity between the Member States, but have a profound impact upon domestic policy making. EU politics is domestic politics and needs to be treated as such.
>
> There is a major domestic democratic deficit with regard to the EU. For example, a British MEP, Chris Davies, discovered that in one session of the

---

25 Provision is, therefore, made for greater involvement of civil society in both law-making and it instigation as well as a greater presence for national parliaments.

Westminster Parliament during which there had been 92 council meetings attended by a minister, only 79 questions were asked by MPs (compared to some 40,000 raised on other matters). Some countries do better – a Danish parliamentary grand committee meets almost weekly to take evidence from ministers before every EU council. But they remain the exception. Likewise, apart from the Euroskeptic parties, MEPs are rarely elected for their position on Europe. To the extent people bother at all, domestic issues tend to dominate. As a result, domestic debates on the EU have a tendency only to surface at times of referenda on treaty changes and so turn on a simple 'in' or 'out,' 'yes' or 'no,' rather than subtler differences of opinion over the kind of Europe citizens might want.

The Constitutional Treaty did contain some positive proposals in this regard. For example, it imposed an obligation on the Commission to keep national parliaments adequately informed of EU developments and gave them a limited role in policing infractions of subsidiarity (Protocol on the Role of National Parliaments in the EU). Of course, how far such measures become a real resource for more informed discussion of EU politics at the domestic level is a matter for national politicians themselves. Voting in the Council of Ministers was to have been made transparent. This too was a welcome step, for it would prevent governments claiming they were not a party to potentially unpopular policies that were 'imposed' by nameless others. Instead, they would be obliged to defend their positions. They could also point out the votes that had gone their way and make more of them. Both these measures could be adopted voluntarily and immediately by the institutions concerned, with no need for any Treaty change at all.

Even such limited measures are sometimes criticized for being largely negative – a way of constraining further integration. That need not be the case. They may also work to give integration greater legitimacy through possessing and mobilizing domestic support. Long term, it can also help forge transnational linkages. By making national politicians aware of common interests with colleagues representing constituencies with similar profiles elsewhere, and highlighting the ideological as well as the national divisions that surround most EU policy decisions, a genuine EU party system is far more likely to develop. In this regard, direct elections to the European Parliament were (and remain) premature and the blocking at the Convention of a formal meeting of national parliamentarians to discuss EU policy a mistake. More generally, national political parties as the organizations that represent millions of voters ought to be regular parts of the EU's consultation process. Great emphasis is laid these days on consulting with civil society organizations. Yet most of those selected have no formal mechanisms of accountability with regard to the citizens they claim to represent – indeed, many have extraordinarily low levels of membership. However, the organizations that do have these mechanisms and comparatively high levels of active support remain on the side lines, unmentioned in any official document on the topic.[26]

26 R. Bellamy, 'The European Constitution is Dead: Long Live European Constitutionalism, (2006) 13 *Constellations* 181, 186–7 (Blackwell Publishing).

4. Recasting the borders of the EU

(i)   The European Union and enlargement

Since December 2005, the European Union has enlarged from twenty-five Member States to twenty-seven with Romania and Bulgaria joining on 1 January 2007. Their membership betrayed, however, some of the tensions over increased membership of the Union, and suggested that membership, in future, might be more partial and more contingent than previously. The Accession Treaty provides for the monitoring by the Commission of both States for a period of three years after accession in three fields – justice and home affairs, internal market and economic policy.[27] If there is a deterioration in the economic situation in those States or they fail to meet their legal obligations, the Commission may adopt measures against these States, notably suspending their rights in these fields. The Commission indicated, shortly before their membership, that with regard to Bulgaria particular areas of concern that it would monitor were corruption, food safety, police cooperation, money laundering and agricultural controls. In respect of Romania, it will monitor its tax regime, agricultural controls and judicial system.[28] Whilst these provisions are temporary, these States are subject to a degree of administrative control and supervision that suggests on the one hand a lack of full confidence in their membership, and restricted membership rights on the other.

This hesitancy is also present in enlargement negotiations with States wishing to accede. In October 2005, accession negotiations opened with Croatia and with the Former Yugoslav Republic of Macedonia two months later. Along with Turkey, there are therefore three candidate States, who, if admitted, could take the total of Member States to thirty. Negotiations with the largest State, Turkey, suggest that there might be less of an appetite for enlargement than previously. In December 2006, negotiations between the Union and Turkey were disrupted over the refusal by Turkey to admit ships or planes flying the Cypriot flag into its ports or airports. This measure was influenced in part by a perception that the European Union was not doing sufficient to improve the lot of the Turkish Cypriot community in the north of Cyprus. As a consequence the European Union decided that there would be no negotiations in eight fields[29] and it would not consider negotiations in any field closed until this matter was resolved. Whilst negotiations have continued since, they have done so at a snail's pace.

---

27 Act of Accession of the Republic of Bulgaria and Romania to the European Union, Protocol concerning the conditions and arrangements for admission of the republic of Bulgaria and Romania to the European Union, articles 36–39, OJ 2005, L 157/3.

28 EC Commission, *Monitoring report on the state of preparedness for EU membership of Bulgaria and Romania*, COM (2006) 549. The first reports were published in July 2007. EC Commission, *Reports on Bulgaria's and Romania's progress on accompanying measures following Accession*, COM(2007) 377 and 378.

29 These were free movement of goods, right of establishment and freedom to provide services, financial services, agriculture and rural development, fisheries, transport policy, customs union and external relations.

(ii)   Variable geometry

The other feature of the last two years is an increased resort to 'variable geometry' arrangements whereby not all Member States participate in common policies, but only those who wish to or are actually able to participate. A hallmark has been that no use is made of the generalised procedures provided by EU law. Instead a series of sector-specific arrangements are concluded, some within the Union legal framework and others outside.

The most longstanding example of variable geometry are the Schengen Conventions of 1985 and 1990. Concluded between thirteen of the EU-15 Member States plus Norway and Iceland, these provide for the abolition of frontier checks, a common external frontier and cooperation in the fields of migration of non-EU nationals, crime and policing. Initially developed on an intergovernmental basis, they were incorporated into EU law by the Treaty of Amsterdam with the result that all the measures adopted under them are now EU instruments. Whilst they are presently subject to the controls and transparency of EU law, their problematic nature lies in their having hog-wired the process so that EU law has adopted fairly unquestioningly a corpus of law developed between civil servants with little public debate or parliamentary or judicial controls. This problem has exacerbated as Schengen has expanded. In December 2007, a further nine EU Member States acceded to the Convention. All were new Member States, with provision made for the three remaining new Member States, Cyprus, Romania and Bulgaria, to join when ready.

The second danger posed by Schengen is that it provides a template for further secretive, intergovernmental arrangements between limited numbers of States, who know others will subsequently join them as there will be significant exclusionary costs if they do not (in the case of Schengen, these included free movement to or from other Member States as well as access to information networks about criminals and irregular migrants). In May 2005 the Prüm Convention was signed between Austria, Belgium, France, Germany, Luxembourg, Netherlands and Spain.[30] This provides for greater exchange of data and integration of networks between the signatories as well as for greater cooperation between security agencies. It takes the idea of a pan-European security agency further than any EU measure but has been developed completely outside its structures.

The third type of measure relates to Economic and Monetary Union and membership of the eurozone. This differs from other measures in that members can exclude others from joining if they do not meet the criteria for membership, in this case whether their economies are strong enough to join the third stage of economic and monetary union and have the euro as their currency. The problematic nature of this

---

30 Despite its not being an EU document, the Convention has been published by the Council. EU Council, *Prüm Convention*, EU Council Doc. 10900/05. For interesting analysis see R. Bossong, 'The European Security Vanguard? Prüm, Heiligendamm and Flexible Integration Theory' LSE/Challenge Working Paper January 2007, http://lse.ac.uk/Depts/intrel/pdfs/EFPU%20Challenge%20Working%20Paper%207.pdf

became apparent when both Slovenia and Lithuania applied for membership from 1 January 2007. Whilst Slovenia was allowed to join and adopt the euro as its currency, Lithuania was blocked by the Commission and other Member States on the grounds that its level of inflation was too high. This move was perceived as divisive and unfair by a number of the new Member States as Lithuania met all the other criteria, which at the time was not true of a number of existing members of the eurozone. On 1 January 2008, Malta and Cyprus also joined the eurozone, taking its number to fifteen.

The final form of variable geometry to emerge was at the Treaty of Lisbon. This was the so-called 'à la carte' geometry where Member States pick which policy fields to engage with and do not participate in others where they do not wish to enter into common arrangements. One argument is that this allows States to free ride, demanding sacrifices of other States, while being unprepared to make any of their own in return. As already discussed, at Lisbon, it was agreed that the United Kingdom and Ireland would enlarge their 'opt in' so that it covers the whole of the area of freedom, security and justice. For immigration, asylum, judicial cooperation in criminal or civil matters and policing, where the EU wants to adopt a measure, these two States must notify the other States of whether they wish to adopt the measure.

The other criticism of such arrangements is that they generate legal uncertainty. An example of this is the previously discussed Protocol on the Application of the Charter of Fundamental Rights to Poland and the United Kingdom. It does not give either of these states 'opt-outs' from the Charter but instead provides that the Charter cannot be used to extend judicial review of national measures in their territories or to render certain social rights justiciable if they are not justiciable in their national laws. This arrangement has raised numerous questions. If the Court of Justice interprets a Directive in the light of a Charter provision, is the Directive to have one meaning for the United Kingdom and Poland and another for the other twenty-five States? As the Charter largely brings together different human rights treaties within a single instrument, can courts use these other treaties to extend judicial review and have social rights invoked before them in these two States? Finally, the Protocol acknowledges that national measures in these two States can be struck down for violation of Charter provisions on condition that the Charter does not 'extend' this power of review. The meaning of this is a complete mystery. And, in this, it provides an appropriate way to end the chapter on the nature of the Union and its democratic qualities. These continue to remain open-ended, and it is their open-endedness that contributes to the Union as a place in which to experiment and debate.

The EU institutions

1. Introduction

The thrust of the Lisbon Treaty is concerned with institutional reform. The bulk of its institutional reforms, moreover, are identical to those proposed in the failed Constitutional Treaty. On the one hand, the Lisbon Treaty sets out, formally at least, increased powers for the European Council, the European Parliament and the Court of Justice. Its other concern is the internal organisational reform of the institutions to make them both more effective and, in some cases, more transparent and accountable.

2. Resetting the inter-institutional balance

(i)   The European Council as agenda-setter

Provision is currently made in the TEU for the European Council to provide the necessary impetus and political guidelines for the development of the Union. Beyond this general statement of its functions, it has extensive powers in the second pillar of the Union. The Treaty also sets out its membership as consisting of the Heads of State or government of the Member States and the President of the Commission. Provision is made for an element of accountability in its being required to submit a report to the European Parliament after each of its meetings as well as an annual report on the progress of the Union.[1]

The Lisbon Treaty sets out a change of gear for the European Council. For the first time it is formally recognised as an institution of the Union.[2] Its agenda-setting powers are set out in a more prescriptive fashion and it is provided with more detailed mechanisms to realise these. The European Council is therefore no longer confined to setting out guidelines for the Union, but is now to define its directions and priorities.

> **Article 15(1) LTEU** The European Council shall provide the Union with the necessary impetus for its development and shall define the general political directions and priorities thereof. It shall not exercise legislative functions.

This agenda-setting is limited by the final sentence, which indicates that the European Council is not to trespass on the Commission's traditional prerogatives to propose legislation. Instead, the suggestion is that it is now to steer, direct and prompt the general course of the Union far more actively than previously. To this effect, a number of new mechanisms have been created.

The first is the establishment of an elected President of the European Council. Elected by qualified majority for a once renewable two and a half year term,[3] the President will sit as an additional member of the European Council.[4] Its tasks are to:

- chair and drive forward the work of the European Council whilst endeavouring to facilitate consensus and cohesion within it;
- ensure the preparation and continuity of the work of the European Council in cooperation with the President of the Commission, and on the basis of the work of the General Affairs Council;
- present a report to the European Parliament after each of the meetings of the European Council;
- Ensure the external representation of the Union on issues concerning its common foreign and security policy, without prejudice to the powers of the High Representative of the Union for Foreign Affairs and Security Policy.[5]

The mission of the President has both an *ex ante* and an *ex post* dimension. *Ex ante*, it is to organise, coordinate and secure direction for the European Council, building alliances and facilitating agendas. *Ex post*, it is mandated to secure follow-up, seeing that European Council decisions are implemented. Its success will be dependent on a number of factors. While setting the policy agenda for the Union and building consensus around this looks like a significant task, there is no provision made for the President to have a significant administration of their own. There is also the question of its relationship with the different Member States. Expected to be the

---

1 Article 4 TEU.   2 Article 13 LTEU.   3 Article 15(5) LTEU.
4 Article 15(2) LTEU.   5 Article 15(6) LTEU.

servant of national governments, there will inevitably be a tension between the larger Member States, who will expect the President to pay more attention to their greater economic weight and larger populations, and the smaller Member States, who will expect the President to treat all Member States equally regardless of size. Finally, there is the President's relationship with the supranational institutions, notably the Commission. They are expected to cooperate with each other, but the essential structure of the relationship is a competitive one. Each will have an agenda-setting role and will be keen to assert its preferences and prerogatives.

The second innovation is the formalisation of the General Affairs Council. Since June 2002, the General Affairs and External Relations Council, comprised of national foreign ministers, has met alternately as the General Affairs Council and as the External Relations Council. As the former, it considers matters that affect a number of Union policies and is responsible for coordinating work done by the other Council configurations, and for handling dossiers submitted by the European Council. This position is formalised by the Lisbon Treaty, which states that it shall ensure consistency in the work of the different Council configurations, and prepare and ensure the follow-up to meetings of the European Council, in liaison with the Presidents of the European Council and the Commission.[6] It is, therefore, to shadow the President of the European Council in preparing and implementing European Council decisions. It also has a policing mission in ensuring that the different configurations of the Council all row in the same direction and that this direction is the one ordained by the European Council.

The challenges for the General Affairs Council are its degree of institutionalisation and its ability to assert influence over the other Councils. The initial draft for the Constitutional Treaty proposed a permanent General and Legislative Affairs Council based in Brussels comprised of Ministers of Europe which would assume the role performed by the General Affairs Council.[7] This proposal was rejected by the national governments who were concerned that such a Council might become too autonomous and powerful. Yet the original initiative suggests that Foreign Ministers meeting every now and then in Brussels may not have the required level of interest and resources to do the job expected of them. The other concern is whether, given the jealousy that national ministers exercise over their portfolios, the General Affairs Council will have the necessary authority. Will, for example, a powerful economics minister listen to his foreign minister?

The final issue concerns the relationship between the system of rotating presidencies and the new Presidency. The rotating presidencies will continue, albeit under a different format. Pre-established groups of three Member States will hold it jointly for eighteen months, with each Member State holding the chair for six months.[8] There

---

6 Article 16(6) LTEU.   7 Article 23(1) DCT.

8 The system for rotating presidencies is contained in Declaration 9 LTEU on Article 16(9) LTEU concerning the European Council decision on the exercise of the Presidency.

will be a rotation of the Presidency between all the Member States with membership of each Presidency taking account of the diversity and geography of the Union.[9] The Presidency will chair all the Council configurations, the COREPER and secure the continuity and smooth operation of the Council. This begs the question of the division of duties as both the rotating Presidency and the European Council Presidency seem responsible for steering the direction of the Union. To be sure, they might liaise and row in the same direction, but there is also a danger of competition, with each pushing for different priorities. In such circumstances, it is unclear who is to take the lead.

(ii)   European Parliament

The largest growth in the European Parliament's powers is in the legislative arena, and this will be dealt with in the update for chapter 4. The other significant development is in the field of the budget. Article 312(2) LTFEU provides that a five-year multi-annual framework for expenditure setting out the limits on total expenditure and ceilings for each heading of expenditure is to be set by the Council after obtaining the consent of the European Parliament. An annual budget shall be agreed by the EU institutions. This is to be bound by the multi-annual framework and to be based on individual institutions' estimates of expenditure. Within these constraints, the co-decision procedure is to be used to set the budget.[10] The new provision on the multi-annual framework lifts to Treaty status existing practice. More significantly, the use of the co-decision procedure for the annual budget both brings the budget within a unified procedure, and increases the Parliament's powers as its current powers depend on the types of expenditure. The consequence is a new situation where the European Parliament is now a fully equal player alongside the Member States in the setting of the budget and has an annual power to veto it. Whilst it is unlikely that this will be deployed in a destructive sense to bring the Union to a halt, there is a good chance that the shadow of the veto will hang over the Member States, allowing the Parliament to influence the movement of money to policies which accord with its own set of priorities – be it agriculture, regional aid, development or R & D.

(iii)   The European Court of Justice

A new basis for the jurisdiction of the Court of Justice is provided. It is, in principle, to have a general jurisdiction over both the LTEU and the LTFEU.[11] It is then excluded from three fields:

---

9 The sequence is set out in Decision 2007/5/EC, Euratom determining the order in which the office of the President is held, OJ 2007, L 1/11. From July 2008, it will be France, Czech Republic, Sweden, Spain, Belgium, Hungary. The Decision sets out the Order until June 2020.

10 Article 314 LTFEU.   11 Article 19(1) LTEU.

- It shall not have jurisdiction in the field of the common foreign and security policy.[12]
- In judicial cooperation in criminal matters and police cooperation, it shall have no jurisdiction to review the validity or proportionality of operations carried out by the police or other law-enforcement services of a Member State or the exercise of the responsibilities incumbent upon Member States with regard to the maintenance of law and order and the safeguarding of internal security.[13]
- If measures are taken to expel a Member State the Court of Justice can rule on the procedure but not the substance of the grounds for expulsion.[14]

This jurisdiction over new fields, most notably policing and judicial cooperation in criminal matters, is likely to change perceptions of the Court of Justice. The fields of law covered by the area of freedom, security and justice – immigration, asylum, penal law, policing law, and, arguably, anti-discrimination law – constitute the daily bread of national judicial systems in a way that other areas of Union law do not. Fields such as environmental, financial services, transport or broadcasting law are, of course, significant but they are for the most part played out in national ministries and regulatory agencies. To date, the legislation in the field of freedom, security and justice has not featured much before the Court of Justice due to most of it only having been agreed after 2000.[15] As the case law of the Court of Justice develops in this field, the Lisbon Treaty could be seen as a watershed in the sense that the Court is playing a far more prominent role in cases with high symbolic resonance.

The salience of the Court and the likelihood of its being drawn into ever more contentious fields have been reinforced by its being granted wider possibilities of judicial review. Most notably, there is the power for it to review the European Council, with all the corollary implications of a supranational institution telling twenty-seven heads of government that they have acted illegally.[16] There is also the opportunity for a wider array of actors to challenge legislative and administrative acts before the Court. The Committee of the Regions now has the power to challenge measures that affect its prerogatives and to challenge measures on grounds of a violation of the subsidiarity principle.[17] Equally significant are the rules on locus standi for private parties, which have been relaxed to allow a broader array of actors to challenge EU acts before the Court.[18]

---

12 Article 24(1) LTEU; Article 275 LTFEU.   13 Article 276 LTFEU.   14 Article 269 LTFEU.
15 For example, if one looks at the equal opportunities legislation, Directive 2000/43/EC, OJ 2000, L 180/22 and Directive 2000/78/EC establishing a general framework for equal treatment in employment and occupation OJ 2000, L 303/16. There have been only three judgments by the Court of Justice on the latter and none on the former. This is likely to change. There were four references in 2006 on the latter and one on the former in 2007. On the likely impact on workload see D. Chalmers, 'Judicial authority and the Constitutional Treaty' (2005) 4 *I-CON* 448, 455–63.
16 Article 263(1) LTFEU.
17 Article 263(3) LTFEU and Protocol No 2 on the Application of the Principles of Subsidiarity and Proportionality, Article 8.
18 Article 263(4) LTFEU.

3. Institutional reforms

(i)   The Commission

The changes to the Commission's internal organisation contained in the Lisbon Treaty are, in essence, the same as those proposed in the Constitutional Treaty.

First, the President of the Commission is made more clearly 'first amongst equals'. In particular, whilst at present the President requires the consent of the College to dismiss an individual Commissioner, the Lisbon Treaty makes it a matter exclusively of their prerogative.[19] Although this reflects the practice since 2004,[20] there is now formal institutionalisation of the President's unique position to 'hire and fire' members of their team.[21] Such a power is likely to loom over Commissioners and awareness of it may lead them to anticipate their preferences, or be particularly susceptible to their intervention. This will create particular challenges for the Commission as it reaches the end of its term. If the President wishes to be re-nominated, they will be especially keen to ensure their 'team' does not offend the players with the power to reappoint them, namely the national governments and the European Parliament, with all the corollary implications for the independence of the Commission.

The potential for conflicts of interest either because of individual Commissioners' reliance upon the President for their career development, or because of their reliance on external institutions for their progression, raises the question of the standard of behaviour to be expected of them. This was addressed in *Cresson* where the Court of Justice considered the meaning of the requirement in Article 213(2) EC that Commissioners act independently and in the general interest.[22] In this case, the French Commissioner, Edith Cresson, had hired her dentist to be her personal adviser on a contract as a visiting scientist, notwithstanding that her chef de cabinet had seen this person as ill-qualified for any post. Disciplinary proceedings were subsequently taken against her by the Commission to withdraw some of her pension entitlements on the grounds of a violation of Article 213(2) EC. The Court of Justice found that the Commission action was justified. However, it suggested a degree of leeway for Commissioners.

> 71. It is . . . the duty of Members of the Commission to ensure that the general interest of the Community takes precedence at all times, not only over national interests, but also over personal interests.

---

19 Article 17(6)(c) LTEU.
20 This is currently contained in the Code of Conduct that all Commissioners must sign on taking office. EC Commission, *Code of Conduct for Commissioners*, SEC (2004) 1487/2, 1.2.1.
21 Commissioners are hired through the making of a proposal by the President and the European Council, which must then be ratified by QMV in the European Council and by the European Parliament, Article 17(7) LTEU.
22 Case C-432/04 *Commission v Cresson* [2006] ECR I-6387.

72. While the Members of the Commission are thus under an obligation to conduct themselves in a manner which is beyond reproach, it does not, however, follow that the slightest deviation from those standards falls to be censured under Article 213(2) EC. A breach of a certain degree of gravity is required.

The Court indicated that a breach would be of sufficient gravity where the action by the Commissioner was manifestly inappropriate, as was the case in *Cresson*. Though there was little elaboration on what this phrase means it would suggest that only the most outrageous conduct will lead to a violation of Article 213(2) EC.

The second reform the Lisbon Treaty makes is a reduction in the number of Commissioners to two thirds of the number of Member States.[23] As stated in the initial edition of this book, the choice of number seems to be an unhappy compromise between representativity and administrative efficiency. This impression is confirmed by virtue of the fact that the European Council can change this number by a unanimity vote should it so wish, and the new formula not entering into effect until 2014, with the current formula of one Commissioner per Member State operating until then. Undoubtedly, perceptions of the Commission will alter once not all Member States are individually represented. There will also be particular pressure on the Institution to react to the interests and desires of non-represented Member States so as not to appear partisan. The pressures were apparent in a Declaration attached to the Treaty of Lisbon, which stated that when not all Member States would have nationals in the Commission, special attention should be paid to relations of full transparency between the Commission and all Member States, and that the Commission had to take all necessary measures to ensure that the political, economic and social realities in all Member States were taken into account.[24]

The third reform is the institution of the office of the High Representative of the Union for Foreign Affairs and Security Policy. Designated as the Union Foreign Minister in the Constitutional Treaty, the High Representative is responsible for the conduct of the Union common foreign and security policy and its security and defence policy, albeit they are to act under the mandate of the Council.[25] They are a member of the Commission, take part in the work of the European Council,[26] and chair the Foreign Affairs Council.[27] The intention of this 'double hat' is to create a more integrated and coordinated external policy,[28] as well as to give the EU a more salient international profile; non-EU leaders know who to call if they want to contact 'Europe'. Saddling the Commission and the Council, they are subject to a double chain of accountability. They are appointed, by QMV, by the European Council with the agreement of the President of the Commission.[29] They are dismissed in the same manner,[30] and so are the only member of the Commission who cannot be dismissed unilaterally by

23 Article 17(5) LTEU.   24 Declaration 10 on Article 17 LTEU.   25 Article 18(2) LTEU.
26 Article 15(2) LTEU.   27 Articles 17(4) and 18(3) LTEU.   28 Article 18(4) LTEU.
29 Article 18(1) LTEU.   30 Article 17(6) LTEU.

the President of the Commission. If the Parliament passes a motion of censure over the whole Commission, the President must resign with the other Commission members.[31] Alongside these competing lines of accountability, there are also questions about the extent of their authority. The President of the European Council has an external role, and a number of individual Commissioners will have portfolios with a strong external dimension (eg neighbourhood policy, trade, environment, energy and development). Whilst the powers of the President of the European Council are formally subject to those of the High Representative,[32] and it is likely that there will be a similar relationship between the President and individual Commissioners, it is however inconceivable that they have a monopoly of authority over external action, and this raises the potential for turf wars and difficulties in coordination.

(ii)   The Council

The organisational measures proposed by the Constitutional Treaty for the Council are retained in the Lisbon treaty with one significant difference.

The first set of reforms relate to the configurations of the Council. As mentioned above, the Lisbon Treaty divides the General Affairs and External Relations Council into two configurations. The General Affairs Council will ensure consistency in the work of the different Council configurations and prepare and ensure follow-up to the European Council meetings,[33] while the External Relations Council (now called the Foreign Affairs Council) is to elaborate the Union's external actions.[34] The Seville European Council also provided for eight other Council configurations.[35] The Lisbon Treaty provides for this to be revisited through the European Council adopting a decision by QMV on the Council configurations other than the General Affairs and Foreign Affairs Council.[36] Moreover, there is clearly a feeling that this should be urgently revisited with it being provided that, pending such a European Council decision, the General Affairs Council may take such a decision by simple majority vote.[37]

The second amendment concerns public deliberations in the Council. At Seville, it was agreed that Council debates under the co-decision procedure would be open to the public. This was extended by the Lisbon Treaty to all legislative acts with the consequence that all Council meetings will be divided into two parts, one dealing with legislative and the other with non-legislative activities.[38] The public will only have access to the former. The basis for this division is unclear, and there is a certain ambivalence attached to the prospect of opening the Council to the public. Whilst greater publicity might seem desirable, there is both a danger of showboating as well as a risk that the main deals will be made by a few select partners in smoky rooms to avoid the scrutiny of the public eye.

---

31 Article 17(8) LTEU.   32 Article 15(6) LTEU.   33 Article 16(6) LTEU.   34 *Ibid.*
35 See pp. 101–102 of the main text.   36 Article 236(a) LTFEU.
37 Protocol No 10 on Transitional Provisions, Article 4.   38 Article 16(8) LTEU.

The third reform consists of the main difference between Lisbon and the Constitutional Treaty. It concerns the weighting and thresholds for Qualified Majority Voting. The thresholds changed with the accession of Romania and Bulgaria on 1 January 2007. Measures proposed by the Commission now require 255 out of 345 possible votes in order to be adopted, and at least 14 States must vote in favour of it. If a measure is not proposed by the Commission, in addition, at least two thirds of the Member States, eighteen, must vote in favour of it. In either case, any Member States can ask to verify that States representing at least 62 per cent of the total EU population supported the measure. The respective votes and population sizes are:

State	Votes	Population
Germany	29	82 mill
United Kingdom	29	59.4 mill
France	29	59.1 mill
Italy	29	57.7 mill
Spain	27	39.4 mill
Poland	27	38.6 mill
Romania	14	21.8 mill
Netherlands	13	15.8 mill
Greece	12	10.6 mill
Czech Rep	12	10.3 mill
Belgium	12	10.2 mill
Hungary	12	10 mill
Portugal	12	9.9 mill
Sweden	10	8.9 mill
Austria	10	8.1 mill
Bulgaria	10	7.8 mill
Slovakia	7	5.4 mill
Denmark	7	5.3 mill
Finland	7	5.2 mill
Lithuania	7	3.7 mill
Ireland	7	3.7 mill
Latvia	4	2.4 mill
Slovenia	4	2 mill
Estonia	4	1.4 mill
Cyprus	4	0.8 mill
Luxembourg	4	0.4 mill
Malta	3	0.4 mill

The Lisbon Treaty sought to adopt the formula established in the Constitutional Treaty under which there would be a Qualified Majority if 55 per cent of the members of the Council comprising at least fifteen Member States who represented at least 65 per cent of the population voted for the measure. In addition, for a measure to be blocked, at least four Member States must vote against it.[39] Poland was particularly unhappy with the new formula for QMV and sought to have it renegotiated.[40] The consequence was an agreement that there would be no change until 31 October 2014 and the new formula would only enter fully into force on 1 April 2017.[41] Between those dates, a single Member State can ask for the existing formula to be used.[42] Perhaps even more significantly, a Declaration was added indicating a new blocking minority. Under the formulation agreed, if 45 per cent of the Member States, or four Member States representing 35 per cent of the population, did not agree to a measure, it could not be adopted by QMV, as 55 per cent of the States representing 65 per cent of the population must support the measure.[43] The Declaration indicates that in the period between 1 October 2014 and 31 March 2017, if 75 per cent of that figure (33.75 per cent and 26.25 per cent) indicate their opposition to a measure, it shall not be adopted, but 'discussed'. The figure from 1 April 2007 is 55 per cent of the blocking minority (24.75 per cent and 19.25 per cent respectively). This suggests the possibility of a much higher threshold for QMV where a measure can essentially be blocked by either a quarter of the States or three States representing 20 per cent of the population.

(iii)   The European Parliament

The accession of Bulgaria and Romania led to an increase in the size of the European Parliament to 785 MEPs with Bulgaria having 18 and Romania 35 MEPs. The Lisbon Treaty provides that the European Parliament should not exceed 750 members and that the representation will be on the basis of degressive proportionality whereby the principle of per head representation is combined with the principle that the larger the population of a Member State the lower the weighting per head. Additionally, it was agreed in the Lisbon Treaty that no State should receive less than 6 MEPs and no State may have more than 96 MEPs.[44] In October 2007, the Constitutional Affairs Committee of the European Parliament made a distribution of seats for each national territory on the basis of this principle, and negotiations proceeded on the basis of these calculations.[45] This proved uncontroversial for all States except Italy, who opposed it on the grounds that it would now have less MEPs than France and the United Kingdom. A compromise was agreed whereby the President of the European

---

39 Article 16(4) LTEU.
40 On the differences in respective influence between the Treaty of Nice and the new formula see D. Cameron, 'The stalemate in the Constitutional IGC' (2004) 5 *EUP* 373, 383.
41 Article 16(4) and (5) LTEU.   42 Protocol No 10 on Transitional Provisions, Article 2.
43 Declaration No 7 on Article 16(4) LTEU and Article 205(2) TFEU.   44 Article 14(2) LTEU.
45 The allocation of seats would be 96 (Germany); 74 (France); 73 (United Kingdom); 72 (Italy); 54 (Spain); 51 (Poland); 33 (Romania); 26 (Netherlands) 22 (Greece, Portugal, Belgium, Czech Republic, Hungary); 20 (Sweden); 19 (Austria); 18 (Bulgaria); 13 (Denmark, Slovakia, Finland); 12 (Ireland, Lithuania); 9 (Latvia); 8 (Slovenia); 6 (Luxembourg, Malta, Cyprus, Estonia).

Parliament would not count towards the total and the extra MEP would be awarded to Italy so that, like the United Kingdom, it would have 73 MEPs.[46]

(iv)   The Court of Justice

The reforms to the Court of Justice relate to designation, appointments and internal procedures.[47]

With regard to designation, the Court of First Instance is to be re-named the General Court. Although its powers are not affected by this renaming, a change in emphasis on the nature of its workload is intended. The renaming is meant to reflect this court's position as the central EU administrative court and as the body with central judicial oversight over the specialised judicial panels, as well as its being a target for an increasing number of preliminary references. The new name would suggest that, in workload at least, the General Court rather than the Court of Justice will be the hub of the Union judiciary.

On the question of membership, the procedures for appointment of judges and Advocates General to the Court and General Court have been altered. At the *Future of Europe* Convention it was proposed that a panel with the task of giving an opinion on the quality of candidates be established as a way of safeguarding the quality of the judges and protecting against over-politicisation of the process of appointment. Such a panel is formally instituted by the Lisbon Treaty. It shall comprise seven persons chosen from among former members of the Court of Justice and the General Court, members of national supreme courts and lawyers of recognised competence, one of whom shall be proposed by the European Parliament. Its role shall be to give opinions on the suitability of candidates.[48] These opinions are likely to have considerable force. It would be very difficult for a candidate to be appointed following a negative opinion of the Panel without the authority of that judge being heavily undermined. In that regard, the membership of the Panel is surprising. In particular, it is unclear why it should be composed of former members of the Court of Justice, who will have a vested interest in protecting their legacy. A further reform of note is that the number of Advocates General is to be increased from eight to eleven, with Poland having the right to a permanent Advocate General.[49]

---

46 Declaration No 4 on the composition of the European Parliament.
47 On the latter see the updates to chapter 7.
48 Article 255 LTFEU. For earlier discussions, see *Final Report of the Discussion Circle of the Court of Justice*, CONV 734/03.
49 Declaration No 38 on Article 252 LTFEU regarding the number of Advocates-General.

4

European Union law making

CONTENTS

1. Introduction

Both the Constitutional Treaty and the Lisbon Treaty were concerned with the modalities of Union law-making and its legitimacy. Reform in this field has been particularly intense. This has been brought about not only by the Treaty reform process, but also by institutional and judicial developments, which have led to significant changes in determining the appropriate legal base for Union legislation: the practice of the co-decision procedure, comitology, and 'variable geometry', the process by which a select number of Member States develop Union law.

2. Legal bases for Union legislation

In the *Environmental Crimes* judgment, it will be remembered, the Court ruled that where a measure appeared to fall within the scope of more than one pillar of the TEU, it would not look at the predominant aim and content of the measure – the test for determining the legal base within the EC pillar – but simply at whether the measure fell within EC competencies.[1] If so, the measure should be legally based upon the EC Treaty

---

1 Case C-176/03 *Commission v Council* [2005] ECR I-7879.

since Article 47 TEU stated that the EC Treaty was not to be affected by other TEU provisions. This provoked a great deal of concern amongst national governments as it created the possibility that the EC Treaty would crowd out the other two pillars. In the judgment, to which the discussion now turns, where a measure appeared to fall within both the EC and the third pillar, an unprecedented nineteen national governments intervened to argue that the measure should be adopted under the third pillar. In the *Ship-Source Pollution* judgment the European Parliament and Commission challenged a Framework Decision that provided for Member States to criminalise ship source pollution where it breached Directive 2005/35/EC on ship source pollution and where it caused serious damage to the environment. The Framework Decision also provided a series of minimum criminal penalties for such conduct.

Case C-440/05 *Commission v Council*, Judgment of 23 October 2007

52. Under Article 47 EU, none of the provisions of the EC Treaty is to be affected by a provision of the EU Treaty. The same rule is laid down in the first paragraph of Article 29 EU, which introduces Title VI of the EU Treaty, entitled 'Provisions on police and judicial cooperation in criminal matters'.

53. It is the task of the Court to ensure that acts which, according to the Council, fall within the scope of Title VI do not encroach upon the powers conferred by the EC Treaty on the Community . . .

54. It is therefore necessary to determine whether or not the provisions of Framework Decision 2005/667 affect the Community's competence under Article 80(2) EC, in that they could have been adopted on the basis of that provision, as submitted by the Commission.

55. It should be borne in mind, firstly, that the common transport policy is one of the foundations of the Community, since Article 70 EC, read together with Article 80(1) EC, provides that the objectives of the Treaty are, in matters of transport by rail, road or inland waterway, to be pursued by the Member States within the framework of that policy . . . Next, it should be noted that, under Article 80(2) EC, the Council may decide whether, to what extent and by what procedure appropriate provisions may be laid down for sea transport . . . and the procedural provisions of Article 71 EC are to apply.

. . . .

60. Moreover, since requirements relating to environmental protection, which is one of the essential objectives of the Community . . . , must, according to Article 6 EC, 'be integrated into the definition and implementation of . . . Community policies and activities', such protection must be regarded as an objective which also forms part of the common transport policy. The Community legislature may therefore, on the basis of Article 80(2) EC and in the exercise of the powers conferred on it by that provision, decide to promote environmental protection . . .

66. Although it is true that, as a general rule, neither criminal law nor the rules of criminal procedure fall within the Community's competence . . . the fact remains that when the application of effective, proportionate and dissuasive criminal penalties by the competent national authorities is an essential measure for combating serious environmental offences, the Community legislature may require the Member States to introduce such penalties in order to ensure that the rules which it lays down in that field are fully effective . . .

67. In the present case, the Court finds, firstly, that the provisions laid down in Framework Decision 2005/667 – like those of Framework Decision 2003/80, at issue in the proceedings which gave rise to the judgment in Case C-176/03 *Commission* v *Council* – relate to conduct

which is likely to cause particularly serious environmental damage as a result, in this case, of the infringement of the Community rules on maritime safety.

68. Secondly, it is clear from the third, fourth, fifth, seventh and eighth recitals in the preamble to Directive 2005/35, read in conjunction with the first five recitals in the preamble to Framework Decision 2005/667, that the Council took the view that criminal penalties were necessary to ensure compliance with the Community rules laid down in the field of maritime safety.

69. Accordingly, since Articles 2, 3 and 5 of Framework Decision 2005/667 are designed to ensure the efficacy of the rules adopted in the field of maritime safety, non-compliance with which may have serious environmental consequences, by requiring Member States to apply criminal penalties to certain forms of conduct, those articles must be regarded as being essentially aimed at improving maritime safety, as well as environmental protection, and could have been validly adopted on the basis of Article 80(2) EC.

70. By contrast, and contrary to the submission of the Commission, the determination of the type and level of the criminal penalties to be applied does not fall within the Community's sphere of competence.

In *Ship Source Pollution* the Court of Justice tried to establish an uneasy quid pro quo. On the one hand, it attempted to protect its interpretation of Article 47 TEU, that where a measure falls within the aegis of the EC Treaty and one of the other pillars, the EC Treaty takes precedence. On the other hand, it recognised that the price for securing this interpretation was that it must set the limits of the EC Treaty. It therefore acknowledged that the EC Treaty cannot be used to determine the type and levels of criminal penalties. The difficulty here is, of course, that the Court would be under increased pressure to define the limits of the EC Treaty. Whilst no bad thing, such an exercise is likely to be fraught with legal uncertainty.

The Lisbon Treaty attempts to deflate the debate. Article 47 TEU is abolished. Instead, the first provisions of both the LTEU and the LTFEU indicate that the Treaties are to be of the same legal value.[2] In all instances, the Court will have to look at the predominant aim and content of the measure, and ascribe it accordingly to the appropriate legal base. The question of uncertainty will still hang over this area. For the reality is that a single legal measure will often address multifarious matters (e.g. environmental, single market as well as penal questions). To decide that a measure is more about one matter than another is a highly contrived exercise, which inevitably involves a select foregrounding of certain features of the measure at the expense of others.

3. Union primary legislation

The two central developments concerning EU primary legislation since 2005 have been firstly, the effects of enlargement from fifteen to twenty-seven Member States and secondly, the Treaty of Lisbon. The potential impact of the enlargements was given as a justification for the new institutional reforms proposed by Lisbon. A welter

---

2 Article 1 LTEU and 1(2) LTFEU respectively.

of research since the 2004 enlargement, excellently synthesised by Helen Wallace,[3] suggests, however, that the addition of ten Member States may have changed how decisions are made, but has not clogged up the system as might have been anticipated.

There has been a modest reduction in the volume of legislation (definitive legislative acts) adopted. Over the period 1999–2003 an average of around 195 legislative acts were adopted each year (but only 164 in 2002 and 165 in 2003); around 230 were adopted in 2004 (with a surge in April 2004 just before the EU15 became the EU25); some 130 were adopted in 2005: and 153 in 2006. Data need to be added for non-legislative decisions, increasingly important in fields such as foreign policy and some aspects of justice and home affairs, where activity levels have been high. Mattila reports that some 942 acts other than legislative decisions were agreed between May 2004 and December 2006.[4] Of the 360 legislative decisions adopted between May 2004 and December 2006 some 43 were identified as revisions to existing legislation to incorporate the new member states.[5] Settembri reports that decisions taken show an increase in 'ordinary' or 'minor' subjects, and a decrease of 11 per cent in what he classifies as the more 'important' topics.[6]

There has also been a drop in the proportion of proposals tabled by the Commission that are accepted by the Council: 2003:40 per cent; 2004:44 per cent; 2005:32 per cent, but it should be borne in mind that there is a time lag between proposal and decision. There has been a reduction in the time lag between proposal and decision on both those subject to the unanimity rule and those based on qualified majority voting (QMV) treaty articles. This is so especially for decisions under the consultation procedures with the European Parliament (EP), including many on agricultural issues, where the data indicate a 5 per cent reduction in the time taken to reach agreement.

Issues subject to co-decision take somewhat longer than before. (Settembri notes that during the one-year period which he covers this means some 22 per cent more days).[7] Interestingly, however, a rising proportion of decisions subject to co-decision have been reached at first reading: 2003:34 per cent; 2004:45 per cent; 2005:64 per cent; 2006:59 per cent. In 2006 a revised joint declaration was adopted by the EU institutions, designed to improve the efficiency of the co-decision procedure.

---

3 H. Wallace, 'Adapting to Enlargement of the European Union: Institutional Practice since May 2004' (2008, TEPSA, Brussels) 2–4.

4 M. Mattila, 'Voting and coalitions in the Council after enlargement' in D. Naurin and H. Wallace (eds.) *Unveiling the Council of the European Union: Games Governments Play in Brussels* (Palgrave: Basingstoke, 2008).

5 S. Hagemann and J. De Clerck-Sacchse, *Old Rules, New Game: Decision-Making in the Council of Ministers after the 2004 Enlargement* (CEPS: Brussels, 2007).

6 P. Settembri, *The surgery succeeded. Has the patient died? The impact of enlargement on the European Union*, paper presented at the Global Fellows Forum, NYU Law School, New York: 5 April 2007 accessible at: www.nyulawglobal.org/fellowsscholars/documents/gffsettembripaper.pdf

7 *Ibid.*

The long-established norm of reaching most decisions by consensus-building has persisted since enlargement (Dehousse and Deloche-Gaudet, 2006), on decisions taken under QMV as well as by definition on those requiring unanimity[8] – Mattila (reports that around 90 per cent were by consensus for both legislative and other acts. In 2004 and 2005, in particular, a larger than usual proportion of legislative decisions reached were on issues subject to the unanimity rule. Mattila reports that 76 per cent of legislative decisions reached were subject to the QMV rule, and that of these 82 per cent were reached without explicit contestation, that some 97 per cent of decisions agreed and subject to the unanimity rule were uncontested and also that some 91 per cent of non-legislative acts were agreed without explicit contestation.[9]

All this might suggest that, in terms of the levels of legislation, business continues as usual in the EU. However, this has been achieved at a price. Agreement is now usually reached earlier in the process, namely before the first reading rather than after the second, and informal processes of consensus-building, in particular the trialogue, have acquired an added prominence. One way of seeing this is that the negotiations in the trialogue before the first reading provide a situation in which the three institutions have an equal status. The negotiations are based on the Commission proposal and it, together with the Council representatives, can defeat any Parliament amendment. Similarly, the European Parliament and the Council can together significantly rewrite a Commission proposal. Finally, as the Council can only introduce its own amendments by unanimity, the Commission and Parliament are often placed in a strong negotiating position to assert a common agenda.

This formal-institutional analysis is, however, simplistic. It ignores that one of the central legitimating structures in parliamentary law-making is its 'publicity'. Legislation is debated and negotiated in public thereby presenting an opportunity for accountability, reflection and deliberation. Informal deals short-circuit this. They also undermine the culture of internal pluralism and limit the possibility of checks and balances within each Institution. The European Parliament, for example, is a body which now articulates a wide variety of interests and viewpoints. If legislation is agreed after only one reading, with its representatives in the trialogue only talking to the chairs of the relevant Committees or the heads of the main political groups, then the majority of its members are being kept out of the loop.

The other concern is that generated by the culture of consensus described by Wallace. The desire to give something to everyone has led to an increase in the length of legislative documents by an average of 15 per cent.[10] Apart from this making

8 R. Dehousse, F. Deloche-Gaudet and O. Duhamel (eds.) *Élargissement: Comment l'Europe s'adapte*, (Paris: Sciences Po, Les Presses, 2006).
9 Supra n. 4.
10 E. Best and P. Settembri, 'Legislative output after enlargement: similar number shifting nature' in E. Best *et al.* (eds.) *The institutions of the Enlarged European Union: Changes and Continuity* (Elgar: Cheltenham, 2008).

legislation more complex and difficult to apply, there must also be concerns about the coherence of such an approach. There is a danger that lengthy legislation contains an unhealthy number of qualifications, thereby limiting its ability to meet its own objectives. There is also the possibility that it is full of exemptions benefiting select interest groups who have succeeded in making their voices heard.

These concerns were not directly addressed in the Lisbon Treaty, and the new institutional dynamics are unacknowledged. Instead, the central concern in the Treaty has been to grant the European Parliament more legislative powers. The co-decision procedure is extended to govern forty new fields. While eight of these are procedural or institutional and one budgetary, thirty-one are substantive policy fields which are, for the first time, governed by the co-decision procedure. The central developments occur in the fields of:

- Internal market – law-making on services of general economic interest, freedom to provide services, movement of capital to third countries and intellectual property.
- External relations – humanitarian aid and common commercial policy.
- Freedom, security and justice – border checks, immigration, police cooperation and judicial cooperation in criminal matters.
- EMU – multilateral surveillance and the use of the euro.
- Miscellaneous policies – agriculture and fisheries, structural and cohesion policy, transport, space, energy, tourism, sport, civil protection and the European Research Area.

This catalogue of fields indicates both qualitatively and quantitatively a significant extension of the co-decision procedure. Prior to Lisbon, figures suggest that at least as many if not more measures were adopted under the consultation procedure as under co-decision.[11] This will certainly not be the case post Lisbon and this is reflected in the procedure's name being changed to the ordinary legislative procedure.

The European Parliament's position has also been strengthened by amendments to two further provisions. The first provision is the legal base for the adoption of measures outlawing discrimination on grounds of sex, racial or ethnic origin, religion or belief, disability, age or sexual orientation,[12] and the second is that which allows the Union to adopt measures to realise its objectives where other procedures do not provide the necessary powers for it to do so. Both these provisions will no longer be based on the consultation procedure, but on the assent procedure, under which Parliament must positively agree to the adoption or repeal of a measure. The first legal base does not support large quantities of legislation, but significant and iconic legislation in the form of anti-discrimination law. The second generates, by contrast,

---

11 In 2005 and 2006, it was calculated that 281 acts were adopted under consultation and 205 under co-decision. Dataset provided to the author by S. Hix extrapolated from T. König, B. Luetgert and T. Dannwolf (2006) 'Quantifying European legislative research' (2006) 7 *EUP* 555 (available on request).
12 Article 19 LTFEU.

about thirty–forty pieces of legislation per annum, some significant and others less so.[13] If these two procedures, which involve co-equality between the Parliament and the Council, are placed alongside the extension of co-decision, we have a situation in which the Parliament is placed, for the first time, at the centre of the vast majority of significant Union law-making.

4. Enhanced cooperation

The procedures on enhanced cooperation are reorganised only to a minor extent in the Lisbon Treaty. The provision setting out the central principles is Article 20 LTEU.

> **Article 20(1) LTEU** Member States which wish to establish enhanced cooperation between themselves within the framework of the Union's non-exclusive competences may make use of its institutions and exercise those competences by applying the relevant provisions of the Treaties, subject to the limits and in accordance with the detailed arrangements laid down in this Article and in Articles 326 to 334 TFEU.[14]
>
> Enhanced cooperation shall aim to further the objectives of the Union, protect its interests and reinforce its integration process. Such cooperation shall be open at any time to all Member States, in accordance with Article 328 TFEU.
>
> 2. The decision authorising enhanced cooperation shall be adopted by the Council as a last resort, when it has established that the objectives of such cooperation cannot be attained within a reasonable period by the Union as a whole, and provided that at least nine Member States participate in it. The Council shall act in accordance with the procedure laid down in Article 329 TFEU.
>
> 3. All members of the Council may participate in its deliberations, but only members of the Council representing the Member States participating in enhanced cooperation shall take part in the vote. The voting rules are set out in Article 330 TFEU.
>
> 4. Acts adopted in the framework of enhanced cooperation shall bind only participating Member States. They shall not be regarded as part of the acquis which has to be accepted by candidate States for accession to the Union.

The only significant difference is that a minimum of nine rather than eight Member States are now required to trigger enhanced cooperation. Alongside this, there is the Protocol on the Schengen Acquis Integrated into the Framework of the European Union. This Protocol, it will be remembered, provides that the Schengen acquis, which sets out a series of measures on the abolition of internal border checks and heightened policing of external borders, shall form part of Union law. It defines the relationship between those States which have fully accepted the acquis, and non-participating States, notably Ireland and the United Kingdom. Article 4 of the Protocol provides that either of these Member States may request to take part in any part or all of the acquis, so long as all other Member States consent. This is, of course, in contrast, to

---

13 R. Schütze, 'Organized Change towards an "Ever closer Union" Article 308 EC and the limits to the Community's legislative competence' (2003) 22 *YEL* 79.

14 These are identical to the procedures and principles current set out in Articles 11 EC, 27 TEU, 43–45 TEU.

the situation concerning general provisions on Enhanced Cooperation, involvement in which does not require such consent. Article 4 also contrasts with Article 5 of the Protocol, which allows the United Kingdom and Ireland to participate in proposals building upon the acquis without the consent of the other States if they notify them within a reasonable period of time. The relationship between Articles 4 and 5 and the Protocol was considered for the first time in two cases brought by the United Kingdom against two measures. The first case concerned Regulation 2007/2004 establishing the European Agency for the Management of Operational Cooperation at the External Borders of the Member States, and the second addressed the introduction of common security features and biometric identifiers into passports.[15] These Regulations had been adopted under the Schengen Protocol, thereby excluding the United Kingdom. Article 62(2)(a) EC provides for the adoption of EC legislation on the standards and procedures to be applied at checks at the external borders of the Member States. On the face of it, the United Kingdom can participate freely within this procedure, and it was argued this should allow it to participate in the measures.

Case C-77/05 United Kingdom v Council, Judgment of 18 December 2007

57. In so far as the United Kingdom and Ireland were the only Member States which were not parties to the Schengen Agreements that constitute the foundation of that closer cooperation, those two States were in a special situation, which the Schengen Protocol took into account in two respects.

58. First, as Article 4 of the Schengen Protocol provides, that protocol reserves to those two Member States the right to apply at any time to take part in only certain provisions of the acquis in force on the date of the application to take part. Second, that protocol reserves to those Member States, under the second subparagraph of Article 5(1), the option of not taking part in proposals and initiatives to build upon that acquis.

59. While those two provisions thus relate to two different aspects of the Schengen acquis, it cannot however be inferred from that circumstance alone that they must be read independently of each other.

60. As follows from the use by the first subparagraph of Article 5(1) of the Schengen Protocol of the words 'proposals and initiatives to build upon the Schengen acquis', the measures referred to in that provision are based on the Schengen acquis within the meaning of Article 4 of that protocol, of which they constitute merely an implementation or further development.

61. Logically, such measures must be consistent with the provisions they implement or develop, so that they presuppose the acceptance both of those provisions and of the principles on which those provisions are based.

62. It follows that the participation of a Member State in the adoption of a measure pursuant to Article 5(1) of the Schengen Protocol is conceivable only to the extent that that State has accepted the area of the Schengen acquis which is the context of the measure or of which it is a development.

---

15 Case C-77/05 *United Kingdom v Council*, Judgment of 18 December 2007. Case C-137/05 *United Kingdom v Council*, Judgment of 18 December 2007.

63. In those circumstances, since Article 4 of the Schengen Protocol provides for the possibility of the United Kingdom and Ireland joining in the Schengen acquis, those Member States cannot be allowed to take part in the adoption of a measure under Article 5(1) of that protocol without first having been authorised by the Council to accept the area of the acquis on which that measure is based.

64. Furthermore, the above interpretation is in keeping with the purpose both of Article 4 of the Schengen Protocol and of Article 5 of that protocol, and is such as to ensure the full effectiveness of each of those provisions.

65. That interpretation does not in any way interfere with the possibility, reserved to the United Kingdom and Ireland by the second subparagraph of Article 5(1) of the Schengen Protocol, of choosing, even when those Member States have been authorised to accept part or all of the Schengen acquis, not to take part in the adoption of measures implementing or developing the parts of the acquis which they have been authorised to accept . . .

76. In so far as the exercise by the United Kingdom of the option to take part in the adoption of a proposal presented pursuant to the provisions of Title IV is not, in accordance with Article 3(1) of the Protocol on Title IV, subject to compliance with any condition other than the notification period laid down by that provision, the classification of Regulation No 2007/2004 as a measure developing provisions of the Schengen acquis had a direct effect on the rights of that Member State.

77. Consequently, and by analogy with what applies in relation to the choice of the legal basis of a Community act, it must be concluded that in a situation such as that at issue in the present case the classification of a Community act as a proposal or initiative to build upon the Schengen acquis within the meaning of the first subparagraph of Article 5(1) of the Schengen Protocol must rest on objective factors which are amenable to judicial review, including in particular the aim and the content of the act . . . .

83. It should be recalled . . . that both the title of the Schengen Agreement and the fourth recital in its preamble and Article 17 of the agreement show that its principal objective was the abolition of checks on persons at the common borders of the Member States and the transfer of those checks to their external borders. The importance of that objective in the context of the Schengen Agreements is underlined by the place occupied in the Implementing Convention by the provisions on the crossing of external borders, and by the fact that, under Articles 6 and 7 of that convention, checks at external borders are to be carried out in accordance with uniform principles, with the Member States having to implement constant and close cooperation in order to ensure that those checks are carried out effectively.

84. It follows that checks on persons at the external borders of the Member States and consequently the effective implementation of the common rules on standards and procedures for those checks must be regarded as constituting elements of the Schengen acquis.

85. Since . . . . Regulation No 2007/2004 is intended, as regards both its purpose and its content, to improve those checks, that regulation must be regarded as constituting a measure to build upon the Schengen acquis within the meaning of the first subparagraph of Article 5(1) of the Schengen Protocol.

This reasoning is open to criticism on a number of fronts. The relationship between the Schengen Protocol and the legal bases governing the area of freedom, security and justice is expressed in particularly poor terms. The Schengen Convention and its acquis govern not just external border controls, but also visa policy, asylum, immigration, policing as well as conditions of residence of non-EU nationals. In principle, following this judgment, the United Kingdom and Ireland cannot participate in any of these fields unless other Member States consent as these are governed by the Schengen acquis. This is not only highly exclusionary and at odds with the general tenet of enhanced cooperation but it seems, bizarrely, that the Protocol takes precedence over the Treaty provisions rather than the other way around. The argument the Court makes about coherence is an odd one. Although the Court does not like it when a Member State refuses to participate in the original acquis, but then expresses interest in participating in subsequent measures which build upon it, it is perfectly happy with the converse, namely a Member State participating in the original acquis, but not in all subsequent measures.

5. Comitology

The central concern of recent years has been the question of how to increase the European Parliament's powers of scrutiny over the procedures.[16] As early as 2002, the Commission proposed to submit the Commission's delegated powers to the joint supervision of the European Parliament and the Council.[17] The Constitutional Treaty also gave both parties the right to revoke any delegation and to object to any delegated measure. Following the non-ratification of the Constitutional Treaty, the Parliament increased its campaign for greater powers, most notably in fields governed by the co-decision procedure. Delegation by the Commission in such fields served to deprive the Parliament of its power of co-legislation. There was also a technical question about whether such delegation was lawful since Article 202 EC only allows delegation of measures taken by the Council, whereas measures taken under co-decision are, of course, adopted by both the Council and the Parliament.

In 2006, a compromise was reached with the establishment of a fourth procedure, the regulatory committee with scrutiny in Decision 2006/512.[18] The procedure applies only to delegated legislation amending legislation which implements a measure adopted under co-decision either by supplementing or repealing the existing measure.

As with the other procedures, the Commission submits a draft to the Committee. The first change occurs where the Committee approves it by qualified majority. The normal regulatory committee procedure would assume the draft to be adopted. Under

---

16 For a good discussion of the background and content of the 2006 reform see G. Schusterschitz and S. Kotz, 'The comitology reform of 2006: increasing the power of the European Parliament without changing the Treaties' (2007) 3 *European Constitutional Law Review* (*ECLR*) 68.
17 EC Commission, Proposal for a Council Decision amending Decision 1999/468/EC laying down the procedures for the exercise of implementing powers conferred on the Commission, COM (2002) 719.
18 Decision 2006/512/EC amending Decision 1999/468/EC laying down the procedures for the exercise of implementing powers conferred on the Commission, OJ 2006, L 200/11.

the regulatory committee with scrutiny, the measure is forwarded to the Council and the Parliament. Either may, within three months, veto the measure on one of three grounds:

- it exceeds the implementing powers provided in the basic instrument;
- it is not compatible with the aim or the content of the basic instrument;
- it does not respect the principles of subsidiarity or proportionality.[19]

If the measure is not in accordance with the view of the Committee or it issues no opinion, the following procedure applies:

> **Article 5a (4) (a)** The Commission shall without delay submit a proposal relating to the measures to be taken to the Council and shall forward it to the European Parliament at the same time;
> (b) the Council shall act on the proposal by a qualified majority within two months from the date of referral to it;
> (c) if, within that period, the Council opposes the proposed measures by a qualified majority, the measures shall not be adopted. In that event, the Commission may submit to the Council an amended proposal or present a legislative proposal on the basis of the Treaty;
> (d) if the Council envisages adopting the proposed measures it shall without delay submit them to the European Parliament. If the Council does not act within the two month period, the Commission shall without delay submit the measures for scrutiny by the European Parliament;
> (e) the European Parliament, acting by a majority of its component members within four months from the forwarding of the proposal in accordance with point (a), may oppose the adoption of the measures in question, justifying their opposition by indicating that the proposed measures exceed the implementing powers provided for in the basic instrument or are not compatible with the aim or the content of the basic instrument or do not respect the principles of subsidiarity or proportionality;
> (f) if, within that period, the European Parliament opposes the proposed measures, the latter shall not be adopted. In that event, the Commission may submit to the Committee an amended draft of the measures or present a legislative proposal on the basis of the Treaty;
> (g) if, on expiry of that period, the European Parliament has not opposed the proposed measures, the latter shall be adopted by the Council or by the Commission, as the case may be.

The bottom line of this convoluted procedure is that either the Council or the Parliament can always veto any Commission draft on the grounds that it exceeds the implementing powers provided in the basic instrument, is not compatible with its aim or content, or violates the subsidiarity or proportionality principles. In addition, if the draft is not approved by the Committee, the Council may oppose the measure by qualified majority or propose an alternative measure on any ground it wishes.

19 Article 5a(3)(b). The Council votes by qualified majority and the Parliament by a majority of its component members.

This raises a number of contradictions. The clear message from the 'regulatory committee with scrutiny' is that Committees are poor guardians of the subsidiarity and proportionality principles. In addition, they have scant regard to the scope and content of the parent instrument. If that is so, the question has to be asked why this procedure is confined to amending measures that fall under the co-decision procedure since the issue seems a general one that could occur anywhere within the comitology system. The other contradiction of the procedure is the high voting thresholds for the Parliament and Council, an absolute and qualified majority respectively, to veto measures or, in the Council's case, adopt alternatives. This can lead to a situation where a draft can be adopted even where it does not command the majority of support of both the Council and Parliament members who voted on it – this seems wrong, particularly where objections centre either on violation of the subsidiarity principle or on exceeding the powers granted to the Commission.

The procedures will be further revised if the Lisbon Treaty comes into effect. The Treaty proposes a further reform of comitology, which echoes exactly the reforms suggested by the Constitutional Treaty.

> **Article 290 (1) LTFEU** A legislative act may delegate to the Commission the power to adopt non legislative acts to supplement or amend certain non-essential elements of the legislative act.
>
> The objectives, content, scope and duration of the delegation of power shall be explicitly defined in the legislative acts. The essential elements of an area shall be reserved for the legislative act and accordingly shall not be the subject of a delegation of power.
>
> 2. Legislative acts shall explicitly lay down the conditions to which the delegation is subject; these conditions may be as follows:
>
> (a) the European Parliament or the Council may decide to revoke the delegation;
>
> (b) the delegated act may enter into force only if no objection has been expressed by the European Parliament or the Council within a period set by the legislative act.
>
> For the purposes of (a) and (b), the European Parliament shall act by a majority of its component members, and the Council by a qualified majority

The new framework places the Parliament on an equal footing with the Council. It allows conditions to be inserted into any parent instrument permitting either institution to revoke the delegation or to veto any piece of delegated legislation – a practice one can imagine taking place as a matter of course. Unlike the regulatory procedure, in the case of scrutiny, the reasons for revocation or veto do not have to be limited to those outlined above. If this is so, Article 290 LTFEU is an indictment of the current situation. It suggests no real trust in the Committees to act as a check on the Commission, in allowing either of the institutions to veto a measure irrespective of the Committees' views.

The new procedures will depend a great deal upon the capacity of the Council and the Parliament to monitor the activities of the Commission in terms of its delegation of legislation. The complexity and amount of legislation suggest that this could be a daunting task, particularly in light of the European Parliament's limited resources. This, combined with the high voting thresholds and the limited time available to them to take a decision, suggests that these seemingly wide-ranging formal powers might be of rhetorical rather than practical value.

6. The democratic deficit and the legislative process

(i)   Representative democracy

A central feature of the Lisbon Treaty is that the Union is to be recast around certain principles of democracy, most notably that of representative democracy.

> **Article 10(1) LTEU** The functioning of the Union shall be founded on representative democracy.
> 2. Citizens are directly represented at Union level in the European Parliament. Member States are represented in the European Council by their Heads of State or Government and in the Council by their governments, themselves democratically accountable either to their national Parliaments, or to their citizens.

This provision is a little odd as its principles of representation are unclear. Representation relies upon the idea of some prior public or political community, which is then represented by institutions, which are also to be representative of it. Although Article 10 LTEU acknowledges that there is no exclusive European political community observed simply through the representation of European citizens by the European Parliament, it does suggest that two particular entities be represented: the European citizen and the Member State. This implies that the only political communities are those of European citizens and of national governments. This is a highly attenuated view of representative democracy and political community. On this view the United Nations comes close to a world representative democracy, as States are represented and arguably, the citizens of the world through its 'universally' applicable human rights instruments. This is highly contentious. No mention is made in the LTEU of local, regional or national representative democracy, nor of the ideas of political community and political membership constituted by these. Yet, in *Brunner*, the German Constitutional Court observed that the principle of representative democracy was constituted most axiomatically at a national level and this was institutionalised most centrally in national parliament.[20]

The Lisbon Treaty does provide for an increased role for national parliaments. Significantly, this is in a separate provision, suggesting that they are not to be at the heart of the Union, but are instead to remain secondary players.

---

20 *Brunner v TEU* [1994] 1 *CMLR* 57.

Article 12 LTEU National Parliaments contribute actively to the good functioning of the Union:

(a) through being informed by the institutions of the Union and having draft legislative acts of the Union forwarded to them in accordance with the Protocol on the role of national Parliaments in the European Union;

(b) by seeing to it that the principle of subsidiarity is respected in accordance with the procedures provided for in the Protocol on the application of the principles of subsidiarity and proportionality;

(c) by taking part, within the framework of the area of freedom, security and justice, in the evaluation mechanisms for the implementation of the Union policies in that area, in accordance with Article 70 TFEU, and through being involved in the political monitoring of Europol and the evaluation of Eurojust's activities in accordance with Articles 88 and 85 of that Treaty;

(d) by taking part in the revision procedures of the Treaties, in accordance with Article 48 of this Treaty;

(e) by being notified of applications for accession to the Union, in accordance with Article 49 of this Treaty;

(f) by taking part in the interparliamentary cooperation between national Parliaments and with the European Parliament, in accordance with the Protocol on the role of national Parliaments in the European Union.

The provision details, very helpfully, the roles of national Parliaments in the European Union.

First, the Lisbon Treaty provides for greater involvement in the pre-legislative and legislative processes. A new Protocol on the Role of National Parliaments in the EU has been established, which augments their position in a number of ways.

- All draft legislative acts will be sent directly to national parliaments, rather than to national governments to pass on to national Parliaments.
- National parliaments will also be sent the annual legislative programme, as well as any policy or legislative planning instrument.
- All agendas and minutes of Council meetings will be sent to national parliaments.
- An eight-week period will elapse between a draft legislative act being sent to national parliaments and its being placed on the agenda of the Council.

Arguably the most significant and most controversial of these is the eight-week period introduced to give national parliaments time to consider legislative drafts and have an input in the process. There is considerable doubt about whether it will be sufficient.[21] To put this in perspective, the Commission allows a period of eight weeks for private parties to make submissions in its consultative procedures.[22] Considering that national parliaments represent a wider array of interests and are

---

21 House of Lords European Union Committee, *The Treaty of Lisbon: An Impact Assessment* (2008, 10th Report, TSO) paras. 11.50–11.53.

22 See n. 31.

charged with more significant responsibilities, giving them the same time period to intervene seems unjustified. Notwithstanding this, the Commission's policy of dealing directly with national parliaments seems to have borne some fruit. Since 2006, it has instigated a procedure whereby it sends its proposals directly to national parliaments, who also return their opinions straight to the Commission.[23] Between October and December 2006 the Commission received 167 opinions from 27 national assemblies in 17 Member States concerning 82 Commission documents. However, whilst the number of opinions were substantial, four Chambers – the Czech Senate, the German Bundesrat, the French Senate and the UK House of Lords – were responsible for ninety-two of these.[24] These are all second Chambers, and their predominance suggests both a danger of asymmetric representation where assemblies with stronger capacity or interest are more actively involved, as well as a problem of benign neglect, where the more powerful first chambers are notable by their absence.

More generally, the reforms are conservative when compared to some of the ideas discussed at the *Future of Europe* Convention. In particular, the Working Party on National Parliaments suggested that where a national parliament opposed a measure, a 'reserve' be indicated on the Council agenda setting this out.[25] This might be introduced via the Council's Rules of Procedure, but has not been introduced as a Treaty amendment. In like vein, whilst the Protocol makes provision for the annual legislative strategy to be forwarded to national parliaments, there is no provision for their involvement in its formulation.

The second set of reforms involves a greater monitoring role for national parliaments. The most salient role is that of policing the legislative process for compliance with the subsidiarity principle.[26] This is dealt with in more detail in chapter 5, but, in brief, national parliaments can issue reasoned opinions indicating that a proposal does not comply with the subsidiarity principle. If sufficient national parliaments indicate their opposition on these grounds, there is an onus on the EU institutions to justify the measure and consider withdrawing it. They are also to have a reinforced role in the field of freedom, security and justice. They are to be involved in Union evaluation of national implementation of Union policies in this field as well as in the evaluation and scrutiny of the two Union institutions unique to this field – Eurojust, which is responsible for coordinating investigations and prosecutions, and Europol, a body established to assist and coordinate the transnational policing of crime.

The third set of reforms concern the role of national parliaments in the 'constitution-making' of the Union. They are to be notified of any application for

---

23 EC Commission, *A Citizens' Agenda – Delivering Results for Europe*, COM (2006) 211 final.
24 *General Report on the Activities of the European Union 2007* (2008, EC Commission, Brussels) 229–30.
25 Final Report of Working Group IV on National Parliaments CONV 353/02, para 20.
26 Protocol on the Role of National Parliaments in the European Union, Article 3.

Union membership by a European State. Perhaps more central is their new role in any revision of the Treaties. A new ordinary revision procedure is established whereby any national government, the Commission or the Parliament can propose amendments to the Treaties limiting or enlarging competencies. These will be examined by the European Council who may then establish a Convention to determine the amendments to the Treaties, which must then be ratified by the Member States.[27] This Convention shall comprise, inter alia, representatives of national parliaments. There is also provision made for a simplified revision procedure. This allows the European Council to move any procedure which is currently subject to a unanimity vote to a qualified majority vote without the need for ratification by all the Member States. In such circumstances, national parliaments will be notified and if any national parliament objects the amendment will not take place.[28]

The final reform set out in Article 12(f) LTEU concerns the role of COSAC. It is formally granted one additional role that it has in practice exercised for some time, namely promoting the exchange of information and best practice.[29] In order to ascertain how the principle of subsidiarity is interpreted by the different national parliaments, in 2007, COSAC asked them all to vet two Commission proposals for compliance with the principle, one proposal on the applicable law in matrimonial matters, and the other on the liberalisation of postal services. It also carried out a survey on practice and opinions about the new Commission mechanism establishing direct dialogues with national parliaments.[30] Although seemingly minor, this new formal role for COSAC institutionalises an important transformation. It has become a more pro-active and salient forum for coordinating and instigating national parliament activities, concerned not so much with fostering European integration as safeguarding their prerogatives and securing the subsidiarity principle. Whilst this is no doubt to be welcomed, it provides further support for the vision that national parliaments are not to be agenda-setters and equals of the other bodies involved in the making of Union law and policy, but are instead simply there as reactive bodies to secure existing national status quos. Bracketing national parliaments in this manner creates an unhealthy dialectic and underplays their potential for a more pro-active contribution to the integration project.

(ii) Participatory democracy

The Lisbon Treaty formalises the processes set in motion by its 2001 Governance agenda in which the Commission commits itself to engage with civil society and

---

27 Article 48(3) LTEU.   28 Article 48(7) LTEU.
29 Protocol on the Role of National Parliaments in the European Union, Article 10.
30 *Seventh bi-annual report: Developments in European Union Procedures and Practices Relevant to Parliamentary Scrutiny* (COSAC, Brussels, May 2007).

consult widely prior to making its legislative proposals. The three underlying principles are participation, transparency and pluralism in the consultations.

> **Article 11(1) LTEU** The institutions shall, by appropriate means, give citizens and representative associations the opportunity to make known and publicly exchange their views in all areas of Union action.
> 2. The institutions shall maintain an open, transparent and regular dialogue with representative associations and civil society.
> 3. The European Commission shall carry out broad consultations with parties concerned in order to ensure that the Union's actions are coherent and transparent.

These principles were fleshed out in the 2002 Commission Communication on General Standards and Minimum Principles for Consultation.[31] Here, the Commission imposed responsibilities on both itself and those lobbying. The Commission's responsibilities are as follows:

> **The content of consultation is to be clear**: The Commission should set out a summary of the context, scope and objectives of consultation, including a description of the specific issues open for discussion or questions with particular importance for the Commission. It should make available details of any hearings, meetings or conferences, as well contact details and information on deadlines. It should provide explanation of the Commission processes for dealing with contributions, what feed-back to expect, and details of the next stages involved in the development of the policy.
>
> **Relevant parties should have an opportunity to express their opinions**: In its consultations, the Commission should ensure adequate coverage of those affected by the policy, those who will be involved in implementation of the policy, or bodies that have stated objectives giving them a direct interest in the policy. In determining the relevant parties for consultation, it should take into account the impact of the policy on other policy areas, the need for specific experience, expertise or technical knowledge, the need to involve non-organised interests. It should consider the track record of participants in previous consultations as well as the need for a proper balance between representatives of social and economic bodies, large and small organisations or companies, wider constituencies (such as churches and religious communities) and specific target groups (for example women, the elderly, the unemployed, or ethnic minorities).
>
> **The Commission should publish consultations widely**: This is via the web portal, 'Your Voice in Europe'[32] which is the Commission's single access point for consultation.

---

31 EC Commission, 'General principles and minimum standards for consultation of interested parties by the Commission', COM(2002) 704. See D. Obradovic and J. Vizcaino, 'Good governance requirements concerning the participation of interest groups in EU consultations' (2004) 43 *CMLR* 1049.
32 http://ec.europa.eu/yourvoice/consultations/index_en.htm

Participants are to be given sufficient time to respond: The Commission should allow at least eight weeks for reception of responses to written public consultations and 20 working days notice for meetings.

Acknowledgement and adequate feedback is to be provided: Receipt of contributions should be acknowledged and the results displayed on websites. Explanatory memoranda accompanying legislative proposals following a consultation process must include the results of these consultations, an explanation as to how these were conducted and how the results were taken into account in the proposal.

The Communication also imposes some responsibilities on lobbyists. Representative institutions must set out which interests they represent and how inclusive that representation is. If they fail to do so, their submission, though not disqualified, will be treated as an individual submission and given less weight. In a review of the procedure, the Commission identified the thinness of these responsibilities as the central weakness. It has therefore committed itself to establishing a voluntary register for lobbyists.[33] Membership will only be available to those who observe a Code of Conduct for Lobbyists, which will involve a far greater disclosure of information about the lobbyist and the organisations they represent and include sanctions for non-compliance. Whilst membership is voluntary, the clear implication is that the Commission will listen more carefully to those on the register as it can be surer about their credibility.

The Lisbon Treaty also establishes one innovatory mechanism of participatory democracy, that of the citizens' initiative.

> **Article 11(4) LTEU** Not less than one million citizens who are nationals of a significant number of Member States may take the initiative of inviting the European Commission, within the framework of its powers, to submit any appropriate proposal on matters where citizens consider that a legal act of the Union is required for the purpose of implementing the Treaties.

The precise modalities governing this initiative, such as the number of Member States from which the citizens must come and the normative force of this invitation, will be set out by Union legislation.[34] Undoubtedly, the devil will be in the detail as these conditions may limit the force of the citizens' initiative and the ease with which it can be deployed. The ethos of the citizens' initiative is to bring Europe closer to its citizens through the institutions being more responsive to particular claims. There is a tension between this and the ethos of representative democracy because the citizens' initiative is not representative of anything more than its one million signatures. Insofar as these can be easily collected by newspapers, websites, trade

---

33 EC Commission, Follow-up to the Green Paper 'European transparency initiative', COM (2007) 127.
34 Article 24 LTFEU.

associations or social movements, it allows – if the Commission is required to act on these – a variety of civil society actors to hijack the legislative process to the disadvantage of representative institutions, such as the Council, national parliaments and the European Parliament. There is also a danger that the Commission will be led to disregard the general good by responding specifically to the interests represented in the initiative, which may, after all, constitute around only 2 per cent of the Union population.

5

Sovereignty and federalism: the authority of EU law and its limits

1. Introduction

EU law has followed three trajectories in this field in recent years. First, the Lisbon Treaty sought to recodify and strengthen the principles underpinning the sovereignty of EU law, namely the primacy of Union law over national law, the competence of the Union to determine the limits and nature of its authority and the fidelity principle requiring all public institutions to secure its effective application and enforcement.[1] In recodifying them, new language is used, recasting the principles in creating new possibilities for legal interpretation and construction. The second development is the increasing contestation of the authority of Union law by national constitutional courts, most notably those of the new Member States. The States acceding since 2004 have all had to consider the authority of Union law within their respective territories, and this has necessarily provoked a rethinking of the subject in general terms that extends beyond the region. The third trajectory is a desire by Member States to give greater institutional bite to the subsidiarity principle both by placing stronger ex ante controls on the enactment of EU legislation, and by involving national parliaments more extensively in the policing of the principle.

---

1 See pp. 185–6 of the main text.

2. Sovereignty of Union law

(i)   The primacy of Union law

The Lisbon Treaty has no equivalent of Article I-13 of the Constitutional Treaty which set out the principle of primacy of Union law over national law in the main text of the Treaty. Instead, a Declaration is attached to the Treaties.

> **Declaration 17** The Conference recalls that, in accordance with well settled case law of the Court of Justice of the European Union, the Treaties and the law adopted by the Union on the basis of the Treaties have primacy over the law of Member States, under the conditions laid down by the said case law.

An Opinion of the Council Legal Service was also attached, which provides only sparse information.

> **Opinion of the Council Legal Service, EU Council Doc 11197/07, 22 June 2007**
>
> It results from the case-law of the Court of Justice that primacy of EC law is a cornerstone principle of Community law. According to the Court, this principle is inherent to the specific nature of the European Community. At the time of the first judgement of this established case-law (Costa/ENEL, 15 July 1964, Case 6/64) there was no mention of primacy in the treaty. It is still the case today. The fact that the principle of primacy will not be included in the future treaty shall not in any way change the existence of the principle and the existing case-law of the Court of Justice.

A minimalist interpretation of these documents is that nothing can be read into the Lisbon Treaty's failure to introduce a primacy provision. They provide a reassurance of continuity that the tradition of primacy established since *Costa* is uninterrupted.[2] A more integrationist interpretation would take note of this being the first time that the *Costa* case law of the Court of Justice has been explicitly endorsed and ratified by all Member States. Such ratification perhaps not only gives the interpretation greater legitimacy, but renders the conclusion that the primacy of Union law can no longer be relegated as merely the view of the Court of Justice, but now represents the political consensus as to the status of Union law.

Even if this latter interpretation is more persuasive, there still remains the question of its implications. It seems constitutionally inappropriate that a treaty ratification exercise could supplant processes of constitution-making or constitutional adjudication which have determined the basic norms and constitutive principles guiding national legal and political systems. Although it may be unlikely that the Declaration can be seen as determinative of the status of Union law, it nevertheless seems a powerful message to constitutional courts. It suggests that not only do national governments

2 Case 6/64 *Costa v ENEL* [1964] ECR 585.

wish to accord primacy to Union law, but also, insofar as the Lisbon Treaty has gone through the ratification processes, so do national parliaments. Pursuant to this, were a national constitutional court to deny the primacy of Union law, it would be placing itself in an institutionally isolated position.

(ii)   The allocation of competencies

The Lisbon Treaty takes up an ambition of the Constitutional Treaty to catalogue Union competencies, both to secure greater transparency in the Union's activities, as well as to set out a clearer division between Union and national competencies.[3] In Article 2 LTFEU the different types of competence enjoyed by the Union are detailed explicitly for the first time.

> **Article 2 (1) LTFEU** When the Treaties confer on the Union exclusive competence in a specific area, only the Union may legislate and adopt legally binding acts, the Member States being able to do so themselves only if so empowered by the Union or for the implementation of acts of the Union.
>
> 2. When the Treaties confer on the Union a competence shared with the Member States in a specific area, the Union and the Member States may legislate and adopt legally binding acts in that area. The Member States shall exercise their competence to the extent that the Union has not exercised its competence. The Member States shall exercise their competence again to the extent that the Union has decided to cease exercising its competence.
>
> 3. The Member States shall coordinate their economic and employment policies within arrangements as determined by this Treaty, which the Union shall have competence to provide.
>
> 4. The Union shall have competence, in accordance with the provisions of the Treaty on European Union, to define and implement a common foreign and security policy, including the progressive framing of a common defence policy.
>
> 5. In certain areas and under the conditions laid down in the Treaties, the Union shall have competence to carry out actions to support, coordinate or supplement the actions of the Member States, without thereby superseding their competence in these areas. Legally binding acts of the Union adopted on the basis of the provisions in the Treaties relating to these areas shall not entail harmonisation of Member States' laws or regulations.

The subsequent provisions set out which policies fall within each type of competence. The central ones are:

> **Exclusive competence**: customs union; the establishing of the competition rules necessary for the functioning of the internal market; monetary policy for the Member States whose currency is the euro; (d) the conservation of marine biological resources under the common fisheries policy; common commercial policy.[4]

---

3 F. Mayer, 'Competences—reloaded? The vertical division of powers in the EU and the new European constitution' (2005) 3 *I-CON* 493.
4 Article 3 LTFEU.

Supporting, coordinating and supplementing action: protection and improvement of human health; industry; culture; tourism; education, vocational training, youth and sport; civil protection; administrative cooperation.[5]

Shared competence: internal market; social policy; economic, social and territorial cohesion; agriculture and fisheries, excluding the conservation of marine biological resources; environment; consumer protection; transport; trans-European networks; energy; area of freedom, security and justice; common safety concerns in public health matters.[6]

This categorisation has inevitably encountered certain policies which are not easily compartmentalised in such a manner. The consequence is that there is a little untidiness and tradition which seems to have served as the central basis for the allocation of competencies. In line with the Court of Justice's case law,[7] therefore, the Union will have exclusive competence in the field of international agreements, but only if certain conditions are met, namely either a Union legislative act provides for them, they are necessary to enable the Union to exercise its internal competence, or their conclusion may affect common rules or alter the scope of these. Similarly, the field of public health is a matter of shared competence for the purpose of alleviating certain common safety concerns stipulated in the Treaty,[8] but otherwise the Union is only to take supporting action. Four fields: development, humanitarian aid, research and development and space, are treated as fields of shared competence, but Union legislation on such matters is to be accorded no preemptive effect so that it does not prevent Member States exercising their competences.[9]

A stronger criticism is that the provisions send contradictory messages about the question of competence creep. The explicit listing of competencies evinces an intention to guard against possible creep. A Protocol on the Exercise of Shared Competence was also adopted which seeks to confine the doctrine of preemption. It provides that Member States will be prevented from legislating only on those elements of the field on which the Union has already acted, leaving Member States the freedom to adopt legislation on unlegislated elements of the field. Against this, however, the category of shared competences seems to be treated as a residual category, with Article 4(1) LTFEU stating that the Union and Member States shall share competences in all fields not listed as exclusive or supporting, coordinating or supplementing. The consequence is that if the Union decides to develop legislation in fields where it is currently active, such as social exclusion or pensions, that possibility would still be open to it.

5 Article 6 LTFEU.   6 Article 4(2) LTFEU.
7 Opinion 1/94 *Re World Trade Agreement* [1994] ECR I-5267.
8 These concerns are set out in Article 168(4) LTFEU. The Union may legislate on human organs, veterinary measures and quality standards for medicinal products.
9 Article 4(3) and (4) LTFEU.

(iii) The fidelity principle

The fidelity principle has been recast by the Lisbon Treaty in Article 4(3) LTEU.[10] The significant innovation is a new first paragraph which states that 'pursuant to the principle of sincere cooperation, the Union and the Member States shall, in full mutual respect, assist each other in carrying out tasks which flow from the Treaties'. The new paragraph does three things. First, it formalises and encrypts in the Treaty the case law of the Court of Justice on the duty of cooperation. This emphasises that the duty is a general one, binding all public institutions in the Union and is based upon mutuality. Each institution must assist the others to meet their responsibilities under Union law.[11] Secondly, it introduces the idea of 'mutual respect'. This suggests a countervailing principle under which each institution must not transgress upon the prerogatives of the other. This would imply, for example, that if the duty of cooperation currently imposes a responsibility on national courts not to assess a potentially anti-competitive practice being considered by the Commission,[12] there may be a corollary obligation on the Commission to leave to national authorities assessment of practices more appropriately considered by them.[13] The final novelty is that the duty of cooperation applies to tasks that 'flow from the Treaties'. This is a more open-ended concept than the duty's merely applying to the tasks arising from fulfillment of Treaty obligations. Notably, it suggests that the duty of cooperation applies to projects such as the Lisbon Strategy whose ambitions both build upon and extend beyond the Treaties.

3. Contesting EU legal sovereignty: primacy and the national courts

The Lisbon Treaty, through its Declaration, gave institutional support to the Court of Justice's view of the European Union as a sovereign legal order. Much will depend on how the national constitutional courts interpret it. In the main text, we considered how the most popular view amongst the national constitutional courts of the EU-15, following the judgment of the German Constitutional Court in *Brunner v TEU*,[14] was that of qualified constitutional sovereignty. This doctrine has three tenets:

- The final arbiters of the relationship between national law and Union law and on the authority of national law are national courts.

---

10 The provision was set out on p. 13 of the updates.
11 Case C-2/88 Imm. *Zwartveld and Others* [1990] ECR I-3365.
12 Case C-344/98 *Masterfoods v HB Ice Cream* [2000] ECR I-11369.
13 This is, of course, established by the Commission Notice on Cooperation within the network of competition authorities, OJ 2004, C 101/43, para 8. The argument here is that there is now a Treaty obligation on the Commission not to get involved or subsequently call into question a national decision.
14 *Brunner v TEU* [1994] 1 *CMLR* 57.

- Nevertheless, in accordance with the Court of Justice's case law, Union law will be accorded primacy over national statutes and national courts' case law. In this way, the sovereignty of Union law will be recognised.
- National constitutional courts reserve the right to strike down Union law if it breaches the doctrine of conferred powers, violates fundamental rights or is incompatible with substantive doctrines central to the constitutional order of that State.

The enlargements of 2004 and 2007 suggested a more heterogeneous reaction, particularly as constitutional courts in many post-Communist states have come to be seen, and see themselves, as important bulwarks against both crude populism and against unaccountable networks of civil servants.[15] Independent responses to the sovereignty of EU law were to be expected, and already evident in the decision of the Polish Constitutional Tribunal on the accession of Poland to the European Union. The Tribunal refused to acknowledge the sovereignty of Union law but, nevertheless, gave Union law primacy over Polish statutes on the ground of the former's status as international law. Other courts of the new Member States have refused to follow this orthodoxy.[16]

In Case 17/04 the Hungarian Constitutional Court had to consider a 2004 Hungarian law which fined anybody engaged in speculation in agricultural products in the period prior to Hungarian accession to the EU.[17] Speculation was assumed to have taken place where agricultural contracts were entered into after 1 January 2004 or where there was a sudden jump in the size of a farmer's inventories. The law was based on an EC Regulation designed to prevent profiteering as a consequence of the subsidies that would accrue to Hungarian farmers from EU membership and which would be based on the volume of their production. The difficulty was that both the Regulation and the Hungarian law came into force on 1 May 2004 and, therefore, were retroactive in that they punished acts that were lawful at the time they were committed.

Notwithstanding the identical phrasing of the EU Regulation and the Hungarian statute, the Constitutional Court treated it as a wholly internal matter. The Court made no reference to EU law. Instead, the Hungarian law was found to violate Article 2(1) of the Hungarian Constitution on the grounds that it violated the principle of legal certainty. Whilst there was a desire not to question directly the supremacy of EU law, at the same time the Constitutional Court refused to look at the wider EU context and the effects its ruling would have on the general operation of EU law. This approach constituted a challenge to the substance of EU law if not to its formal authority.

---

15 K. Scheppele, 'Constitutional negotiations: political contexts of judicial activism in post-Soviet Europe' (2003) 18 *International Sociology 219*; A. Sajó, 'Learning co-operative Constitutionalism the hard way: the Hungarian Constitutional Court shying away from EU supremacy' (2004) 2 *Zeitschrift für Staats– und Europawissenschaften* 351.

16 An interesting analysis is provided in W. Sadurski, "*Solange, chapter 3*": *Constitutional Courts in Central Europe – Democracy – European Union*, EUI Working Paper 2006/40 (EUI, Florence, 2006).

17 Decision 17/2004 (V. 25.) AB at www.mkab.hu/en/enpage3.htm

A similar ethos was present in a decision of the Cypriot Constitutional Court in *Konstantinou*.[18] Konstantinou was a dual Cypriot-British national, whose surrender was requested by the British authorities on the grounds that he was to be tried for conspiracy to defraud. The basis for the request was the European Arrest Warrant, which requires surrender of individuals in certain circumstances. The Cypriot Constitution, however, prohibits the detention of Cypriot nationals for deportation. The Constitutional Court acknowledged the primacy of EC law, but placed emphasis on the nature of third pillar measures, in particular Framework Decisions, which leave the forms and methods for achieving their aims up to the Member States. The Constitutional Court noted that this gave discretion to the Member States. In this case, it was impossible for the national legislation to implement the European Arrest Warrant as it violated the Cypriot Constitution. Once again, there was a reticence to challenge formally the authority of EU law, but there was substantive evasion. Since the instrument was not directly effective, the Constitutional Court considered that this gave it a measure of judicial discretion not to give effect to EU law where that violated the Constitution.

The most interesting approach has been that of the Czech Constitutional Court. In Pl US 50/04,[19] the Czech Constitutional Court annulled a series of government measures organising the sugar market on the grounds that competence for these had been transferred to the Union. In the judgment, it reflected, for the first time, on the relationship between Union and Czech law.

> In the Constitutional Court's view, this conferral of a part of its [the Czech Republic's] powers is naturally a conditional conferral, as the original bearer of sovereignty, as well as the powers flowing there from, still remains the Czech Republic, whose sovereignty is still founded upon Art. 1 para. 1 of the Constitution of the Czech Republic. In the Constitutional Court's view, the conditional nature of the delegation of these powers is manifested on two planes: the formal and the substantive plane. The first of these planes concerns the power attributes of state sovereignty itself, the second plane concerns the substantive component of the exercise of state power. In other words, the delegation of a part of the powers of national organs may persist only so long as these powers are exercised in a manner that is compatible with the preservation of the foundations of state sovereignty of the Czech Republic, and in a manner which does not threaten the very essence of the substantive law-based state. In such determination the Constitutional Court is called upon to protect constitutionalism (Art. 83 of the Constitution of the Czech Republic). According to Art. 9 para. 2 of the Constitution of the Czech Republic, the essential attributes of a democratic state governed by the rule of law, remain beyond the reach of the Constituent Assembly itself.

18 *Cyprus v Konstantinou* [2007] 3 *CMLR* 42.
19 Pl US 50/04 Sugar Quota Regulation II Judgment of 8 March 2006 at http://angl.concourt.cz/ angl_verze/ doc/p-50-04.php

This formulation, repeated subsequently,[20] qualifies EU legal sovereignty in two ways. Formally, it is something that can be repossessed and is materially limited in that it cannot extinguish the core functions of the Czech State. Substantively, the Czech Constitutional Court will intervene whenever the Union does not act according to the principles of a 'democratic law-based State'. The basis for this is that the constitutional identity of the Czech State rests upon these foundations and there can be no derogation whatsoever from these principles.

This test is more multifaceted and convincing than *Brunner*. The latter, it will be remembered, operates a dualist logic. On the one hand, the German Constitutional Court reasons that the unique presence of a demos at the national level makes it the only context in which democracy is possible and therefore requires that the majority of power be exercised there. On the other hand, the Union is permitted to exercise limited powers subject to certain safeguards, most notably the protection of fundamental rights. The Court, however, leaves the relationship between these logics unexplored. Consequently, no reason is provided for why any power at all should be transferred to the Union as any transfer is necessarily undemocratic. To maintain the stability of the reasoning, important notions such as national community and limited powers are left untested. Something called 'national community' is taken as a sine qua non for democracy, and, in like vein, the Union's extensive powers are assumed to be limited. Both assumptions are highly questionable.

The reasoning of the Czech Constitutional Court, by contrast, is a unitary one. The idea of a democratic law-based State is not troubled by a transfer of power to another democratic law-based State. The basis for retaining a national core of power is not the prerogatives of the national community, but those of the constitutional state. Put simply, the constitutional state acts as a fulcrum that both mediates power between, and provides a check on, other levels of government – a central republican principle. In addition, the idea of a democratic law-based state becomes a constitutive principle of all government. It can call for the transfer of competencies between levels of government where one level is unable to meet the needs of its constituents. It also acts as a basis for each to review the actions of the other according to a common legal ethical syntax. Defined in such broad terms, it is not confined to questions of fundamental rights, but all questions that trouble public lawyers – checks and balances, principles of representation, accountability, deliberation and participation.

4. Federal limits of EU law

Following the failure of the Constitutional Treaty, a number of governments, notably the Dutch and Czech governments, indicated that a strengthening of the mechanisms protecting national competencies and elaborating the subsidiarity principle would be desirable. Two measures were taken at Lisbon in this regard. The first was to try

---

20 Pl US 66/04 *European Arrest Warrant* Judgment of 3 May 2006 at http://angl.concourt.cz/angl_verze/doc/pl-66–04.php

to place some limits on Article 352 LFTEU, the flexibility provision which allows the Union to take legislative measures if action is required to realise its objectives and no other provision has provided the necessary legal base. The other was to bolster the position of national parliaments as guardians of the subsidiarity principle.

(i)   Conferred powers

As observed in the updates to chapter 1,[21] the integration of the pillar system within a single framework has had the effect of enlarging the remit of Article 352 LTFEU. Whilst its current counterpart, Article 308 EC, can be used to take legislative measures to realise the objectives of the Community, Article 352 LTFEU, by contrast, can be deployed to realise the objectives of the Union, a far more multifarious beast. In the Constitutional Treaty, a couple of constraints were established to counter the risks this created, and these are replicated in Article 352(2) and (3) LTFEU:

> **Article 352 (2) LTFEU** Using the procedure for monitoring the subsidiarity principle referred to in Article 5(3) [LTEU], the Commission shall draw national Parliaments' attention to proposals based on this Article.
> 3. Measures based on this Article shall not entail harmonisation of Member States' laws or regulations in cases where the Treaties exclude such harmonisation.

The first provision refers to the procedure for monitoring the subsidiarity principle set out below. It indicates, however, that there are particular risks associated with measures based on Article 352 LTFEU as these either concern matters not explicitly mentioned in the Treaties, or they have no explicit legal base. The Commission is therefore required to bring them to national parliaments' attention. The second provision indicates that Article 352 LTFEU cannot be used to undermine the internal institutional balance within the Treaties by being used in fields which provide only for the adoption of supporting, coordinating or complementary measures.

The Lisbon Treaty adds one further safeguard in Article 352(4) LTFEU by indicating that the procedure cannot be used for measures in the field of the common foreign and security policy. More significant perhaps are two Declarations attached to the Lisbon Treaty. Declaration 41 refers to the Union objectives that Article 352 LTFEU may pursue. It observes that these are not the broad objectives of the Union set out in Article 3(1) LTEU, which refer to 'peace, values and the well-being of peoples'. Instead, they are those set out in Article 3(2), (3) and (5) LTEU.

> **Article 3 (2) LTEU** The Union shall offer its citizens an area of freedom, security and justice without internal frontiers, in which the free movement of persons is ensured in conjunction with appropriate measures with respect to external border controls, asylum, immigration and the prevention and combating of crime.

21 See p. 8.

3. The Union shall establish an internal market. It shall work for the sustainable development of Europe based on balanced economic growth and price stability, a highly competitive social market economy, aiming at full employment and social progress, and a high level of protection and improvement of the quality of the environment. It shall promote scientific and technological advance.

It shall combat social exclusion and discrimination, and shall promote social justice and protection, equality between women and men, solidarity between generations and protection of the rights of the child.

5. In its relations with the wider world, the Union shall uphold and promote its values and contribute to the protection if its citizens. It shall contribute to peace, security, the sustainable development of the Earth, solidarity and mutual respect among peoples, free and fair trade, eradication of poverty and the protection of human rights, in particular the rights of the child, as well as to the strict observance and the development of international law, including respect for the principles of the United Nations Charter.

This is the first time that an attempt has been made to confine Article 352 LTFEU. The objectives are nevertheless wide-ranging and include social justice, intergenerational equity, full employment and the eradication of poverty. They allow for an aggressive deployment of the Article 352 LTFEU procedure. Declaration 42 is intended, however, to prevent this. It states that, in accordance with the case law of the Court of Justice, Article 352 LTFEU:

cannot serve as a basis for widening the scope of Union powers beyond the general framework created by the provisions of the Treaties as a whole and, in particular, by those that define the tasks and the activities of the Union. In any event, this Article cannot be used as a basis for the adoption of provisions whose effect would, in substance, be to amend the Treaties without following the procedure which they provide for that purpose.

At one level, this Declaration does no more than reiterate the ruling of the Court of Justice in *Opinion 2/94* that the provision cannot be used to amend the Treaties.[22] Yet the use of such detailed language and the emphasis by twenty-seven governments that there must be no amendment and that the doctrine of conferred powers be observed carries with it a powerful message, that the procedure is not to be used aggressively and far more thought must be given to the limits of Union competence in the course of its deployment.

(ii)   Subsidiarity

Whilst there exists the possibility for an EU measure to be struck down by the Court of Justice for failure to comply with the subsidiarity principle, this has never happened. There are a number of reasons why this might be so. The test is very complex, but, above all, review of a measure is an ex post process, meaning that if the Court were to strike

22 Opinion 2/94 *Re Accession to the ECHR* [1996] ECR I-1759.

down a measure, it would be telling all the political institutions that their collective assessment of a need for a Union measure was wrong. The Constitutional Treaty placed increased emphasis on *ex ante* controls prior to adoption of the measure by non-judicial bodies, most notably national parliaments. These have all been retained in the Lisbon Treaty, and are set out in the Protocol on the Application of the Principles of Subsidiarity and Proportionality.

The first control, now present in Article 2, is that the Commission should consult widely before making a proposal. This requirement already exists in Union law,[23] but it has been reinforced by a requirement that the Commission consider the local and regional dimension rather than simply whether the Union measure is justified under the subsidiarity principle.

The second control is a duty on the Commission to justify the proposed measure. Once again, such is a duty is not new.[24] The required level of detail in the justification is, however, new as it has incorporated commitments made by the Commission under its Governance agenda.[25]

Protocol on the application of the principles of subsidiarity and proportionality

Article 5 Draft legislative acts shall be justified with regard to the principles of subsidiarity and proportionality. Any draft legislative act should contain a detailed statement making it possible to appraise compliance with the principles of subsidiarity and proportionality. This statement should contain some assessment of the proposal's financial impact and, in the case of a directive, of its implications for the rules to be put in place by Member States, including, where necessary, the regional legislation. The reasons for concluding that an objective of the Union can be better achieved at the level of the Union shall be substantiated by qualitative and, wherever possible, quantitative indicators. Draft legislative acts shall take account of the need for any burden, whether financial or administrative, falling upon the Union, national governments, regional or local authorities, economic operators and citizens, to be minimised and commensurate with the objective to be achieved.

Measures must be justified not merely on the basis of the subsidiarity principle, but must also be in line with the proportionality principle, which requires assessment of the cost of measures, and their impact on businesses, local communities and administrations. To a certain extent, such foresight seems very wise. It is difficult to object to consideration of a measure prior to rather than after its adoption. The challenge is that such impact assessments are necessarily extremely wide-ranging and speculative. The ambiguity and open-endedness of the data will inevitably give the policy-maker considerable discretion, and it is unclear whether these processes are in fact used to validate, rather than to question, prior decisions.[26]

---

23 Protocol to the EC Treaty on the application of the principles of subsidiarity and proportionality, para 9.
24 *Ibid.*, para 4.   25 EC Commission, *Impact Assessment*, COM (2002) 276.
26 On this see C. Radaelli, 'Diffusion without convergence: How political context shapes the adoption of regulatory impact assessment' (2005) 12 *JEPP* 924.

The third control is the 'yellow card' procedure. National parliaments are given the right to adopt reasoned opinions, which shall be taken into account by the EU Institution or Member States proposing the measure. The national parliaments of each Member State are also given two votes, which are shared out between chambers in the case of a bicameral system.

> **Article 7(2)** Where reasoned opinions on a draft legislative act's non-compliance with the principle of subsidiarity represent at least one third of all the votes allocated to the national Parliaments . . ., the draft must be reviewed. This threshold shall be a quarter in the case of a draft legislative act submitted on the basis of Article 76 LTFEU on the area of freedom, security and justice.
>
> After such review, the Commission or, where appropriate, the group of Member States, the European Parliament, the Court of Justice, the European Central Bank or the European Investment Bank, if the draft legislative act originates from them, may decide to maintain, amend or withdraw the draft. Reasons must be given for this decision.

This procedure has been discussed at length in the main text. Some of the concerns raised were, first, that it national parliaments have a 'yellow' rather than a 'red card', so the measure could still be adopted regardless of opposition from national parliaments. Second, national parliaments have no direct access to the Court of Justice to enforce the letter of the law. A more significant problem, in our view, was the high thresholds of opposition required given the particularistic nature of many subsidiarity concerns. This would make it difficult for individual parliaments to lobby support from other national parliaments to achieve the one third or one quarter threshold required.[27]

In spite of this, the Member States decided that the central difficulty with the 'yellow' card procedure was the level of discretion granted to the Commission. They therefore established a further procedure, the 'orange card' procedure.

> **Article 7(3)** Furthermore, under the ordinary legislative procedure, where reasoned opinions on the non-compliance of a proposal for a legislative act with the principle of subsidiarity represent at least a simple majority of the votes allocated to the national Parliaments . . ., the proposal must be reviewed. After such review, the Commission may decide to maintain, amend or withdraw the proposal.
>
> If it chooses to maintain the proposal, the Commission will have, in a reasoned opinion, to justify why it considers that the proposal complies with the principle of subsidiarity. This reasoned opinion, as well as the reasoned opinions of the national Parliaments, will have to be submitted to the Union's legislator, for consideration in the procedure:
>
> (a) before concluding the first reading, the legislator (the European Parliament and the Council) shall consider whether the legislative proposal is compatible with the principle of subsidiarity, taking particular account of the reasons expressed and shared by the majority of national Parliaments as well as the reasoned opinion of the Commission;

---

27 See pp. 228–30 of the main text.

(b) if, by a majority of 55 per cent of the members of the Council or a majority of the votes cast in the European Parliament, the legislator is of the opinion that the proposal is not compatible with the principle of subsidiarity, the legislative proposal shall not be given further consideration.

This new procedure seems unnecessary. It is almost inconceivable that the Commission would take forward a proposal where over half the national parliaments opposed it. As national governments are accountable to national parliaments, it is almost as unimaginable that such a proposal would receive the QMV in the Council. National governments would face the wrath of their parliaments for ignoring their wishes. On its own terms, the procedure is somewhat bizarre. It only applies to the ordinary legislative procedure (co-decision). Yet, if there is a problem with Commission discretion, surely it would generally affect the institution's role in all legislative procedures. The other feature of the procedure that seems a little odd is that it requires a positive majority to vote a measure incompatible with the subsidiarity principle. A more appropriate threshold is that the burden of proof is reversed and a qualified majority in the Council and absolute majority in the Parliament would be needed to vote that the measure satisfied the subsidiarity test.

6

Fundamental rights

CONTENTS	

1. Introduction

Provision for accession of the Union to the European Convention for the Protection of Human Rights and the establishment of a European Union Agency for Fundamental Rights would constitute significant developments in any three-year period. These have, however, been overshadowed by two other developments. The first is the legal recognition of the European Union Charter for Fundamental Rights and Freedoms, initially by the Court of Justice and then in the Lisbon Treaty. Yet there is considerable ambiguity as to the force of this recognition and it has generated significant controversy, with two Member States, Poland and the United Kingdom, requiring the establishment of a special regime. The second development concerns the institutional remit of EU fundamental rights law. The Court and the Lisbon Treaty expressly intimate that Union action currently covered by the third pillar is bound by EU fundamental rights law. As a corollary, there are suggestions of a new test whereby Member States are only bound by EU fundamental rights law when implementing Union law. However, this test has not been clearly established and there are conflicting messages about its meaning.

2. Development of fundamental rights by the political institutions of the European Union

Fundamental rights protection has been based on two pillars in EU law. The Union has committed itself to securing the non-violation of fundamental rights by the Union institutions and Member States when either implementing or acting within the field of Community law. Since the early 1990s, initially in the field of external relations and subsequently internally, it has also developed, arguably controversially, a fundamental rights policy.[1] These two pillars have both been reinforced since 2005. The principle of non-violation was strengthened by the Treaty of Lisbon which provides for the accession of the Union to the European Convention for the Protection of Human Rights and Freedoms.

Article 6(2) LTEU The Union shall accede to the European Convention for the Protection of Human Rights and Fundamental Freedoms. Such accession shall not affect the Union's competences as defined in the Treaties.

A Protocol was attached to the Treaties providing that special arrangements be made for participation by the Union in the Convention's control bodies and to ensure that proceedings by non-Member States and individual applications are correctly addressed to Member States and/or the Union.[2] The Protocol also emphasised that accession to the ECHR would not only not affect the competences of the Union and the powers of its institutions, but that it would also not affect the situation of the Member States, particularly in relation to individual derogations from the Convention or choices of accession to particular Protocols of the ECHR.[3]

The development of an EU fundamental rights policy realised its clearest institutional expression with the establishment of the European Union Agency for Fundamental Rights.[4] The Agency replaces the Union Monitoring Centre on Racism and Xenophobia and the Network of Independent Experts. The objective of the Agency is to provide the Union institutions and Member States when they are implementing Community law with 'assistance and expertise relating to fundamental rights in order to support them when they take measures or formulate courses of action within their respective spheres of competence to fully respect fundamental rights'.[5] To that end it has four central tasks:

- collecting, recording, disseminating and comparing data and research on fundamental rights and developing methods and standards to improve the comparability, objectivity and reliability of that data;
- at the request of EU institutions it can publish opinions for EU institutions and Member States implementing EC law;
- it is to publish both an annual report and thematic reports on fundamental rights issues covered by the areas of its activity, highlighting examples of good practice;

1 See pp. 241–6 of the main text.
2 Protocol relating to Article 6(2) LTEU on the Accession of the Union to the ECHR.
3 The ECHR has five Protocols but not all are signed by all the Member States. Article 15(1) ECHR also allows States to make derogations from particular provisions in times of war or public emergency.
4 Regulation 168/2007/EC establishing a European Union Agency for Fundamental Rights, OJ 2007, L 53/1.
5 *Ibid.*, article 2(1).

- it is to mobilise public awareness of fundamental rights through promoting dialogue with civil society.[6]

The remit and nature of the Agency's work has proved highly controversial. This is reflected in the time taken to bring it into existence. The initial political decision to establish the Agency was taken in December 2003 and its Director, the Dane Morten Kjaerum, was only offered the job in March 2008. It is reflected, more dramatically, in the curbs placed on its powers and institutional practice since its establishment.

The most powerful task of the Agency is the power to give opinions, notably on legislative proposals. The potential normative force of these opinions is unclear. In other fields, the Commission can only derogate from the opinions of the Agency where it can provide a contrary opinion by a body of equal weight and can provide reasons for choosing one over the other.[7] The Commission, as a consequence, invariably follows the Agency's opinions. With fundamental rights teaching on all areas of Union law, the Fundamental Rights Agency is potentially a very powerful body. Yet the Regulation provides that the Agency can only provide opinions on the legality of proposals at the request of the Commission and cannot address the legality of the measure for the purposes of judicial review, or make an assessment as to whether a Member State has met its obligations within the context of an enforcement action.[8] Even though one of its tasks is to consider questions of fundamental rights in assessing the impact of any legislative proposal,[9] there is presently little evidence of the Commission having consulted the Agency.

The Agency also has to work within the aegis of a Multi-annual Framework established by the Union political institutions, which sets out the thematic areas within which it is to function. Its work is either confined by institutional requests, in the case of opinions, or, more generally, by the political agenda of the EU institutions. This inevitably confines not only the Agency activities, but also the type of rights examined by the Agency. The Framework for 2007–2012 is a case in point. It takes a reasonably broad remit, but has excluded analysis of social rights, bioethical rights and the war on terror – all of which are touched upon significantly by Union activities.[10]

The Agency reflects, therefore, very much the debate on the establishment of an EU fundamental rights policy. Its remit, as with the policy, is partial, unsteady and makes

---

6 *Ibid.*, article 4(1).

7 In relation to the European Food Safety Authority see Case T-13/99 *Pfizer Animal Health v Council* [2002] ECR II-3305.

8 Supra n. 4, article 4(2).   9 See p. 261 of the main text.

10 The fields included are racism, xenophobia and related intolerance; discrimination based on sex, race or ethnic origin, religion or belief, disability, age or sexual orientation and against persons belonging to minorities; compensation of victims; the rights of the child; asylum, immigration and integration of migrants; visa and border control; participation of the citizens of the Union in the Union's democratic functioning; information society and, in particular, respect for private life and protection of personal data; access to efficient and independent justice. Decision 2008//203/EC, implementing Regulation (EC) No 168/2007 as regards the adoption of a Multi-annual Framework for the European Union Agency for Fundamental Rights for 2007–2012, OJ 2008, L 63/14, article 2.

distinctions which are hard to justify. Yet, for those who advocate a fundamental rights policy, the establish of an Agency with the legal power to proof all Union legislation for compliance with fundamental rights and with the power to act as a hub for European civil society and awareness on these matters is indeed a powerful step forward.

3. The European Union Charter of Fundamental Rights

(i)   The development of the Charter by the Court

The proclamation of the Charter at the Treaty of Nice by the EU institutions in December 2000 left its status unresolved. Whilst numerous Advocates General and the Court of First Instance had explicitly relied upon it as an authoritative articulation of fundamental rights in EU law, the Court of Justice had been careful to steer clear of the subject.[11] This changed in the *Family Reunification* case. In this judgment, the European Parliament challenged three elements of the Directive on family reunifica-tion, which set out the conditions under which family members of non-EU nationals resident in the Union could join them. The first element challenged was a provision stating that integration requirements could be imposed upon a child over 12 years where the family, resident in the EU, sought her reunification.[12] The second was an exception to the general provision for a right of family reunification for a child of 16 years or younger. The exception provided this rule did not apply to children who were already 15 years old at the time of the submission of the application. The third challenge concerned a provision which stipulated that Member States could require non-EU nationals to have lawfully resided for two years on their territories before their families can join them. The Directive provided in its Preamble that it complied with the right to respect for family life as set out in Article 8 ECHR and Article 7 of the Charter.

Case C-540/03 Parliament v Council [2006] ECR I-5769

35. Fundamental rights form an integral part of the general principles of law the obser-vance of which the Court ensures. For that purpose, the Court draws inspiration from the constitutional traditions common to the Member States and from the guidelines supplied by international instruments for the protection of human rights on which the Member States have collaborated or to which they are signatories. The ECHR has special significance in that respect . . .

36. In addition, Article 6(2) EU states that 'the Union shall respect fundamental rights, as guaranteed by the [ECHR] and as they result from the constitutional traditions common to the Member States, as general principles of Community law'.

37. The Court has already had occasion to point out that the International Covenant on Civil and Political Rights is one of the international instruments for the protection of human

---

11 See pp. 248–52 of the main text.
12 These typically require knowledge of the language and history of the host State as well as a demonstration of commitment to its values.

> rights of which it takes account in applying the general principles of Community law . . . That is also true of the Convention on the Rights of the Child referred to above which, like the Covenant, binds each of the Member States.
>
> 38. The Charter was solemnly proclaimed by the Parliament, the Council and the Commission in Nice on 7 December 2000. While the Charter is not a legally binding instrument, the Community legislature did, however, acknowledge its importance by stating, in the second recital in the preamble to the Directive, that the Directive observes the principles recognised not only by Article 8 of the ECHR but also in the Charter. Furthermore, the principal aim of the Charter, as is apparent from its preamble, is to reaffirm 'rights as they result, in particular, from the constitutional traditions and international obligations common to the Member States, the Treaty on European Union, the Community Treaties, the [ECHR], the Social Charters adopted by the Community and by the Council of Europe and the case-law of the Court . . . and of the European Court of Human Rights'.

The judgment was a hesitant recognition of the status of the Charter. The Directive was unusual in that it explicitly mentioned the Charter, and consequently it could be argued that the Court, in referring to the Charter, was merely following the intention of the legislature. In addition, in the remainder of the judgment, the Court relied predominantly on the case law of the European Convention on Human Rights. The reference to the Charter seemed, therefore, to be little more than rhetorical. In subsequent case law, the Court has begun to rely more clearly on the Charter. In *Unibet*, the Court invoked the Charter – albeit as one of a number of other instruments – even though no reference was made to it in the legal provision under consideration.[13] The most extensive consideration of the Charter was in *Promusciae*. Promusiciae, an association of music producers, asked Telefonica, the large Spanish internet service provider, to hand over the identities and addresses of a number of people it claimed were using the file-sharing programme, KaZaa, to share music in breach of its copyright. The latter refused, arguing that the relevant Community Directives, notably Directive 2002/58, provided for this only in the course of a criminal investigation or for the purpose of safeguarding public security and national defence, and not in civil proceedings. Promusciae invoked the Charter against this, arguing that since it protected that the right to property and to an effective judicial remedy, the Directives had to be applied in the light of these.

> ### Case C-275/06 Promusciae v Telefónica de España, Judgment of 29 January 2008
>
> 61. The national court refers in its order for reference to Articles 17 and 47 of the Charter, the first of which concerns the protection of the right to property, including intellectual property, and the second of which concerns the right to an effective remedy. By so doing, that court must be regarded as seeking to know whether an interpretation of those directives to the effect that the Member States are not obliged to lay down, in order to ensure the

---

13 Case C-432/05 *Unibet* [2007] ECR I-2271.

effective protection of copyright, an obligation to communicate personal data in the context of civil proceedings leads to an infringement of the fundamental right to property and the fundamental right to effective judicial protection.

62. It should be recalled that the fundamental right to property, which includes intellectual property rights such as copyright . . ., and the fundamental right to effective judicial protection constitute general principles of Community law . . .

63. However, the situation in respect of which the national court puts that question involves, in addition to those two rights, a further fundamental right, namely the right that guarantees protection of personal data and hence of private life.

64. According to recital 2 in the preamble to Directive 2002/58, the directive seeks to respect the fundamental rights and observes the principles recognised in particular by the Charter. In particular, the directive seeks to ensure full respect for the rights set out in Articles 7 and 8 of that Charter. Article 7 substantially reproduces Article 8 of the European Convention for the Protection of Human Rights and Fundamental Freedoms signed at Rome on 4 November 1950, which guarantees the right to respect for private life, and Article 8 of the Charter expressly proclaims the right to protection of personal data.

65. The present reference for a preliminary ruling thus raises the question of the need to reconcile the requirements of the protection of different fundamental rights, namely the right to respect for private life on the one hand and the rights to protection of property and to an effective remedy on the other.

66. The mechanisms allowing those different rights and interests to be balanced are contained, first, in Directive 2002/58 itself, in that it provides for rules which determine in what circumstances and to what extent the processing of personal data is lawful and what safeguards must be provided for, and in the three directives mentioned by the national court, which reserve the cases in which the measures adopted to protect the rights they regulate affect the protection of personal data. Second, they result from the adoption by the Member States of national provisions transposing those directives and their application by the national authorities.

67. As to those directives, their provisions are relatively general, since they have to be applied to a large number of different situations which may arise in any of the Member States. They therefore logically include rules which leave the Member States with the necessary discretion to define transposition measures which may be adapted to the various situations possible.

68. That being so, the Member States must, when transposing the directives mentioned above, take care to rely on an interpretation of the directives which allows a fair balance to be struck between the various fundamental rights protected by the Community legal order. Further, when implementing the measures transposing those directives, the authorities and courts of the Member States must not only interpret their national law in a manner consistent with those directives but also make sure that they do not rely on an interpretation of them which would be in conflict with those fundamental rights or with the other general principles of Community law, such as the principle of proportionality . . .

69. Moreover, it should be recalled here that the Community legislature expressly required, in accordance with . . . Directive 2002/58, that the measures referred to in that paragraph be adopted by the Member States in compliance with the general principles of Community law, including those mentioned in Article 6(1) and (2) TEU.

70. In the light of all the foregoing, the answer to the national court's question must be that [the] Directives . . . do not require the Member States to lay down, in a situation such as that in the main proceedings, an obligation to communicate personal data in order to ensure effective protection of copyright in the context of civil proceedings. However, Community

> law requires that, when transposing those directives, the Member States take care to rely on an interpretation of them which allows a fair balance to be struck between the various fundamental rights protected by the Community legal order. Further, when implementing the measures transposing those directives, the authorities and courts of the Member States must not only interpret their national law in a manner consistent with those directives but also make sure that they do not rely on an interpretation of them which would be in conflict with those fundamental rights or with the other general principles of Community law, such as the principle of proportionality.

The salient feature of *Promusciae* was that the Court was prepared to reason in the context of the Charter. It noted that fundamental rights include not just the protection of property rights and effective judicial protection, but also the right to respect for privacy and the guarantee of protection of personal data. Although it does not refer to the Charter with regard to the latter rights, these are both set out in the Charter. *Promusciae* suggests, therefore, that the Charter might lead to a new type of reasoning in which the Court will be less focused on a specific right, and instead use the instrument as a whole to enable it to balance a series of entitlements and concerns.

That said, the manner in which the Charter has come to be invoked by the Court raises a number of concerns. There is, of course, the constitutional point that it has subverted the treaty amendment process. The instrument was too controversial at Nice to be made part of EU law and was still contested by a number of governments at Lisbon in 2007. The Charter is now part of EU law, whether the Lisbon Treaty is ratified or not. A more serious charge is that the Court of Justice has neglected the business of protecting fundamental rights to enable this institutional engineering. The Charter has not been successfully used to protect the interests of those invoking it in any of the cases before the Court. In the *Family Reunification* judgment, the measures challenged were highly illiberal. It is difficult to think of any circumstance, other than that of parental abuse, in which it is right to separate 12-year-old children from their parents. In allowing for the possibility of such a situation being compatible with the right to respect for family life in the same judgment as it has engaged in judicial activism with regard to the Charter, the Court has opened itself to the accusation that it has neglected some of the most vulnerable in order to further integrationist goals – a very serious charge indeed.

(ii)   The Charter and the Lisbon Treaty

Contentiousness with regard to the status of the Charter was reflected in the Lisbon Treaty, which provided for no equivalent to Part II of the Constitutional Treaty, where the full text of the Charter was set out in the substantive body of the Treaty. Instead, the Lisbon Treaty merely provides for a reference to the Charter in the TEU.

Article 6(1) LTEU The Union recognises the rights, freedoms and principles set out in the Charter of Fundamental Rights of the European Union . . . which shall have the same legal value as the Treaties.

The provisions of the Charter shall not extend in any way the competences of the Union as defined in the Treaties.

The rights, freedoms and principles in the Charter shall be interpreted in accordance with the general provisions in Title VII of the Charter governing its interpretation and application and with due regard to the explanations referred to in the Charter, that set out the sources of those provisions.

The failure to include the provisions of the Charter in the main text of the Treaties undermined one of the rationales for its establishment, namely to render more visible the rights it proclaimed. Legal recognition of the Charter is nevertheless significant. The Charter can now more easily and more vigorously be deployed as a standard for judicial review of Union measures and national measures implementing Union law and as an aid to interpreting national and Union measures. Recognition will, moreover, not merely affect judicial duties, but there is also a likelihood that the Charter will be used to justify certain legislative measures and to orient others.

The quality of recognition provided is, however, highly ambiguous. Article 6 LTEU states that the Charter has the same legal value as the Treaties. One interpretation of this is that the Charter is now an autonomous, self-standing source of law generating its own meanings, case law and rules of interpretation. After all, this is what the EU Treaties have done. Another interpretation is based on the proviso in the last paragraph, that due regard must be had to the explanations which set out the sources of individual provisions. These explanations make clear that the Charter is largely a codifying document.[14] Every provision repeats, and therefore reflects, provisions in other international human rights treaties. Such a vision creates a more minimal role for the Charter, which is no different from that provided for in the Court of Justice's case law. It sets out the rights to be recognised, but is not an autonomous basis for their development. Instead, regard is to be had to the prior sources of law.

This will be one of the most pressing matters to be decided by the Court of Justice if the Lisbon Treaty comes into effect, not merely because it relates to the interpretation of the Charter, but also because it affects the nature of the obligations of two Member States, Poland and the United Kingdom. These States had particular reservations about the Charter, and a Protocol on the Application of the Charter of Fundamental Rights to Poland and the United Kingdom was appended to the Lisbon Treaty.

Article 1(1) The Charter does not extend the ability of the Court of Justice of the European Union, or any court or tribunal of Poland or of the United Kingdom, to find that the laws, regulations or administrative provisions, practices or action of Poland or of the United Kingdom are inconsistent with the fundamental rights, freedoms and principles that it reaffirms.

14 Explanations Relating to the Charter of Fundamental Rights of the European Union, CHARTE 4473/00.

> 2. In particular, and for the avoidance of doubt, nothing in Title IV of the Charter creates justiciable rights applicable to Poland or the United Kingdom except in so far as Poland or the United Kingdom has provided for such rights in its national law.
>
> **Article 2** To the extent that a provision of the Charter refers to national laws and practices, it shall only apply to Poland or the United Kingdom to the extent that the rights or principles that it contains are recognised in the law or practices of Poland or of the United Kingdom.

The Protocol does not give these two States an 'opt-out', as is widely misreported. Instead, the Charter cannot 'extend' the ability of any court to declare the practices of these States illegal. If an interpretation of the Charter merely codifies international human rights obligations that are already present in EU law, then the caveat has almost no value. If, by contrast, the Charter is accorded a more autonomous meaning of its own, then there is a significant danger of interpretive chaos. In references from Poland and the United Kingdom, the Court would take a minimalist interpretation of a provision, but it might take a different interpretation in references from other Member States. It is not clear how this would create a coherent body of case law. The situation in which the Court rules on the validity of Union measures forming the basis of national implementing measures is also murky. Since striking down the Union measure would also be striking down the national measures based upon it, must it apply the same logic to the other twenty-five Member States as it applies to the United Kingdom and Poland?

This suggests the Charter's legal force should be understood to have a minimalist interpretation. This implication is reinforced elsewhere. Article 6 LTEU indicates that the Charter cannot be used to extend the competences of the Union, which would militate against too autonomous an interpretation. In addition, Article 52(3), in Title VII of the Charter,[15] provides that where Charter provisions correspond to rights guaranteed by the ECHR, their meaning and scope shall be the same as those in the ECHR.

A further question is raised in Article 1(2) of the Protocol. This states that, with respect to Poland and the United Kingdom, the rights in Title IV are not justiciable and cannot be used as a basis for judicial review or independent dispute resolution. These rights are 'solidarity' rights, and are largely concerned with labour protection, but also include wider social rights such as the right to health care and social assistance, as well as Union policies committing themselves to a high level of environmental and consumer protection. On the face of it, the insistence on this is strange since these rights currently cannot be invoked in an autonomous manner as a means to review EU and national measures.[16]

Yet the Lisbon Treaty suggested the possibility for change here as it removed the safeguards in the Constitutional Treaty distinguishing between provisions expressing

---

15 For discussion of the issues surrounding Title VII see pp. 258–61 of the main text.
16 The Court has thus accorded a mild interpretive force to the Community Charter of the Fundamental Social Rights of Workers 1989 – the basis for most of these rights – but no more. Case C-151/02 *Landeshauptstadt Kiel v Jaeger* [2003] ECR I-8389.

rights and those expressing principles.[17] Principles were not self-standing bases for review, but were merely judicially cognisable with regard to legislation implementing them. The distinction has now been removed. However, it is not clear whether the same legal force will be given to each provision, or whether, in the light of the extremely diffuse nature of some provisions, this distinction will be reinvented on an ad hoc basis by the Court of Justice. This removal has not only generated considerable uncertainty, but opened up the possibility for a very wide scope of review by the Court of Justice.

4. Fundamental rights and the institutional scheme of the Treaties

Historically, fundamental rights have been a Community law doctrine. It binds the Community institutions and Member States when implementing or acting within the field of EC law. However, Article 6 TEU talks of the Union respecting fundamental rights, and one would expect fundamental rights to be particularly acute in the third pillar of the TEU, which concerns policing and judicial cooperation in criminal matters. The question of the bite of fundamental rights in the third pillar was undoubtedly an open question due to the Court of Justice not having had an opportunity to consider the matter due to its limited jurisdiction under the third pillar. In Common Position 2001/931/CFSP, adopted under both the second and third pillars in response to the attacks of 11 September, the Member States agreed to afford each other the widest possible assistance in preventing and combating terrorist acts, and to exploit their widest powers against organisations in the Annex. One such organisation was Segi, which was seen as part of the Basque separatist organisation, ETA. Segi's alleged leaders were imprisoned in early 2002 in Spain. They argued, inter alia, that the Common Position was illegal as it violated their fundamental right to an effective judicial remedy. The Court of First Instance dismissed their challenge and they appealed to the Court of Justice.

> ## Case C-355/04P Segi et al. v Council, Judgment of 27 February 2007[18]
>
> 50. It is true that, as regards the Union, the treaties have established a system of legal remedies in which, by virtue of Article 35 EU, the jurisdiction of the Court is less extensive under Title VI of the Treaty on European Union than it is under the EC Treaty . . . It is even less extensive under Title V. While a system of legal remedies, in particular a body of rules governing non-contractual liability, other than that established by the treaties can indeed be envisaged, it is for the Member States, should the case arise, to reform the system currently in force in accordance with Article 48 EU.
>
> 51. Nevertheless, the appellants cannot validly argue that they are deprived of all judicial protection. As is clear from Article 6 EU, the Union is founded on the principle of the rule

---

17 Article II-112(5) CT.

18 A parallel judgment was given on the same day in Case C-354/04P *Gestoras Pro Amnistía et al. v Council*, Judgment of 27 February 2007. See S. Peers, 'Salvation outside the church: judicial protection in the third pillar after the Pupino and Segi judgments' (2007) 44 *CMLR* 883.

of law and it respects fundamental rights as general principles of Community law. It follows that the institutions are subject to review of the conformity of their acts with the treaties and the general principles of law, just like the Member States when they implement the law of the Union.

52. Here it is to be noted that Article 34 EU provides that the Council may adopt acts varying in nature and scope. Under Article 34(2)(a) EU the Council may 'adopt common positions defining the approach of the Union to a particular matter'. A common position requires the compliance of the Member States by virtue of the principle of the duty to cooperate in good faith, which means in particular that Member States are to take all appropriate measures, whether general or particular, to ensure fulfilment of their obligations under European Union law (see *Pupino*, paragraph 42). Article 37 EU thus provides that the Member States are to defend the common positions '[w]ithin international organisations and at international conferences in which they take part'. However, a common position is not supposed to produce of itself legal effects in relation to third parties. That is why, in the system established by Title VI of the EU Treaty, only framework decisions and decisions may be the subject of an action for annulment before the Court of Justice. The Court's jurisdiction, as defined by Article 35(1) EU, to give preliminary rulings also does not extend to common positions but is limited to rulings on the validity and interpretation of framework decisions and decisions, on the interpretation of conventions established under Title VI and on the validity and interpretation of the measures implementing them.

53. Article 35(1) EU, in that it does not enable national courts to refer a question to the Court for a preliminary ruling on a common position but only a question concerning the acts listed in that provision, treats as acts capable of being the subject of such a reference for a preliminary ruling all measures adopted by the Council and intended to produce legal effects in relation to third parties. Given that the procedure enabling the Court to give preliminary rulings is designed to guarantee observance of the law in the interpretation and application of the Treaty, it would run counter to that objective to interpret Article 35(1) EU narrowly. The right to make a reference to the Court of Justice for a preliminary ruling must therefore exist in respect of all measures adopted by the Council, whatever their nature or form, which are intended to have legal effects in relation to third parties . . .

54. As a result, it has to be possible to make subject to review by the Court a common position which, because of its content, has a scope going beyond that assigned by the EU Treaty to that kind of act. Therefore, a national court hearing a dispute which indirectly raises the issue of the validity or interpretation of a common position adopted on the basis of Article 34 EU, as is the case in this instance for part of Common Position 2001/931 and in any event for Article 4 thereof and the Annex thereto, and which has serious doubts whether that common position is really intended to produce legal effects in relation to third parties, would be able, subject to the conditions fixed by Article 35 EU, to ask the Court to give a preliminary ruling. It would then fall to the Court to find, where appropriate, that the common position is intended to produce legal effects in relation to third parties, to accord it its true classification and to give a preliminary ruling.

55. The Court would also have jurisdiction to review the lawfulness of such acts when an action has been brought by a Member State or the Commission under the conditions fixed by Article 35(6) EU.

56. Finally, it is to be borne in mind that it is for the Member States and, in particular, their courts and tribunals, to interpret and apply national procedural rules governing the exercise of rights of action in a way that enables natural and legal persons to challenge before the courts the lawfulness of any decision or other national measure relating to the drawing up of an act of the European Union or to its application to them and to seek compensation for any loss suffered.

In the final paragraph of the extract, the judgment makes clear that, in the third pillar, EU fundamental rights law binds not just Union institutions, but also Member States implementing Union law. *Segi* was unusual, however, in that fundamental rights law was used to protect the EU institutions from challenge. The more conventional situation arose in *Advocaten voor de Wereld*.[19] This case involved a challenge by a Belgian NGO to Framework Decision 2002/584/JHA, establishing the European Arrest Warrant. The Arrest Warrant abolished the principle of dual criminality for thirty-two offences. For these offences, a State is required to surrender an individual to the State issuing a warrant even if the alleged acts do not constitute an offence on its territory. Advocaten voor de Wereld argued that this violated fundamental rights in two ways. First, it breached the non-discrimination principle by making an arbitrary distinction between these and other offences not included. Second, it violated the principle of legality under which offences and penalties must be clearly defined. The Court emphasised that Union institutions and Member States implementing Union law were subject to review for compliance with EU fundamental rights law. It ruled that there had been no breach. The non-discrimination principle had not been violated as a distinction could be made between these offences and other offences by virtue of their seriousness which could justify a difference in treatment. There was no breach of the legality principle as the offences were required to be clearly defined in the legislation of the issuing State, who would have to respect fundamental rights.

In both these judgments, it is noteworthy that the Court stated that EU fundamental rights law bound Union institutions and Member States *implementing* Union law. This is different from and, in some respects, narrower than the traditional formulation since *ERT*,[20] which referred to Member States *acting within the field* of EC law. More saliently still, the former is also the formulation adopted by the Lisbon Treaty. Article 6 LTEU refers to Chapter VII of the Charter. There, Article 51(1) states that the Charter only binds Member States when they are implementing Union law. It is notable here that the Court has only referred to that formulation twice since the signing of the Constitutional Treaty.[21]

However, there is ambiguity as to the meaning of this. The Explanations of the Secretariat suggest that 'implementing' is synonymous with 'acting within the field of'.[22] Any Member State action falling within the field of Union law would therefore be caught by EU fundamental rights law. By contrast, the Czech Government lodged a Declaration to the Lisbon Treaty stating that the Charter only binds Member States when they are implementing Union law, and not when they are adopting

19 Case C-303/05 *Advocaten voor de Wereld v Leden van de Ministerraad*, Judgment of 3 May 2007.
20 Case C-260/89 *ERT v DEP* [1991] ECR I-2925.
21 Case C-36/02 *Omega v Oberbürgermeisterin der Bundesstalt Bonn* [2004] ECR I-9609; Case C-441/02 *Commission v Germany*, Judgment of 27 April 2006.
22 Explanations Relating to the Charter of Fundamental Rights of the European Union, CHARTE 4473/00, 46–7.

and implementing national law independently from Union law.[23] This would suggest a narrower test whereby EU fundamental rights law binds Member States only when they are transposing, implementing or enforcing Union law. This uncertainty is unfortunate and gives the impression of poor draftsmanship with regard to this dimension of the Lisbon Treaty.

---

23 Declaration by the Czech Republic on the Charter of Fundamental Rights of the European Union, article 1.

7

Judicial relations in the European Union

CONTENTS	
1. Introduction	75
2. Integration of the reference procedures	75
3. Preserving the unity of Union law	78

1. Introduction

The central theme in developments in EU judicial relations has been the bolstering of the institutional authority of the Court of Justice through expanding the remit of the preliminary reference procedure and reaffirming the Court's central position within it. The Lisbon Treaty followed the template set out by the Constitutional Treaty and replaced the current three procedures with a single preliminary ruling procedure. In practical terms, this will make it much easier for references to be made in the area of freedom, security and justice, and it will mean an end to the exceptional procedures limiting who can make such references. Alongside this, the Court of Justice has reiterated in recent case law the duty of referral for national courts, against whose decisions there is no judicial remedy, and amplified the consequences and penalties where they fail to refer. In so doing, it indicated that the extra cases it received would not be used as a justification for decentralisation of the judicial system. Instead, the workload would be managed through internal procedural reforms. It remains to be seen whether these will be sufficient.

2. Integration of the reference procedures

Subject to the general limits placed on the jurisdiction of the Court,[1] following the Lisbon Treaty all Union law will be subject to a unitary framework modelled on that currently provided by Article 234 EC.

---

1 See pp. 22–3 of the updates.

Article 19(3)(b) LTEU The Court of Justice of the European Union shall, in accordance with the Treaties . . . (b) give preliminary rulings, at the request of courts or tribunals of the Member States, on the interpretation of Union law or the validity of acts adopted by the institutions. .

Article 267 LTFEU The Court of Justice of the European Union shall have jurisdiction to give preliminary rulings concerning:

(a) the interpretation of the Treaties;
(b) the validity and interpretation of acts of the institutions, bodies, offices or agencies of the Union.

Where such a question is raised before any court or tribunal of a Member State, that court or tribunal may, if it considers that a decision on the question is necessary to enable it to give judgment, request the Court to give a ruling thereon.

Where any such question is raised in a case pending before a court or tribunal of a Member State against whose decisions there is no judicial remedy under national law, that court or tribunal shall bring the matter before the Court.

If such a question is raised in a case pending before a court or tribunal of a Member State with regard to a person in custody, the Court of Justice of the European Union shall act with the minimum of delay.

The Treaty dispenses with the procedures set out in Article 68 EC for Title IV on Visas, Asylum, Immigration and other Policies Related to Free Movement of Persons and Article 35 TEU for Title VI on Police and Judicial Cooperation in Criminal Matters. The former, it will be remembered, confines the power to refer to national courts against whose decision there is no judicial remedy. The latter gives Member States a right to opt-in through a Declaration to the reference procedure in the field of policing and judicial cooperation in criminal matters. Member States could decide whether the power to refer should be granted to all courts or merely those against whose decisions there is no judicial remedy. Concerns were expressed about these procedures on a number of fronts:[2]

- The possibilities for the development of Union law and its uniformity in these fields were constrained as the circumstances in which references could be made were highly limited.[3]
- The procedures were considered to undermine judicial protection of individuals where lower courts were prevented from making a reference. These could not declare an EU measure invalid by virtue of the *Fotofrost* doctrine,[4] and equally could not refer the matter to the Court of Justice.

2 With the exception of Ireland and the United Kingdom, all EU-15 States have fully opted in. Spain only allows courts of last resort to make references. Of the new Member States, the Czech Republic, Hungary, Latvia, Slovenia and Lithuania have opted in. OJ 2008, L 70/23.
3 EC Commission, *Adaptation of the provisions of Title IV EC Treaty relating to the jurisdiction of the Court of Justice with a view to ensuring more effective judicial protection*, COM (2006) 346.
4 Case 314/85 *Foto-Frost* [1987] ECR 4199.

- The Court's docket in the field of policing and judicial cooperation was highly imbalanced. Whilst its rulings bound all courts in the Union, it could only receive references from courts in seventeen Member States.

Although the amendments act to counter these criticisms, they bring their own challenges. These are alluded to in the final paragraph, which has no counterpart in Article 234 EC. It provides for the Court of Justice to act with a minimum of delay if a person is in custody. The EU institutions have already implemented this through a Council Decision amending the Court Rules of Procedure to create a new 'urgent procedure' which applies only in the area of freedom, security and justice.[5] This procedure allows, on the one hand, for a national court to request that a reference jump the queue and be heard urgently, and, on the other hand, provides for certain procedural short cuts to be taken in such circumstances. Its presence is an admission both that the Court has more work than it can currently handle, and that the new procedure will expose the Court to significantly more references, and exacerbate the situation. Although it is clearly unacceptable for a person's time in custody to be extended on account of judicial backlog, the fast track procedure will lead to further problems.

First, immigration, asylum and criminal law, the fields in which this procedure will be deployed, also form the mainstay of national judicial activity in a manner unparalleled by any other area of EU law. Enabling the Court of Justice to be easily accessible in these fields, with resolution possible in a matter of days, while the restrictions on access are maintained in other fields, will unbalance its docket. There is a real danger it will become, in practice, a criminal and asylum court with other cases being treated in a residual manner.

Second, the short cuts in procedure pose a number of risks. The opinion of the Advocate General can be dispensed with and restrictions may be placed on the rights of Member States and EU institutions to make submissions. In extreme circumstances, there will, in fact, only be an oral procedure. Whilst the case for urgency is appreciated, a situation where the Court is making authoritative rulings in fields as important as this is a recipe for bad law.

Third, there is the question of abuse of judicial discretion. Since 2000, there has been provision for an expedited and accelerated procedure, which contains none of these procedural short cuts.[6] The urgent procedure will work in the same way, with the national court requesting it and the Court of Justice deciding whether to grant the request. The Court has approved the request in only 3/51 cases[7] and in relation to

---

5 Decision 2008/79 EC, Euratom amending amending the Protocol on the Statute of the Court of Justice, OJ 2008, L 24/42.
6 E. de la Serre, 'Accelerated and expedited procedures before the EC Courts: a review of the practice' (2006) 43 *CMLR* 783.
7 *Annual Report of the Court of Justice 2007* (2008, Luxembourg) Table 15.

the urgent procedure, it has issued a communication indicating that it will consider the question of 'urgency' on a case by case basis.[8]

3. Preserving the unity of Union law

The *Köbler* judgment indicated that a State can be liable in damages if a national court against whose decisions there is no judicial remedy misinterprets a point of EC law in a sufficiently serious manner, or fails to refer where the point of law is not already resolved by case law of the Court of Justice, or where it is not so clear that there is no reasonable doubt as to its interpretation.[9] This draconian, and for many national courts unprecedented, form of judicial accountability has led to two changes.

The first is a direct alteration, calling for a rethink of the *Köbler* principle. In *Traghetti*, the Italian Court of Cassation, the top civil court, had ruled in a dispute between ferry operators that a subsidy granted to one based in the Mezzogiorno region of Italy did not violate EC law on State aids as it followed the Court of Justice's settled case law. Traghetti, the ferry operator bringing the proceedings, had meanwhile gone into liquidation. Its administrator considered that the Court of Cassation had misapplied the law and brought an action for damages. However, Italian law excluded liability for damage where any infringement was the result of a court of last instance's interpretation of the law or assessment of the facts and evidence. In cases where liability was permitted, there was also a requirement for intentional fault and serious misconduct on the part of the court.

> ### Case C-173/03 Traghetti del Mediterraneo v Italian Republic [2006] ECR I- 5177
>
> 33. Analogous considerations linked to the need to guarantee effective judicial protection to individuals of the rights conferred on them by Community law similarly preclude State liability not being incurred solely because an infringement of Community law attributable to a national court adjudicating at last instance arises from the interpretation of provisions of law made by that court.
>
> 34. On the one hand, interpretation of provisions of law forms part of the very essence of judicial activity since, whatever the sphere of activity considered, a court faced with divergent or conflicting arguments must normally interpret the relevant legal rules – of national and/or Community law – in order to resolve the dispute brought before it.
>
> 35. On the other hand, it is not inconceivable that a manifest infringement of Community law might be committed precisely in the exercise of such work of interpretation if, for example,

---

8 'Information Note on references from national courts for a preliminary ruling: Supplement following the implementation of the urgent preliminary ruling procedure applicable to references concerning the area of freedom, security and justice' http://curia.europa.eu/en/instit/txtdocfr/txtsenvigueur/noteppu.pdf <1 April 2008>

9 Case C-224/01 *Köbler* [2003] ECR I-10239.

the court gives a substantive or procedural rule of Community law a manifestly incorrect meaning, particularly in the light of the relevant case-law of the Court on the subject . . ., or where it interprets national law in such a way that in practice it leads to an infringement of the applicable Community law.

36. As the Advocate General observed in point 52 of his Opinion, to exclude all State liability in such circumstances on the ground that the infringement of Community law arises from an interpretation of provisions of law made by a court would be tantamount to rendering meaningless the principle laid down by the Court in the *Köbler* judgment. That remark is even more apposite in the case of courts adjudicating at last instance, which are responsible, at national level, for ensuring that rules of law are given a uniform interpretation.

37. An analogous conclusion must be drawn with regard to legislation which in a general manner excludes all State liability where the infringement attributable to a court of that State arises from its assessment of the facts and evidence.

38. On the one hand, such an assessment constitutes, like the interpretation of provisions of law, another essential aspect of the judicial function since, regardless of the interpretation adopted by the national court seised of a particular case, the application of those provisions to that case will often depend on the assessment which the court has made of the facts and the value and relevance of the evidence adduced for that purpose by the parties to the dispute.

39. On the other hand, such an assessment – which sometimes requires complex analysis – may also lead, in certain cases, to a manifest infringement of the applicable law, whether that assessment is made in the context of the application of specific provisions relating to the burden of proof or the weight or admissibility of the evidence, or in the context of the application of provisions which require a legal characterisation of the facts.

40. To exclude, in such circumstances, any possibility that State liability might be incurred where the infringement allegedly committed by the national court relates to the assessment which it made of facts or evidence would also amount to depriving the principle set out in the *Köbler* judgment of all practical effect with regard to manifest infringements of Community law for which courts adjudicating at last instance were responsible.

42. With regard, finally, to the limitation of State liability to cases of intentional fault and serious misconduct on the part of the court, it should be recalled, as was pointed out in paragraph 32 of this judgment, that the Court held, in the *Köbler* judgment, that State liability for damage caused to individuals by reason of an infringement of Community law attributable to a national court adjudicating at last instance could be incurred in the exceptional case where that court manifestly infringed the applicable law.

43. Such manifest infringement is to be assessed, inter alia, in the light of a number of criteria, such as the degree of clarity and precision of the rule infringed, whether the infringement was intentional, whether the error of law was excusable or inexcusable, and the non-compliance by the court in question with its obligation to make a reference for a preliminary ruling under the third paragraph of Article 234 EC; it is in any event presumed where the decision involved is made in manifest disregard of the case-law of the Court on the subject (*Köbler*, paragraphs 53 to 56).

44. Accordingly, although it remains possible for national law to define the criteria relating to the nature or degree of the infringement which must be met before State liability can be incurred for an infringement of Community law attributable to a national court adjudicating at last instance, under no circumstances may such criteria impose requirements stricter than that of a manifest infringement of the applicable law, as set out in paragraphs 53 to 56 of the *Köbler* judgment.

Aside from reaffirming *Köbler*, *Traghetti* indicates that liability is to be determined on the basis of a competence-based rather than fault-based test. That is to say liability will be incurred not necessarily where a national court of last resort flouts EC law, but instead where it fails to interpret EC law in the manner that one would expect of a reasonable court. To be sure, it is too simplistic to argue that the test is merely one of whether a court could reasonably have come to the interpretation it did, and if not then the State is liable for damages. Yet the test, namely whether the interpretation was manifestly inappropriate, is not so different from the standard applied to the notionally competent court. The relevant question would then be how far the national court must fall below that standard in order to attract State liability. On this basis, an action for State liability will involve an action before a court of first instance attacking, in the majority of cases, the most senior court in the land for behaving not just incompetently but very incompetently! This raises all kinds of questions about conflict of interest and about the actual competence of the junior court to hear the action.

The second change to *Köbler* is a more indirect one questioning the circumstances in which national courts are obliged to refer. In particular, national courts have raised the question of whether they can ever declare a Union measure invalid. In *Schul*,[10] a Dutch court of last resort was required to consider a charge levied on Brazilian sugar imported into the Netherlands on a basis of a Commission Regulation. It noted that in this instance, an identical pricing structure was used as regards a measure in the poultry sector, and was ruled illegal by the Court of Justice: the Council had suggested one pricing structure (the representative price) and the Commission had exceeded its delegated power by using a different one (cif price). On the basis of the identical nature of the cases, the national court asked whether it could strike down the measure currently before it. The Court of Justice refused. It noted that there was no analogy with the *CILFIT* judgment, which gives national courts of last resort a margin of discretion in the interpretation of EC law.[11] It repeated its reasoning in *Foto-Frost*.[12] The uniformity of EC law and its procedural rules, by which all Member States and Union institutions have the right to make observations, entailed the conclusion that only it could declare Union acts invalid. The Court noted that this was the case even where an analogous measure had been struck down by it. Even if the measures themselves were the same, the factual and legal context surrounding each measure would be different.

In *Schul*, the Court refuses to soften the obligation on national courts of last resort to refer. Indeed, the Court of Justice even stated that the problem of delay could not be used as an argument for changing the law here. In *IATA*, however, the Court suggested that the matter might be a little more nuanced.[13] The case concerned a

---

10 Case C-461/03 *Schul v Minister van Landbouw, Natuur en Voedselkwaliteit* [2005] ECR I-10513.
11 Case 283/81 *Cilfit* [1982] ECR 3415.   12 Case 314/85 *Foto-Frost* [1987] ECR 4199.
13 Case C-344/04 *R ex parte IATA v Department for Transport* [2006] ECR I-403.

reference from an English court which had received a challenge from the IATA, the central association representing airlines, to Regulation 261/2004, which provided for compensation and assistance to passengers in the event of denied boarding and of cancellation or long delay to long-haul flights. The national court was unconvinced, and the challenge was eventually unsuccessful. It asked about the threshold at which it must refer to the Court of Justice. The latter stated it was not required to refer simply because one party challenged the validity of a measure, and should only do so if it believed an argument as to the invalidity of a measure, raised either by itself or by one of the parties, to be well-founded.

Although *IATA* reaffirms existing case law,[14] it brings a paradox to the fore. Since *Köbler*, we have a system of damages which will punish Member States if national courts against whose decisions there is no judicial remedy do not observe the following schema. They must only refer if they think there is a good chance that an EC measure is invalid. In cases of doubt, they are not required to refer. With regard to interpretation of EC law, they must refer unless there is settled case law or the provision in question is very clear. In other words, where there is doubt, they must refer. Importantly, however, in situations where they have discretion, there are incentives not to refer. The delays of referring will be avoided, and there is no system of penalties. This peculiar distinction in their duties seems to go against the ethos espoused by the Court. Also, it is difficult to believe that if one was devising a schema for mandatory references, one would confine it to cast-iron cases for judicial review of EU institutions, and the interpretation of any ambiguous provision. The consequence is that too few measures will be reviewed and too many arcane disputes subjected to the lengthy procedures of the reference system.

14 The point was actually made in Case 314/85 *Foto-Frost* [1987] ECR 4199.

Accountability and Review of the EU Institutions

1. Introduction

The general theme in recent years has been to open up the EU institutions and make them more accountable. The case law on public access to documents has served to narrow down the exceptions to public access so that not only more activities of the EU institutions are subject to public view, but also the interactions between national governments and the institutions. In addition, the Lisbon Treaty has both sought to increase the number of EU institutions susceptible to judicial review, as well as to relax the rules on standing, particularly for non-privileged applicants. The only field in which contradictory messages have emerged is that of non-contractual liability. On the one hand, the Court seems reluctant to hold EU institutions liable for substantive illegality where these institutions enjoy some discretion, and where their tasks appear in any way complex. In such circumstances, only the most flagrant illegality will incur liability. On the other hand, the Court is severe when it comes to breaches of process and procedure, so that almost any such illegal conduct will attract liability.

2. Transparency

Since 2005, there has been a welter of litigation concerning Regulation 1049/2001/EC, the instrument governing public access to EU institution documents.[1] All these cases have concerned interpretation of the exceptions to the general right of access to documents. On the face of it, this may seem an arcane business; to ponder over

---

1 For the text of the instrument see pp. 324–5 of the main text.

and again the meaning of a particular word in a piece of secondary legislation. Yet it has proved central not only to the remit of the transparency principle, but also to its very meaning. This is because these exceptions do not just provide grounds for EU institutions to refuse individual requests for access. They are formulated in such a way that they can cover whole fields of EU governmental or legislative activity. Debates about the remit of an exception are not therefore simply confined to matters of interpretation, but raise questions as to whether we can be denied access to knowledge about the way in which an entire field of EU law or politics is being conducted. This can be seen more clearly when we look at the three provisions in Regulation 1049/2001/EC attracting the most litigation.

The first is article 4(5), which provides that a Member State may request an EU institution not to disclose a document originating from it without its prior agreement. This exception could cover both the overwhelming proportion of EU legislative negotiations, as well as the administration of EU law carried out by Member States. In respect of EU legislative negotiations, the Commission rarely instigates a legislative proposal off its own bat, but will invariably respond to soundings or initiatives from, *inter alia*, national governments. Likewise, any Commission proposal will be considered by working parties composed of national officials. With regard to the administration of EU law, the Union, with its very limited administrative resources, relies heavily upon national, local and regional administrations to apply and enforce EU law. The prevailing view was that in giving any national government an unconditional veto over any document originating from it, article 4(5) in practice served to foreclose huge areas of EU activity from public view.[2]

This changed in *Sweden v Commission* where Sweden appealed against the *IFAW* decision to the Court of Justice.[3] The Court of Justice held that a national veto over documents originating from a Member State would be incompatible with both the general principle of transparency and the obligation upon EU institutions to disclose the documents provided to them by third parties. Article 4(5) could not therefore be used as a further exception to the right of public access. Instead, it had to be read in the light of article 4(1)–(3) on the substantive grounds for refusing access to a document. Article 4(5) only gave a Member State 'a form of assent confirming that none of the grounds of exception under article 4(1) to (3) is present'. If an EU institution received a request for a national document, it was required to open a dialogue with the Member State, which could only refuse disclosure if it provided reasons why the document fell within one of the exceptions set out in article 4(1)–(3).

The judgment revolutionises the principle of transparency. It indicates that the same substantive principles concerning grounds for disclosure shall apply whatever the provenance of the document. In this way it significantly expands the remit of

---

2 T-76/02 *Messina v Commission* [2003] ECR II-3203; T-168/02 *IFAW v Commission* [2004] ECR II-4135.
3 Case C-64/05P *Sweden v Commission*, Judgment of 18 December 2007. The *IFAW* judgment is discussed at pp. 327–8 in the main text.

the principle in that whole fields of activity in which the predominant players are Member States will now be subject to far greater scrutiny. National governments may not pass documents to EU institutions in order to evade disclosure, nor can they seek to enlarge the exceptions contained in article 4(1)–(3). It is yet to be seen how effective this will be in practice, but is clear that in terms of transparency, it is a significant improvement on the status quo.

The second field of activity is that covered by article 4(2), which allows EU institutions to refuse to disclose documents, inter alia, for 'the purpose of inspections, investigations and audits, unless there is an overriding public interest in disclosure'. This exception covers almost all the work of OLAF, the Community anti-fraud unit, and much of the Commission's work in competition, external trade relations and management of the Union's expenditure. In short, it would allow much of the EU administration to be kept from public view. The Commission, in particular, had been keen for the exception to cover not only on-going inspections, but all inspections, irrespective of how long ago they had taken place. This interpretation has been refused by the CFI, which has stated that the exception cannot apply to inspections, investigations or audits which have been completed.[4] Documents concerning these must be disclosed. This distinction between past and ongoing proceedings suggests a double function of the transparency principle. With regard to past proceedings, transparency is important and is used to secure the accountability of EU institutions, to verify their actions and to enable exposure of any maladministration or illegal conduct that might have occurred. The importance of the principle of accountability provides little if any justification for refusing disclosure of documents. With regard to ongoing proceedings, another value is at stake. Parties sometimes request access to documents as a means of participating in, allaying or disrupting proceedings. Whilst there may be grounds for refusing disclosure of documents, there may also grounds for allowing them. The CFI stated therefore in *Technische Glaswerke Ilmenau* that the discretion to refuse documents with regard to on-going proceedings is limited.[5] Refusal can only take place where there is a reasonably foreseeable risk to the purpose of the inspection, investigation or audit in question and there is no overriding public interest in disclosure. It also stated that an assessment must be made and reasons provided for each individual document requested. Blanket refusals are unacceptable.

3. Judicial review

The theme of expanding the accountability of EU institutions in the field of transparency is mirrored in developments in the field of judicial review. This is reflected, first, in the amendments proposed by the Lisbon Treaty.

4 Joined Cases T-391/03 & T-70/04 *Franchet et al. v Commission* [2006] ECR II-2023.
5 Case T-237/02 *Technische Glaswerke Ilmenau v Commission* [2006] ECR II-5131.

Article 263 LTFEU The Court of Justice of the European Union shall review the legality of legislative acts, of acts of the Council, of the Commission and of the European Central Bank, other than recommendations and opinions, and of acts of the European Parliament and of the European Council intended to produce legal effects vis-à-vis third parties. It shall also review the legality of acts of bodies, offices or agencies of the Union intended to produce legal effects vis-à-vis third parties.

It shall for this purpose have jurisdiction in actions brought by a Member State, the European Parliament, the Council or the Commission on grounds of lack of competence, infringement of an essential procedural requirement, infringement of the Treaties or of any rule of law relating to their application, or misuse of powers.

The Court shall have jurisdiction under the same conditions in actions brought by the Court of Auditors, by the European Central Bank and by the Committee of the Regions for the purpose of protecting their prerogatives.

The new provision widens the range of the bodies and institutions susceptible to judicial review by including the European Council and Union agencies as bodies whose acts can be challenged. As stated in chapter 1, the inclusion of the European Council is potentially significant as the decision to subject the agreements of twenty-seven Heads of Government to judicial challenge is unprecedented and illustrates the symbolic importance attached to the rule of law in the European Union. In a different way, the clarification as to the accountability of Union agencies is of equal significance. In recent years, agencies have proliferated and on 1 April 2008 there were twenty-four Community agencies, six executive agencies and three agencies in the field of policing and judicial cooperation in criminal matters.[6] Though their powers vary considerably, most dominate their fields through establishing technical norms or patterns of coordination between national agencies. There has been particular concern over their accountability, most notably in the field of policing and judicial cooperation in criminal matters.[7]

The practical importance of this amendment will hang on which types of measure are considered amenable to review. The European Council cannot adopt legislative measures and very few agencies have the power to adopt legally binding decisions. If the Court adopts a narrow view in which 'acts' capable of being reviewed must bring about a change in a party's legal position, then most of the activity of these bodies would fall below the radar. This would be a pity as European Council guidelines are intended to inform legal changes, while EU institutions invariably not only follow the expert opinions of agencies in setting out legal norms, but are also obliged to do so unless they can find a substitute expert body and provide reasons for following the opinion of the latter.[8] There are, therefore, strong arguments for the accountability of these activities. There is also legal support for such activities being challengeable.

---

6 There are also three agencies in the field of common foreign and security policy, but, as this field falls outside the jurisdiction of the Court of Justice, these cannot be judicially reviewed.

7 Case C-160/03 *Spain v Eurojust* [2005] ECR I-2077.

8 Case T-13/99 *Pfizer Animal Health v Council* [2002] ECR II-3305.

In *Commission v Council*,[9] the Court held that conclusions adopted by the Council were reviewable acts, insofar as these conclusions decided to hold an institutional procedure, in this case the excessive deficit procedure, in abeyance. If that is so, it would appear that any guideline or opinion is reviewable if it forms part of a decision-making procedure and must take place for a procedure to be started, continued or ceased. This reasoning is supported by *IATA*.[10] In this instance, a joint text decided by the Conciliation Committee within the context of the co-decision procedure was challenged on the grounds that it had exceeded its powers. A joint text is not a legally binding document, but forms part of the co-decision procedure. While the Court found that the Committee had acted lawfully, it had no hesitation in reviewing the joint text and the Committee's behaviour.

The second paragraph of Article 263 LTFEU has introduced one new privileged applicant, the Committee of the Regions, who may review measures for the purpose of protecting its prerogatives. This amendment suggests a reinforced position for the Committee beyond simply a new power of judicial review. To date, there had been nothing to suggest that it was in an analogous position to the European Parliament. Where provision is made for its consultation, it must be consulted if the measure is not to be illegal, as well as re-consulted if the final measure adopted is significantly different from that upon which it was consulted.[11] In the light of the Committee of the Regions now having 'prerogatives' to protect, this may have to be revisited. Failure to consult may now generate legal consequences and so consultation will have to be more systematic and more weight should be given to the Committee's opinions.

The standing of non-privileged applicants has also been altered by the Lisbon Treaty.

> **Article 263(4) LTFEU** Any natural or legal person may, under the conditions referred to in the first and second subparagraphs, institute proceedings against an act addressed to that person or which is of direct and individual concern to them, and against a regulatory act which is of direct concern to them and does not entail implementing measures.
>
> Acts setting up bodies, offices and agencies of the Union may lay down specific conditions (5) and arrangements concerning actions brought by natural or legal persons against acts of these bodies, offices or agencies intended to produce legal effects in relation to them.

The central change has been the abolition of the requirement of individual concern for challenges to regulatory acts. The phraseology is unfortunate and is a left-over from the Constitutional Treaty. Regulatory acts are not defined in the Lisbon Treaty, but were described by the Constitutional Treaty as measures which are 'non legislative' but general in nature and which implement EU legislation or Treaty provisions.[12] They are, in short, quasi-legislation. Article 263(4) LFTEU brings about, therefore,

9 Case C-27/04 *Commission v Council* [2004] ECR I-6649.
10 Case C-344/04 *R v Department of Transport ex parte IATA* [2006] ECR I-403.
11 See pp. 146–9 of the main text.   12 Article I-32(1) CT.

a fundamental shift in the balance of power between the EU administration and the EU judiciary. Whilst the latter is still to have relatively curtailed jurisdiction with regard to genuine legislative measures, they are to have general jurisdiction over any administrative measure, which directly affects private parties. Individuals will not only be able to challenge administrative measures more easily, but there will also be greater judicial scrutiny and involvement with EU administration. This shift is reflected in Article 263(5) LFTEU, an addition to the status quo, which provides for the possibility of even more relaxed rules of standing for reviewing measures of regulatory agencies.

The philosophy of the Lisbon Treaty is that measures taken by non-representative and non-majoritarian institutions – be they the Commission or agencies – should be subject to greater judicial review. This represents an important ideological shift. The arguments in favour of delegating powers to these bodies are those of specialised expertise, decisional efficiency and long-term planning. Extension of judicial over-sight over these bodies suggests a realignment in which these values are to be more strongly constrained by other values of liberal democracy, such as fundamental rights, the giving of reasons and proper consultation.

4. Non contractual liability

It will be remembered that for an individual to sue Union institutions under Article 288(2) EC (Article 340(2) LTFEU following Lisbon) three conditions must be met:

- the rule of EC law breached must confer rights on individuals;
- there must be a sufficiently serious breach of this rule;
- there must be a causal link between the unlawful conduct and the damage suffered by the individual.

For many years, a distinction was made between legislative acts involving economic policy choices and other acts, with a far higher degree of fault required for liability in the case of the former.[13] From *Bergaderm* onwards, the Court has indicated that it will operate a single test which makes no distinction between the types of act being challenged.[14] Instead, the central question would be the amount of discretion avail-able to the EU institution. Simple illegality is sufficient where there is no discretion, but further culpability must be present where the institution enjoys some discretion. The CFI ruled in more detail on the parameters of liability in *Schneider*. Schneider and Legrand were two companies specialising in electrical distribution and low volt-age installations who merged into a single company. They notified the Commission of this, who, under its merger powers, declared the merger incompatible with the common market and ordered a break up of the company. In 2002, the CFI found the

---

13 Case 5/71 *Aktien-Zuckerfabrik Schöppenstedt* v *Council* [1971] ECR 975.
14 Case C-352/98P *Laboratoires Pharmaceutiques Bergaderm* v *Commission* [2000] ECR I-5291. This was reaffirmed in Case T-47/03 *Sison* v *Council*, Judgment of 11 July 2007.

Commission decision to be illegal on two grounds.[15] There were errors in its economic analysis of all the national markets other than the French market. Notwithstanding this, the CFI held that the competition effects on the French market were sufficient for the merger to be declared incompatible with the single market. In addition, in its initial statement of objections, the Commission had failed to tell Schneider in sufficiently clear terms what measures it needed to take to avoid the merger being declared illegal. Schneider then sued under Article 288(2) EC:

T-351/03 Schneider v Commission, Judgment of 11 July 2007

116. The system of rules which the Court of Justice has worked out in relation to the non-contractual liability of the Community takes into account, inter alia, the complexity of the situations to be regulated, difficulties in the application or interpretation of the legislation and, more particularly, the margin of discretion available to the author of the act in question . . .

117. Where the institution criticised has only considerably reduced, or even no, discretion, the mere infringement of Community law may be sufficient to establish the existence of a sufficiently serious breach of Community law . . .

118. The same applies where the defendant institution breaches a general obligation of diligence . . . or misapplies relevant substantive or procedural rules . . .

121. In that context, the Commission contends that, if it were to incur financial liability in circumstances such as those of this case, its capacity fully to function as a regulator of competition, a task entrusted to it by the EC Treaty, would be compromised as a result of the possible inhibiting effect that the risk of having to bear damages alleged by the undertakings concerned might have on the control of concentrations.

122. It must be conceded that such an effect, contrary to the general Community interest, might arise if the concept of a serious breach of Community law were construed as comprising all errors or mistakes which, even if of some gravity, are not by their nature or extent alien to the normal conduct of an institution entrusted with the task of overseeing the application of competition rules, which are complex, delicate and subject to a considerable degree of discretion.

123. Therefore, a sufficiently serious breach of Community law, for the purposes of establishing the non-contractual liability of the Community, cannot be constituted by failure to fulfil a legal obligation, which, regrettable though it may be, can be explained by the objective constraints to which the institution and its officials are subject as a result of the provisions governing the control of concentrations.

124. On the other hand, the right to compensation for damage resulting from the conduct of the institution becomes available where such conduct takes the form of action manifestly contrary to the rule of law and seriously detrimental to the interests of persons outside the institution and cannot be justified or accounted for by the particular constraints to which the staff of the institution, operating normally, is objectively subject.

125. Such a definition of the threshold for the establishment of non-contractual liability of the Community is conducive to protection of the room for manoeuvre and freedom of assessment which must, in the general interest, be enjoyed by the Community regulator of competition, both in its discretionary decisions and in its interpretation and application of the

---

15 Case T-310/01 *Schneider* v *Commission* [2002] ECR II-4071.

relevant provisions of primary and secondary Community law, without thereby leaving third parties to bear the consequences of flagrant and inexcusable misconduct. . .

129. In principle, the possibility cannot be ruled out that manifest and serious defects affecting the economic analysis underlying competition policy decisions may constitute sufficiently serious breaches of a rule of law to cause the Community to incur non-contractual liability.

130. However, for such a finding to be made it is first necessary to verify that the rule infringed by the incorrect analysis is intended to confer rights on individuals. Whilst certain principles and certain rules which must be observed in any competitive analysis are indeed rules intended to confer rights on individuals, not all norms, whether of primary or secondary law or deriving from case-law, which the Commission must observe in its economic assessments can be automatically held to be rules of that kind.

131. Next, it must be noted that the economic analyses necessary for the classification, under competition law, of a given situation or transaction are generally, as regards both the facts and the reasoning based on the account of the facts, complex and difficult intellectual formulas, which may inadvertently contain certain inadequacies, such as approximations, inconsistencies, or indeed certain omissions, in view of the time constraints to which the institution is subject. That is even more so where, as in the case of the control of concentrations, the analysis has a prospective element. The gravity of a documentary or logical inadequacy, in such circumstances, may not always constitute a sufficient circumstance to cause the Community to incur liability.

132. Last, it must be borne in mind that the Commission enjoys discretion in maintaining control over Community competition policy, which means that rigorously consistent and invariable practice in implementing the relevant rules cannot be expected of it, and, as a corollary, that it enjoys a degree of latitude regarding the choice of the econometric instruments available to it and the choice of the appropriate approach to the study of any matter (see, for example, regarding the definition of the relevant market, . . . provided that those choices are not manifestly contrary to the accepted rules of economic discipline and are applied consistently.

133. However, it is unnecessary in this case to decide whether the three foregoing considerations support the view that the defects in the economic analysis of the expected effects of the transaction on the relevant sectoral markets outside France go beyond the threshold at which the Community must be held to have incurred non-contractual liability.

134. The defects in the analysis of the impact of the transaction on national sectoral markets outside France found by the *Schneider I* judgment cannot have had any effect on the finding finally arrived at by the Commission in the incompatibility decision that the transaction was incompatible with the common market.

135. Even in the absence of that breach of Community law, the Commission would not have been in a position to authorise the transaction as proposed at that time, since . . . the errors found did not in themselves suffice to call in question the objections which the Commission had raised in respect of each of the French sectoral markets . . .

152. In this case, a manifest and serious breach . . . of the regulation stems from the fact of the Commission's drafting, as in this case, a statement of objections in such a way that, as is apparent from the *Schneider I* judgment, the applicant could not ascertain that, if it did not submit corrective measures conducive to reducing or eliminating the support between its positions and those of Legrand in the French sectoral markets, it had no chance of securing a declaration that the transaction was compatible with the common market.

153. Thus, the corrective measures submitted by Schneider in September 2001, which included Legrand's withdrawal from the market in components for panel-boards throughout

the EEA, were not objectively capable of resolving the specific problem of the support provided, on the French sectoral markets in low-voltage electrical equipment perceived at wholesale level, by Schneider's dominant position in the sector of components for distribution and final panel-boards to Legrand's leading position in the ultraterminal equipment segments.

154. That breach of the rights of the defence is neither justified nor accounted for by the particular constraints to which Commission staff are objectively subject. The fault at issue, the existence and extent of which are not contested by the Commission, therefore imposes upon the Community a duty to make good the harmful consequences.

155. The defendant's argument as to the difficulty inherent in undertaking a complex market analysis under a very rigid time constraint is irrelevant, since the fact giving rise to the damage under consideration here is not the analysis of the relevant markets contained in the statement of objections or the incompatibility decision but the omission from the statement of objections of a reference which was of the essence as regards its consequences and the operative part of the incompatibility decision, which did not involve any particular technical difficulty or call for any additional specific examination that could not be carried out for reasons of time and the absence of which cannot be attributed to a fortuitous or accidental drafting problem that could be compensated for by a reading of the statement of objections as a whole.

156. It follows that the breach of Schneider's rights of defence is to be regarded in this case as a manifest and serious disregard by the Commission of the limits to which it is subject and, as such, constitutes a sufficiently serious breach of a rule of law intended to confer rights on individuals.

In determining the standard for liability of EU institutions, the Court could have used a risk-based test. This would have involved the Court deciding, in conditions of uncertainty, whether EU institutions or private parties would be better equipped to bear responsibility for the costs of things going wrong. Instead, the Court chose to apply a fault-based test. The virtues of such a test are that it carries with it a duty of care on the part of EU institutions to those affected by their actions. This test is not, however, without its own challenges. There is a danger that the acknowledgment of a breach of this duty of care through the payment of damages might negatively impact on others reliant upon EU funds, considering that such damages have to be paid out of public funds, the most part of which would otherwise go to the needy. Another challenge facing the fault-based test is the question of the required level of fault for determining liability. In this regard, EC law suggests a paradoxical standard. With regard to substantive obligations, only the most flagrant violations of clear obligations or arbitrary conduct will incur liability – a very narrow fault test indeed. As regards matters of process, the situation is reversed, with relatively small failures to observe due process or rights of defence being likely to lead to liability. The difficulty with this is that it provides incentives for EU institutions to focus on process in their activities at the expense of substance.

The enforcement of European law

CONTENTS

1. Introduction

The first significant development in this field has been the attempt to give more bite to the Article 228 EC procedure, which allows the Court of Justice to impose fines on Member States who have not complied with a prior Article 226 EC ruling. The changes in Commission practices as well as reforms introduced in the Lisbon Treaty suggest that the procedure will be deployed more frequently, with more easily imposable, more draconian penalties. The other development concerns the application of EC law in national courts. In particular, it concerns the question as to whether the doctrine of effective judicial protection of EC law is an autonomous legal doctrine separate from other EC law doctrines such as direct effect, indirect effect and the State liability. The Court does indeed seems to be moving to a position where this is the case. This has consequences for the legal entitlements parties enjoy before courts, as it suggests some level of protection even where this is not afforded by these latter doctrines.

2. Strengthening the powers of the Court of Justice to sanction Member States

The Article 228 EC procedure allowing for the sanctioning and fining of Member States who are not complying with EC law was established at Maastricht. As of 1 April 2008, only seven Member States had appeared before the Court under the procedure. Considering that all cases were decided against the Member States, and that five of these cases took place in the last three years, its non-deployment seems to be, above all, a matter of political will. Undoubtedly, another reason for its lack of use is the lengthy nature of the procedure. The Commission must jump through a number of procedural hoops to bring an Article 226 EC action, obtain a ruling against the Member State, and then, where necessary, repeat the same process under Article 228 EC.

At the *Future of Europe* Convention, it was suggested that Article 226 EC and Article 228 EC be amalgamated in a single procedure mirroring the current Article 226 EC power so that the Court of Justice would not only be able to declare that a Member State had acted illegally, but simultaneously, would have the power to impose a fine.[1] This was not adopted by the Constitutional Treaty. Instead, two amendments were made, which have been reproduced in the Lisbon Treaty.

> **Article 260(2) LTFEU** If the Commission considers that the Member State concerned has not taken the necessary measures to comply with the judgment of the Court, it may bring the case before the Court after giving that State the opportunity to submit its observations.
>
> It shall specify the amount of the lump sum or penalty payment to be paid by the Member State concerned which it considers appropriate in the circumstances.
> If the Court finds that the Member State concerned has not complied with its judgment it may impose a lump sum or penalty payment on it . . .
> 3. When the Commission brings a case before the Court pursuant to Article 258[2] on the grounds that the Member State concerned has failed to fulfil its obligation to notify measures transposing a directive adopted under a legislative procedure, it may, when it deems appropriate, specify the amount of the lump sum or penalty payment to be paid by the Member State concerned which it considers appropriate in the circumstances.
>
> If the Court finds that there is an infringement it may impose a lump sum or penalty payment on the Member State concerned not exceeding the amount specified by the Commission. The payment obligation shall take effect on the date set by the Court in its judgment.

The first change is in Article 260(2) LTFEU. The Commission must still await non-compliance with a prior Court judgment before instigating the procedure, but there is no longer a need for it to issue a reasoned opinion or await Member State compliance with that opinion before taking the case before the Court. Issuing a formal notice and giving the Member State the opportunity to submit its observations is sufficient. It is difficult to predict the effects of this. Taken as a whole, the enforcement procedure is still very cumbersome in light of all the stages to go through in the initial enforcement action. Yet the distance between a declaration of non-compliance with EC law by the Court and the imposition of a fine has been telescoped. The consequence is that while the bite of the Court's judgments on non-compliance is likely to be strengthened, Member States can still play the system in the period prior to the judgment.

The second amendment, set out in Article 260(3) LTFEU, allows the Court of Justice to impose a fine at the initial moment of declaring a Member State non-compliant with EU law (as suggested by the Convention), but only in relation to failure to notify

---

1 Final Report of the Discussion Circle on the Court of Justice, CONV 636/03, 10–11.
2 This is the Article 226 EC procedure renumbered under the LTFEU.

non-transposition of Directives. In this way, an amalgamated procedure has been introduced, but confined to the most limited of circumstances, namely a procedural failure. It is notable that the procedure does not appear to be available for non-transposition or poor transposition of a Directive, but only with regard to the formal process of notification.

There is a third amendment introduced by Lisbon, which is not found in the Constitutional Treaty. It is set out in the final paragraph of Article 260(3) LTFEU, which states that the Court cannot impose a fine in excess of that suggested by the Commission. This is the reverse of the current position in which the Court considers that the Commission's guidelines or suggestions do not bind it any way.[3] This amendment in the Lisbon Treaty casts new importance on the guidelines announced by the Commission on 13 December 2005.[4] These were adopted in the light of the *Commission v France* judgment,[5] which established that Article 228 EC allows for the simultaneous imposition of a daily penalty accruing from the date of the Article 228 EC judgment and a lump sum penalty, accruing from the date of the initial Article 226 EC judgment. The Commission's Communication states that, as a general rule, it will press for both a daily penalty and a lump sum fine.

With regard to the daily penalty, it establishes a two stage formula. The first stage is a daily flat rate of €600 per day multiplied by a coefficient for seriousness (on a scale 1–20) and a coefficient for duration (on a scale 1–3). The coefficient for duration will be 0.10 for each month of continued infringement after the Article 228 EC judgment. The co-efficient for seriousness is determined by the importance of the provision breached[6] and the impact on particular and general interests. The second stage will apply a multiplier, *n*, to the amount reached in the first stage. This multiplier is based on the capacity of the State to pay and its votes in the Council, and ranges from 0.36 for Malta to 25.40 for Germany.

With regard to the lump sum, the Communication suggests a minimum sum for each Member State based on the degree of fault of the State in not complying with the initial judgment. These range from €180,000 for Malta to €12,700,000 for Germany. In addition, to calculate the lump sum a daily rate will be applied if its amount exceeds that of the minimum sum. This rate, which starts from the date of the Article 226 EC judgment, is €200 per day multiplied by the same coefficient for seriousness and by the same *n* multiplier as that described in the paragraph above.

The Commission acknowledges that these formulae must operate in the light of the proportionality principle. There may be times, therefore, when it departs from them.

---

3 The Court imposed, therefore, a higher penalty than that suggested by the Commission in Case C-70/06 *Commission v Portugal*, Judgment of 10 January 2008.
4 EC Commission, *Application of Article 228 EC*, SEC (2005) 1658.
5 Case C-304/02 *Commission v France* [2005] ECR I-6263.
6 Importance is determined not by whether it is a Treaty provision or secondary legislation but by the perceived nature of the rules, so violations of fundamental rights or economic rights are always treated as very serious breaches. *Ibid.*, para 16.1.

It may simply demand a lump sum penalty where the Member State has taken all the necessary measures, but where some time is needed for the results to be realised. Similarly, it acknowledges that more lenient treatment may be appropriate where a Member State has made 'best efforts' to comply, or it has taken all practical steps but is still not yet fully compliant. There may also be times where the Commission suspends penalties in order to take time to verify whether compliance has taken place, or where it seems practicable only to award periodic penalties based on monthly intervals. The proportionality principle cuts both ways, however, and can be used to increase penalties. The Communication, therefore, indicates that where there are several heads of infringement, the Commission will require both the lump sum and the daily penalty to be applied to each head separately.

3. The duty to apply EC law in national courts

An ongoing debate has taken place about whether the basis for application of EC law in national courts has come about as a result of a series of discrete doctrines (direct effect, indirect effect, State liability), or whether there is an independent more general duty to apply EC law derived from the principle of supremacy.[7] The latter view argues that the doctrine of supremacy produces certain exclusionary effects, in particular it prevents a national law being invoked in a national court when it conflicts with EC law. Primacy therefore acts as a shield against national actions which violate EC law. Primacy cannot, however, generate independent actions of its own as it has no substitutionary effects.[8] These are provided autonomously by the doctrines of direct effect, indirect effect and State liability.

The basis in the case law for this latter view had been the *CIA* and *Unilever* judgments,[9] which allowed a Directive, Directive 83/189/EC, to be invoked in a dispute between two private parties by providing that national laws could not be invoked against one because these laws had not followed the procedures in Directive 83/189/EC, which requires that they be notified to the Commission, and not be implemented pending examination. The suspension of these laws was, however, highly contingent. Simple breach of Directive 83/189/EC was insufficient. In addition, the national law had to be hindering, directly or indirectly, the marketing of the goods under dispute. In other words, two features had to be combined to prevent the application of the national laws: non compliance with the Directive, and transgression of the principle of free movement.

---

7 For an excellent discussion of the debates see M. Dougan, 'When worlds collide: competing visions of the relationship between direct effect and supremacy' (2007) 44 *CMLR* 931.
8 For articulators of this view see T. Tridimas, 'Black, white and shades of grey: Horizontality of directives revisited' (2002) 21 *YBEL* 327; K. Lenaerts and T. Corthaut, 'Of birds and hedges: the role of primacy in invoking norms of EU Law' (2006) 31 *ELR* 287.
9 Case 194/94 *CIA v Signalson* [1996] ECR I-2201; Case C-443/98 *Unilever v Central Food* [2000] ECR I-7535. On these see pp. 499–501 of the main text.

This combination of factors, the absence of explicit reasoning by the Court, as well as the lack of follow-up in subsequent cases led many, including the authors of this textbook, to conclude that there was insufficient support for this view. However, the case of *Unibet* has resurrected the debate. Unibet, a British gambling company, sought to advertise its internet gambling in the Swedish media. These gambling activities contravened Swedish law, and the Swedish authorities obtained injunctions and initiated criminal proceedings against those who had provided advertising space to Unibet. No action was brought against Unibet itself. Unibet, however, brought an action for a Declaration that the Swedish law violated Article 49 EC, which provides for the right to provide services. In Swedish law, no possibility exists for an individual to bring a self-standing action for a Declaration that a Swedish statute is illegal in the absence of a specific legal relationship. The Swedish court asked whether effective protection of an individual's rights in EC law required the creation of a new independent remedy permitting an action for a Declaration that a national law is illegal.

Case C-432/05 Unibet v Justitiekanslern, Judgment of 13 March 2007

37. It is to be noted at the outset that, according to settled case-law, the principle of effective judicial protection is a general principle of Community law stemming from the constitutional traditions common to the Member States, which has been enshrined in Articles 6 and 13 of the European Convention for the Protection of Human Rights and Fundamental Freedoms . . . and which has also been reaffirmed by Article 47 of the Charter of fundamental rights of the European Union, proclaimed on 7 December 2000 in Nice (OJ 2000 C 364, p. 1).

38. Under the principle of cooperation laid down in Article 10 EC, it is for the Member States to ensure judicial protection of an individual's rights under Community law . . .

39. It is also to be noted that, in the absence of Community rules governing the matter, it is for the domestic legal system of each Member State to designate the courts and tribunals having jurisdiction and to lay down the detailed procedural rules governing actions for safeguarding rights which individuals derive from Community law . . .

40. Although the EC Treaty has made it possible in a number of instances for private persons to bring a direct action, where appropriate, before the Community Court, it was not intended to create new remedies in the national courts to ensure the observance of Community law other than those already laid down by national law . . .

41. It would be otherwise only if it were apparent from the overall scheme of the national legal system in question that no legal remedy existed which made it possible to ensure, even indirectly, respect for an individual's rights under Community law . . .

42. Thus, while it is, in principle, for national law to determine an individual's standing and legal interest in bringing proceedings, Community law nevertheless requires that the national legislation does not undermine the right to effective judicial protection . . .

43. In that regard, the detailed procedural rules governing actions for safeguarding an individual's rights under Community law must be no less favourable than those governing similar domestic actions (principle of equivalence) and must not render practically impossible or excessively difficult the exercise of rights conferred by Community law (principle of effectiveness) . . .

44. Moreover, it is for the national courts to interpret the procedural rules governing actions brought before them, such as the requirement for there to be a specific legal relationship

between the applicant and the State, in such a way as to enable those rules, wherever possible, to be implemented in such a manner as to contribute to the attainment of the objective, referred to at paragraph 37 above, of ensuring effective judicial protection of an individual's rights under Community law . . .

47. In that regard, it is to be noted, as is apparent from the case-law referred to at paragraph 40 above and has been argued by all the governments which have submitted observations to the Court and by the Commission of the European Communities, that the principle of effective judicial protection does not require it to be possible, as such, to bring a free-standing action which seeks primarily to dispute the compatibility of national provisions with Community law, provided that the principles of equivalence and effectiveness are observed in the domestic system of judicial remedies.

48. Firstly, it is apparent from the order for reference that Swedish law does not provide for such a free-standing action, regardless of whether the higher-ranking legal rule to be complied with is a national rule or a Community rule . . .

53. It is necessary . . . to establish whether the effect of the indirect legal remedies provided for by Swedish law for disputing the compatibility of a national provision with Community law is to render practically impossible or excessively difficult the exercise of rights conferred by Community law.

54. In that regard, each case which raises the question whether a national procedural provision renders the application of Community law impossible or excessively difficult must be analysed by reference to the role of that provision in the procedure, its progress and its special features, viewed as a whole, before the various national instances . . .

55. It is apparent from the order for reference that Swedish law does not prevent a person, such as Unibet, from disputing the compatibility of national legislation, such as the Law on Lotteries, with Community law but that, on the contrary, there exist various indirect legal remedies for that purpose.

56. Thus, firstly, the Högsta domstolen states that Unibet may obtain an examination of whether the Law on Lotteries is compatible with Community law in the context of a claim for damages before the ordinary courts.

57. It is also clear from the order for reference that Unibet brought such a claim and that the Högsta domstolen found it to be admissible.

58. Consequently, where an examination of the compatibility of the Law on Lotteries with Community law takes place in the context of the determination of a claim for damages, that action constitutes a remedy which enables Unibet to ensure effective protection of the rights conferred on it by Community law.

59. It is for the Högsta domstolen to ensure that the examination of the compatibility of that law with Community law takes place irrespective of the assessment of the merits of the case with regard to the requirements for damage and a causal link in the claim for damages.

60. Secondly, the Högsta domstolen adds that, if Unibet applied to the Swedish Government for an exception to the prohibition on the promotion of its services in Sweden, any decision rejecting that application could be the subject of judicial review proceedings before the Regeringsrätten, in which Unibet would be able to argue that the provisions of the Law on Lotteries are incompatible with Community law. Where appropriate, the competent court would be required to disapply the provisions of that law that were considered to be in conflict with Community law.

61. It is to be noted that such judicial review proceedings, which would enable Unibet to obtain a judicial decision that those provisions are incompatible with Community law, constitute a legal remedy securing effective judicial protection of its rights under Community law.

62. Moreover, the Högsta domstolen states that if Unibet disregarded the provisions of the Law on Lotteries and administrative action or criminal proceedings were brought against it by the competent national authorities, it would have the opportunity, in proceedings brought before the administrative court or an ordinary court, to dispute the compatibility of those provisions with Community law. Where appropriate, the competent court would be required to disapply the provisions of that law that were considered to be in conflict with Community law.

63. In addition to the remedies referred to at paragraphs 56 and 60 above, it would therefore be possible for Unibet to claim in court proceedings against the administration or in criminal proceedings that measures taken or required to be taken against it were incompatible with Community law on account of the fact that it had not been permitted by the competent national authorities to promote its services in Sweden.

64. In any event, it is clear from paragraphs 56 to 61 above that Unibet must be regarded as having available to it legal remedies which ensure effective judicial protection of its rights under Community law. If, on the contrary, as mentioned at paragraph 62 above, it was forced to be subject to administrative or criminal proceedings and to any penalties that may result as the sole form of legal remedy for disputing the compatibility of the national provision at issue with Community law, that would not be sufficient to secure for it such effective judicial protection.

65. Accordingly, the answer to the first question must be that the principle of effective judicial protection of an individual's rights under Community law must be interpreted as meaning that it does not require the national legal order of a Member State to provide for a free-standing action for an examination of whether national provisions are compatible with Article 49 EC, provided that other effective legal remedies, which are no less favourable than those governing similar domestic actions, make it possible for such a question of compatibility to be determined as a preliminary issue, which is a matter for the national court to establish.

The significance of *Unibet* is masked by the lengthy reasoning and the Court of Justices' conclusion that there is little wrong with the Swedish system of judicial protection. However, three important steps are taken in the judgment.

First, notwithstanding that Article 49 EC is directly effective,[10] the reasoning of direct effect is not deployed. The Court does not state that Unibet must have a remedy by reason of the direct effect of the provision. Instead, a completely autonomous line of reasoning is used. Unibet has a right to effective remedies equivalent to those available for breaches of domestic law of a similar nature due to its entitlement to effective judicial protection of its rights. This last phrase, effective judicial protection of its rights, is a principle both independent from EC legal doctrines, and which is the starting point for the Court's ensuing reasoning.

Second, whilst the doctrine of effective judicial protection of rights does not establish a free-standing Community action of first resort, it does, *inter alia*, establish a Community action of last resort. If, directly or indirectly, the national system of judicial remedies provides no avenue for an individual to seek protection of their rights before a court, be it through review of an administrative decision or an action

---

10 Case 33/74 *Van Binsbergen v Bestuur van der Bedrijsvereniging voor de Metaalnijverheid* [1974] ECR 1299.

for damages, EC law provides for them to bring an independent action, irrespective of prevailing domestic procedures. It states, therefore, that the effectiveness of EC law requires the provision of new remedies if those provided in the domestic system are insufficient.[11] In this, it seems a precursor to the Lisbon Treaty which has now explicitly provided for such a seam of reasoning.

Article 19 (1) LTEU Member States shall provide remedies sufficient to ensure effective legal protection in the fields covered by Union law.

If *Unibet* establishes the doctrine of effective judicial protection as an independent source of reasoning, the question is raised of the relationship between this doctrine and those of direct effect, indirect effect and State liability. The judgment echoes, albeit in a more detailed and explicit manner, the justification provided in the *Francovich* judgment for the creation of the doctrine of State liability. Here the applicants were left with no alternative remedy but to sue the State for the damage caused.[12] This would suggest that these doctrines can be seen as *leges speciales*, operating within the framework of effective judicial protection. Although they operate within its aegis, they take precedence over it. Just as the doctrine of effective judicial protection only comes into effect if there are no satisfactory domestic procedures, likewise it will only be applicable if there are no satisfactory Community procedures, or where these are too limited to secure adequate redress. The doctrine therefore came into being in *Francovich*, thereby leaving behind the doctrine of State liability, and *Unibet* suggests the Court reserves the right to deploy it again.

The third issue concerns the parameters of the doctrine. It all seems to hang on the presence of some prior right in need of protection. However, EC law is very unclear as to what is understood to be a right. Treaty provisions or Regulations are capable of generating rights. Directives are only capable of generating rights against the State but not, it would appear, against private bodies. Thus, it is suggested that *Unibet* offers a method of reconciling the anomalous cases of *CIA* and *Unilever*. In these cases, it appears as though the Directive contained no substantive rights of its own. It did refer, however, to a more general right, that of the free movement of goods. It was this principle that required effective protection.[13] In *CIA* and *Unilever*, the only form of available judicial protection was to disapply national laws, penalising those who might otherwise benefit from the principle of free movement through the marketing of goods. In these judgments, this principle was treated as self-standing

11 A. Arnull, 'Case C-432/05, Unibet (London) Ltd and Unibet (International) Ltd v. Justitiekanslern,' (2007) 44 *CMLR* 1763, 1773.
12 Joined Cases C-6/90 and C-9/90 *Francovich et al* [1991] ECR I-5357.
13 The idea of legal instruments giving expression to underlying rights present in other instruments is a recurrent one in EC law. For an example of a Regulation giving legal protection to a Directive entitlement, see Joined Cases C-37/06 & C-58/06 *Viamex Agra Handels Gmbh v Hauptzollamt Hamburg-Jonas*, Judgment of 27 January 2008.

and autonomous from particular Treaty provisions.[14] Legal entitlements would thus not only be derived from principles seen as underlying the Treaty, but these principles may also have a slightly wider remit than particular Treaty provisions.

14 Similar reasoning was used in *Mangold* where Directive 2000/78/EC, establishing a general framework for equal treatment in employment and occupation, was seen as securing an underlying principle of non-discrimination, Case C-144/04 *Mangold* [2005] ECR I-9981.

Free movement of goods, the single market and the economic constitution

1. Introduction

The dominant concern inspiring developments in this field has been over the remit of the single market and the type of regulatory procedure that could be justified by it. This has become increasingly important as market regulation and questions of competitiveness and adaptiveness have acquired increased salience in EU policy-making.[1] The other important development concerns the old chestnut of the limits on Article 28 EC, the provision on free movement of goods. There has, by its standards, been relatively little case law on the provision in recent years.[2] However, there have been a few suggestions that the Court may be moving to synthesise its reasoning around a more explicit rationale than is currently the case.

2. The remit of the single market

Two themes have emerged following the first *Tobacco Advertising* judgment. The first is that recourse to Article 95 EC is contingent upon a two-fold test. There is an external dimension in which there must be obstructions or potential obstructions to the functioning of the single market, whose removal require a level of harmonisation. There is also an internal dimension in which the object of the legislation must be to improve the functioning of the single market. The second theme to have emerged

---

1 So-called simplification of the regulatory environment has become a central policy object of the EU Commission, therefore. EC Commission, *Second progress report on the strategy for simplifying the regulatory environment*, COM (2008) 33.
2 On these see P. Oliver and S. Enchelmaier, 'Free movement of goods: recent developments in the case law' (2007) 44 *CMLR* 649.

is a relaxation of not necessarily the letter but the rigor of *Tobacco Advertising I*. In *Biotechnology Patents*, the Court accepted that the measure could be based on Article 95 EC, even though it provided for Member States to restrict biotechnology patents from their markets on grounds of public morality.[3] In *Swedish Match*, the measure was held to be lawful as it was seen as a generally liberalising measure, even though it outlawed altogether the marketing of certain products, in that case snus (the tobacco snuff inhaled in Sweden).[4]

The *Tobacco Advertising II* judgment consolidated these themes. Germany challenged Directive 2003/33, adopted to replace the Directive declared illegal in *Tobacco Advertising I*. The new Directive prohibited advertising of tobacco in all of the printed press other than publications intended for professionals (article 3), on the radio (article 4) and through sponsorship (article 5). Unlike its predecessor, it contained a market access provision, article 8, which prohibited Member States from preventing the free movement of goods and services complying with the Directive.

> ## Case C-380/03 Germany v Parliament and Council [2006] ECR I-11573
>
> 36. Article 95(1) EC establishes that the Council is to adopt measures for the approximation of provisions laid down by law, regulation or administrative action in the Member States which have as their object the establishment and functioning of the internal market.
>
> 37. While a mere finding of disparities between national rules is not sufficient to justify having recourse to Article 95 EC, it is otherwise where there are differences between the laws, regulations or administrative provisions of the Member States which are such as to obstruct the fundamental freedoms and thus have a direct effect on the functioning of the internal market . . .
>
> 38. It is also settled case-law that, although recourse to Article 95 EC as a legal basis is possible if the aim is to prevent the emergence of future obstacles to trade resulting from multifarious development of national laws, the emergence of such obstacles must be likely and the measure in question must be designed to prevent them . . .
>
> 41. It follows from the foregoing that when there are obstacles to trade, or it is likely that such obstacles will emerge in the future, because the Member States have taken, or are about to take, divergent measures with respect to a product or a class of products, which bring about different levels of protection and thereby prevent the product or products concerned from moving freely within the Community, Article 95 EC authorises the Community legislature to intervene by adopting appropriate measures, in compliance with Article 95(3) EC and with the legal principles mentioned in the EC Treaty or identified in the case-law, in particular the principle of proportionality . . .
>
> 56. First, measures prohibiting or restricting the advertising of tobacco products are liable to impede access to the market by products from other Member States more than they impede access by domestic products.
>
> 57. Second, such measures restrict the ability of undertakings established in the Member States where they are in force to offer advertising space in their publications to advertisers established in other Member States, thereby affecting the cross-border supply of services . . .

---

3 Case C-377/98 *Netherlands v Parliament & Council* [2001] ECR I-7079.
4 Case C-210/03 *R v Secretary for State ex parte Swedish Match* [2004] ECR I-11893.

58. Moreover, even if, in reality, certain publications are not sold in other Member States, the fact remains that the adoption of divergent laws on the advertising of tobacco products creates, or is likely to create, incontestably, legal obstacles to trade in respect of press products and other printed publications . . . Such obstacles therefore also exist for publications placed essentially on a local, regional or national market that are sold in other Member States, even if only by way of exception or in small quantities.

59. Furthermore, it is common ground that certain Member States which have prohibited the advertising of tobacco products exclude the foreign press from that prohibition. The fact that those Member States have chosen to accompany the prohibition with such an exception confirms that, in their eyes at least, there is significant intra-Community trade in press products.

60. Finally, the risk that new barriers to trade or to the freedom to provide services would emerge as a result of the accession of new Member States was real.

61. The same finding must be made with regard to the advertising of tobacco products in radio broadcasts and information society services. Many Member States had already legislated in those areas or were preparing to do so. Given the increasing public awareness of the harm caused to health by the consumption of tobacco products, it was likely that new barriers to trade or to the freedom to provide services were going to emerge as a result of the adoption of new rules reflecting that development and intended to discourage more effectively the consumption of tobacco products.

68. It follows from the foregoing that the barriers and the risks of distortions of competition warranted intervention by the Community legislature on the basis of Article 95 EC.

69. It remains to determine whether, in the fields covered by Articles 3 and 4 of the Directive, those articles are in fact designed to eliminate or prevent obstacles to the free movement of goods or the freedom to provide services or to remove distortions of competition . . .

71. The adoption of such a prohibition, which is designed to apply uniformly throughout the Community, is intended to prevent intra-Community trade in press products from being impeded by the national rules of one or other Member State.

72. It should be pointed out that Article 3(1) of the Directive expressly permits the insertion of advertising for tobacco products in certain publications, in particular in those which are intended exclusively for professionals in the tobacco trade.

73. Furthermore, unlike Directive 98/43, Article 8 of the Directive provides that the Member States are not to prohibit or restrict the free movement of products which comply with the Directive. This article consequently precludes Member States from impeding the movement within the Community of publications intended exclusively for professionals in the tobacco trade, inter alia by means of more restrictive provisions which they consider necessary in order to protect human health with regard to advertising or sponsorship for tobacco products.

74. In preventing the Member States in this way from opposing the provision of advertising space in publications intended exclusively for professionals in the tobacco trade, Article 8 of the Directive gives expression to the objective laid down in Article 1(2) of improving the conditions for the functioning of the internal market.

75. The same finding must be made with regard to the freedom to provide services, which is also covered by Article 8 of the Directive. Under this article, the Member States cannot prohibit or restrict that freedom where services comply with the Directive.

76 . . . Articles 3(2) and 4(1) of the Directive, which prohibit the advertising of tobacco products in information society services and in radio broadcasting, seek to promote freedom to broadcast by radio and the free movement of communications which fall within information society services.

77. Likewise, in prohibiting the sponsorship of radio programmes by undertakings whose principal activity is the manufacture or sale of tobacco products, Article 4(2) of the Directive seeks to prevent the freedom to provide services from being impeded by the national rules of one or other Member State.

78. It follows from the foregoing that Articles 3 and 4 of the Directive do in fact have as their object the improvement of the conditions for the functioning of the internal market and, therefore, that they were able to be adopted on the basis of Article 95 EC.

Although it claims only to be a continuation of the case law, *Tobacco Advertising II* liberalises both stages of the test for recourse to Article 95 EC. With regard to the external dimension, although the Court suggests that differences between national legislation are insufficient to activate Article 95 EC and obstacles to trade must also be present or likely, no market analysis is carried out. Indeed, with regard to free movement of services, it is difficult to see what obstacles were present. The Court talks speculatively about public awareness of the risks of tobacco leading to new legislation which may generate possible obstacles to trade. This is pure hypothesis and it is notable that the Court has never struck down a measure on the grounds that the external dimension is not present. The threshold seems therefore to be extremely low.

With regard to the second stage of the test, namely the object of the legislation, the central difference between *Tobacco Advertising I* and *Tobacco Advertising II* was the presence of a market access provision in the latter requiring goods and services complying with the Directive to be allowed to be marketed across the Union. It is, however, questionable whether this provision consists of no more than a paper requirement, as its meaning is unclear. Neither racial hatred nor pornography can be disseminated freely across the Union, even if the medium through which it is distributed does not advertise tobacco. Goods and services will still be subject to other restrictions and therefore the market access provision looks like little more than an adornment on which to hang a more wide-ranging regime restricting tobacco advertising.

The other issue to have arisen since *Tobacco Advertising I* is the type of measure that can be based on Article 95 EC. The judgment stated that Article 95 EC provided no general regulatory power. In *Biotechnological Patents*, the Court stated that Article 95 EC could be used to harmonise intellectual property rights, but left it unclear as to whether it could create them.[5] This has been resolved by the Lisbon Treaty.

Article 118 LTFEU In the context of the establishment and functioning of the internal market, the European Parliament and the Council, acting in accordance with the ordinary legislative procedure, shall establish measures for the creation of European intellectual property rights to provide uniform protection of intellectual property rights throughout the Union and for the setting up of centralised Union-wide authorisation, coordination and supervision arrangements.

5 Case C-377/98 *Netherlands v Parliament & Council* [2001] ECR I-7079.

> The Council, acting in accordance with a special legislative procedure, shall by means of regulations establish language arrangements for the European intellectual property rights. The Council shall act unanimously after consulting the European Parliament.

The question as to whether Article 95 EC could be used not merely to harmonise national laws, but also to set up regulatory institutions was not resolved, however, until the *Smoked Flavourings* judgment. The United Kingdom challenged a 2003 Regulation governing the smoked flavourings that may be used in foods. The Regulation established an authorisation procedure in which the Commission, after a receiving an opinion from the European Food Safety Authority, would decide whether a flavouring could be marketed. The constraints on the Commission were extremely vague. It could only authorise flavourings if they did not risk human health, mislead consumers, and the wood used had not been treated with chemicals in the six months prior to use. The United Kingdom argued this was illegal as Article 95 EC could not be used to establish a new tier of supranational government.

Case C-66/04 United Kingdom v Council & Parliament [2005] ECR I-10533

45 . . . it should be observed that by the expression 'measures for the approximation' in Article 95 EC the authors of the Treaty intended to confer on the Community legislature a discretion, depending on the general context and the specific circumstances of the matter to be harmonised, as regards the harmonisation technique most appropriate for achieving the desired result, in particular in fields which are characterised by complex technical features. 46 That discretion may be used in particular to choose the most appropriate harmonisation technique where the proposed approximation requires physical, chemical or biological analyses to be made and scientific developments in the field concerned to be taken into account. Such evaluations relating to the safety of products correspond to the objective imposed on the Community legislature by Article 95(3) EC of ensuring a high level of protection of health.

47. Finally, it should be added that where the Community legislature provides for a harmonisation which comprises several stages, for instance the fixing of a number of essential criteria set out in a basic regulation followed by scientific evaluation of the substances concerned and the adoption of a positive list of substances authorised throughout the Community, two conditions must be satisfied.

48. First, the Community legislature must determine in the basic act the essential elements of the harmonising measure in question.

49. Second, the mechanism for implementing those elements must be designed in such a way that it leads to a harmonisation within the meaning of Article 95 EC. That is the case where the Community legislature establishes the detailed rules for making decisions at each stage of such an authorisation procedure, and determines and circumscribes precisely the powers of the Commission as the body which has to take the final decision. That applies in particular where the harmonisation in question consists in drawing up a list of products authorised throughout the Community to the exclusion of all other products.

50. Such an interpretation of Article 95 EC is also borne out by the fact that, according to their very wording, paragraphs 4 and 5 of that article recognise that the Commission has

power to adopt harmonisation measures. The reference to that power of the Commission in those paragraphs, read in conjunction with paragraph 1 of that article, indicates that an act adopted by the Community legislature on the basis of Article 95 EC, in accordance with the co-decision procedure referred to in Article 251 EC, may be limited to defining the provisions which are essential for the achievement of objectives in connection with the establishment and functioning of the internal market in the field concerned, while conferring power on the Commission to adopt the harmonisation measures needed for the implementation of the legislative act in question.

Smoked Flavourings indicates that Article 95 EC can be used to establish new regulatory institutions or procedures provided that these respect general EC law doctrines on delegated powers and lead to 'harmonisation', namely common EC rules that open up or improve the functioning of the single market. The Court went one step further in *European Network and Information Security Agency*.[6] The United Kingdom challenged the establishment of this Agency under Article 95 EC on the basis that its central tasks were providing advice and expertise on network and information security to the EU institutions and Member States, and these did not consist of harmonisation within the meaning of Article 95 EC. The Court held that the Agency's establishment was legal as Article 95 EC could be used to establish a Community body responsible for contributing to the implementation of harmonising measures, notably where it facilitated the uniform implementation and application of these measures. Crucial to the assessment of the legality of the Agency was determining the proximity of the link between its tasks and the harmonisation measures in question. In this instance, the Court found that there was a close link. Much of the harmonisation in the field of Information Communication Technology concerned itself with the challenge of network and information security. In the Court's view, the development of common methodologies, best practice and risk assessment contributed to the objectives of this legislation, as did the development of cooperation between the institutional actors involved in this field.

Article 95 EC is increasingly being used not only to create common rules, but to establish a new tier of government involved with risk assessment and management, quasi-legislation and network coordination. A formal reading of the provision might lead to the conclusion that the Court is engaging in interpretive gymnastics here. However, even if that were the case, there would be strong justification for it. Increasingly, as liberalisation of the single market has taken place, the EU has had to turn its focus to management of the single market and its attendant risks. This entails development of a panoply of regulatory techniques which are heterogeneous, responsive and provide added value to those already deployed by the Member States. In this regard, simply saying that the Union has the power to change common rules every time a new risk emerges would seem to be both unwieldy and insufficient.

---

6 Case C-217/04 *United Kingdom v Council & Parliament* [2006] ECR I-3771.

3. Harmonisation and the non-market values of Member States

It will be remembered that a distinction is made between those Member States wishing to derogate from EU measures based on Article 95 EC at the time of the adoption of the measure and those wishing to derogate subsequently. Both require an authorisation from the Commission, which must verify that the measures do not constitute a form of arbitrary discrimination or a disguised restriction on trade. The grounds for derogation do, however, differ. With regard to the former, Article 95(4) EC states that they must be based on grounds of major needs, referred to in Article 30 EC, or related to protection of the natural or working environment. With regard to the latter, Article 95(5) states that a measure can only be introduced on the basis of new scientific evidence relating to the protection of the natural or working environment on grounds of a problem specific to that Member State. In the main text we argued that Article 95(5) was highly restrictive. The example given was Commission Decision 2003/653/EC, which dismissed a new study provided by the Austrian government of the dangers of GMOs on the grounds that the study did no more than refer to previous work.[7] Austria challenged this arguing that its unique eco-systems, sizeable organic production and large number of small farms made it a special case worthy of protection under Article 95(5) EC. The challenge was dismissed by the CFI[8] and Austria appealed to the Court of Justice.[9] The Court held that the three conditions in Article 95(5) EC – new evidence, problems specific to a Member State and a ground relating to the natural or working environment – were cumulative. If any one of them could not be proved by the Member State, a derogation could not be granted. The Court neither considered the question of organic production nor of small-scale farms, suggesting that these were not the sort of problems envisaged in Article 95(5) EC. On the question of the special nature of Austrian eco-systems, the Court, dismissing the appeal, noted no scientific evidence had been adduced to establish this. The case illustrates the narrowness of the exception. It is not simply that the conditions are cumulative. It is that scientific evidence, which by its nature makes universal statements, must relate to problems specific to that State. This will be difficult to prove and will lead to a situation where theoretically a Member State could bring forth new scientific evidence showing an EU measure to be harmful, but still be unable to derogate because its claims are generally true – clearly nonsensical!

4. The remit of Article 28 EC

In recent years, the case law on the remit of Article 28 EC has fragmented into three strands. First, national measures discriminating overtly or covertly against imports were held to fall within Article 28 EC. Second, indistinctly applicable measures fell

---

7 See pp. 490–1 of the main text.
8 Joined Cases T-366/03 and T-235/04 *Land Oberösterreich and Austria* v *Commission* [2005] ECR II-4005.
9 Joined Cases C-439/05P and C-454/05P *Land Oberösterreich and Austria* v *Commission*, Judgment of 13 September 2007.

within Article 28 EC if they related to the characteristics of a product. A third category had also developed in which measures fell within Article 28 EC if, even though indistinctly applicable, they were liable to impede the access of imports more than the access of domestic products. The relationship and the presence of a common rationale between these three strands of reasoning were unclear. The basis for the third line of reasoning was particularly opaque. It was not clear whether it was concerned to prevent discrimination between imports and domestic products, discrimination between established products and market entrants, or was concerned with measures that were unnecessarily restrictive.

Some light on this issue has been shed in *Alfa Vita Vassilopoulos*. The case concerned a Greek law which required those wishing to sell 'bake-off' bread to have a license on the grounds that all bakers had to have a licence. Bake-off bread was frozen bread that needed to be thawed and reheated before being sold. Traditionally, licensing laws have not been seen as product requirements and relate instead to the question of who can sell the good, rather than the nature of the good itself.[10] Yet the law clearly placed this bread, which had already been baked, at a disadvantage by putting it in the same situation as bread which had yet to be baked. It also seemed an unnecessarily restrictive measure, as the process in question was a simple one of reheating the bread.

Joined Cases C-158/04 & C-159/04 Alfa Vita Vassilopoulos v Elliniki Dimosio [2006] ECR I-8135

Opinion of Advocate General Poiares Maduro

21. A characteristic of 'bake-off' bread is that it has already gone through certain stages of bread production, such as kneading and the first stage of baking. In those circumstances, making it subject to manufacturing requirements identical to those imposed upon fresh bread clearly leads to unnecessary costs, such that marketing is thereby rendered more onerous and therefore more difficult. Furthermore, those costs particularly concern frozen products which, by their nature, are intended to be preserved and transported, particularly from other Member States. Therefore, it seems clear to me that with regard to imported products the legislation at issue is in fact discriminatory and accordingly constitutes a barrier to intra-Community trade . . . .

39. The fact remains that, in the context of the establishment of an internal market, the fundamental objective of the principle of free movement of goods is to ensure that producers are put in a position to benefit, in fact, from the right to carry out their activity at a cross-border level, while consumers are put in a position to access, in practice, products from other Member States in the same conditions as domestic products. Such was the intention of the Treaty draftsmen; such has been the approach of the Court which has implemented it.

40. However, it appears to me that it would be neither satisfactory nor true to the development of the case-law to reduce freedom of movement to a mere standard of promotion of trade between Member States. It is important that the freedoms of movement fit into the broader framework of the objectives of the internal market and European citizenship. At present, the freedoms of movement must be understood to be one of the essential elements of

---

10 Case C-391/92 *Commission v Greece* [1995] ECR I-1621; Case C-387/93 *Banchero* [1995] ECR I-4663.

the 'fundamental status of nationals of the Member States'. They represent the cross-border dimension of the economic and social status conferred on European citizens. However, the protection of such a status requires going beyond guaranteeing that there will be no discrimination based on nationality. It means Member States taking into account the effect of the measures they adopt on the position of all European Union citizens wishing to assert their rights to freedom of movement. As the Court pointed out in *Deutscher Apothekerverband*, that requires consideration of a broader scale than a strictly national context.

41. In such circumstances it is obvious that the task of the Court is not to call into question as a matter of course Member States' economic policies. It is instead responsible for satisfying itself that those States do not adopt measures which, in actual fact, lead to *cross-border situations being treated less favourably than purely national situations*.

42. In order to carry out such a review, it is necessary to rely on concrete criteria. Three principal criteria can be drawn from the relevant case-law.

43. Firstly, the Court maintains, in this respect, that any discrimination based on nationality, whether direct or indirect, is prohibited. For example, it is clear that a publicity campaign promoting the purchase of national products to the detriment of intra-Community trade constitutes a breach of Treaty rules.

44. Second, it is established that imposing supplementary costs on goods in circulation in the Community or on traders carrying out a cross-border activity creates a barrier to trade which needs to be duly justified. However, it should be made clear, in this respect, that not every imposition of supplementary costs is wrongful. Some costs can arise from a mere divergence between the legislation of the Member State in which the goods are produced and that of the Member State in which they are marketed. Such costs, which arise from disparities in the laws of the Member States, cannot be considered to be restrictions on freedom of movement. To be considered a restriction on trade, the supplementary cost imposed must stem from the fact that the national rules did not take into account the particular situation of the imported products and, in particular, the fact that those products already had to comply with the rules of their State of origin. Rules relating to the characteristics of products easily fit into this category. Therefore, in my opinion, although the Court has excluded rules relating to selling arrangements from the scope of Article 28 EC, it is because, in general, those rules do not impose such costs. Such was the case of the rules concerning resale at a loss examined in *Keck and Mithouard*, or the rules relating to the prohibition of Sunday trading. Nevertheless, the possibility remains that rules relating to selling arrangements may be adopted without taking into account the particular situation of the imported products. In such a case, it is legitimate to make them subject to Article 28 EC. A system which allowed only traders holding a particular licence to import alcoholic beverages was accordingly held to be contrary to that article since it had the effect of exposing beverages imported from other Member States to supplementary costs.

45. Thirdly, any measure which impedes to a greater extent the access to the market and the putting into circulation of products from other Member States is considered to be a measure having equivalent effect within the meaning of Article 28 EC. A measure constitutes a barrier to access to a national market where it protects the acquired positions of certain economic operators on a national market or where it makes intra-Community trade more difficult than trade within the national market. For example, in *Deutscher Apothekerverband*, the Court considered a measure prohibiting the sale of medicinal products by mail order to be a measure having equivalent effect on the ground that it could impede access to the market for products from other Member States more than it impedes access for domestic products.

46. It seems to me that a consistent approach emerges from this case-law. These three criteria, as they have been applied by the Court, amount in substance to identifying *discrimination against the exercise of freedom of movement*.

47. It is true that rules concerning selling arrangements are prima facie included among measures which do not specifically disadvantage the access and circulation of products from other Member States. However, as the case-law developed by the Court following *Keck and Mithouard* demonstrates, presumptions based on the character of these rules are not sufficient in that regard. In order to ascertain whether Article 28 EC must be applied to such measures, they must be examined in the light of the stated criteria. Provided that the criteria are applied in the light of the objective of combating discrimination affecting cross-border situations, they appear to me both necessary and sufficient to decide, in every case and for all kinds of rules, whether there exists a barrier to trade.

48. In response to a legitimate question on the meaning and scope of the rules relating to the free movement of goods, the Court chose in *Keck and Mithouard* to give an apparently formal answer, by limiting the scope of those rules to certain types of rules according to their subject-matter. It is suggested that this judgment should be understood in the light of the subsequent case-law based on the application of certain substantive criteria. This reply is admittedly not able to remove all the difficulties which the Court may face in assessing each individual case, but it would at least have the advantage of clarifying the method to be followed.

49. If such a direction were followed, it would enable the Court's approach to be the same in all cases relating to the application of Article 28 EC

50. Furthermore, this approach would allow the case-law relating to the freedoms of movement to be harmonised. As pointed out, the distinction laid down in *Keck and Mithouard* is undoubtedly difficult to transpose into the context of the other freedoms of movement. Nevertheless, the considerations which governed the adoption of the decision are to be found in those areas. In all those fields, it seems necessary to define limits to the application of the principles of freedom of movement and to provide a better framework for review by the Court.

51. I would add that such a harmonisation of the systems of free movement seems to me to be essential in the light of the requirements of genuine Union citizenship. It would be desirable for the same system to be applied to all the citizens of the Union wishing to use their freedom of movement or freedom to move services, goods or capital as well as their freedom to reside or to set up the seat of their activities in the Community. Accordingly, any measure liable to impede or make less attractive the exercise of these fundamental freedoms should be held to be contrary to the Treaty. It is not a question of guaranteeing that the exercise of those freedoms is entirely neutral; it may be more or less advantageous for European citizens. It is more a question of ensuring that Member States take into account the extent to which the rules they adopt are liable to affect the position of nationals from other Member States and make more difficult their full enjoyment of the freedoms of movement.

52. If we now apply this new approach to the present cases, it is apparent that the analysis is thereby simplified. As a measure applied without distinction, the Greek legislation satisfies, at first sight, the test of non-discrimination based on nationality. However, as demonstrated in point 21 of this Opinion, this measure clearly creates unnecessary supplementary costs in relation to the marketing of frozen bread from other Member States. It does not, therefore, satisfy the second criterion. Accordingly, it is for the Member State concerned to justify the adopted measure.

The Court of Justice

16. The Court has, however, clarified that measures having equivalent effect to quantitative restrictions and therefore prohibited by Article 28 EC do not include national provisions restricting or prohibiting certain selling arrangements, so long as those provisions apply to

all relevant traders operating within the national territory and so long as they affect in the same manner, in law and in fact, the marketing of domestic products and of those from other Member States . . .

17. In their written observations, the Prefectural Authority and the Greek Government, referring to the *Keck and Mithouard* case-law, claim that the national legislation merely regulates the manner in which 'bake-off' products may be sold, and, consequently, do not come within the scope of application of Article 28 EC.

18. As noted by the Advocate General in point 15 of his Opinion, that categorisation cannot be accepted. An examination of the provisions of the national legislation shows clearly that it aims to specify the production conditions for bakery products, including 'bake-off' products.

19. It is common ground that the principal characteristic of 'bake-off' products is that they are delivered at sales outlets after the main stages of preparation of those products have been completed. At those sales outlets, only a brief thawing and reheating or final baking are carried out. In those circumstances, requiring vendors of 'bake-off' products to comply with all of the requirements imposed on traditional bakeries, including, in particular, the requirement of having a flour store, an area for kneading equipment and a solid-fuel store, does not take the specific nature of those products into account and entails additional costs, thereby making the marketing of those products more difficult. That legislation therefore constitutes a barrier to imports which cannot be regarded as establishing a selling arrangement as contemplated in *Keck and Mithouard*.

The Opinion of Advocate General Maduro is considerably clearer than that of the Court. He argues that the rationale for Article 28 EC, as for all economic freedoms, is that Member States should take into account the effect of their measures on the position of all EU citizens wishing to assert their rights to freedom of movement. This starting point leads to three types of situation falling within Article 28 EC:

- measures discriminating overtly or covertly against imports;
- measures imposing supplementary costs on imports through a failure to take into account the particular situation of the imported products as having already had to comply with the rules of their State of origin;
- measure protecting the acquired positions of established producers.

In its reference to the traditional *Keck* case law, and the fact that this measure is not a selling arrangement, the Court seems to reject the Advocate General's views.[11] Yet, all is not as it seems. The Court does not say that a license to market goods is a product requirement and therefore falls within Article 28 EC. To do so would be both to contradict its prior case law as well as the language of *Keck* which does not mention this as a product characteristic. Instead, the Court finds the measure, due to its discriminatory effects, does not qualify as a selling arrangement. It reinterprets *Keck* to suggest that a precondition of a selling arrangement is that of being non-discriminatory. Furthermore, the Court does not stipulate what must be discriminated

11 Joined Cases C-267/91 & C-268/91 *Keck & Mithouard* [1993] ECR I-6097.

against. It merely notes the supplementary costs of 'bake-off' bread, irrespective of whether this is imported or produced domestically. The reasoning is perfectly consistent with both the second and the third situation offered by Maduro. Yet, if this is so, there is a feeling that the Court is hedging its bets. The language is obtuse, and if the Court had intended to develop a new revitalising synthesis of its case law, one would have expected it to use more ambitious language. This begs the question as to whether it is appropriate for a Court to hedge its bets, given the legal uncertainty induced.

Free movement of capital and Economic and Monetary Union

CONTENTS	

1. Introduction

Litigation in the field of free movement of capital and in particular on the meaning of Article 56(1) EC (Article 63(1) LTFEU following the Lisbon Treaty) has been extensive in the last thirty months. Three issues have been prevalent. The first is the *ratione materiae* of the provision, namely what constitutes a capital movement. The second is what types of restriction on these movements fall within Article 56 EC. Finally, as free movement of capital is the only economic freedom which catches movements between EU and non EU States, the question has arisen whether any distinction should be drawn between these restrictions and those on capital moving within the EU.

By contrast, the Lisbon Treaty only proposed light amendments to the architecture governing Economic and Monetary Union (EMU). Yet it has taken place against a significant shift in which the institutional settlement is less a system in which economic policy is dominated by an independent central bank with errant States punished for running up large budget deficits. Instead, the new settlement is recentred about a European economic government in which there is extensive surveillance by national governments of each other's economies, and common economic agenda-setting is beginning to emerge, most notably through the Eurogroup. This suggests a shift away from central bankers to finance ministers, but also a world in which opting-out of Union economic government is less clear and possibly less available than previously thought.

2. Free movement of capital

The provision on free movement of capital, Article 56(1) EC, only governs restrictions on 'capital movements'. The Court of Justice has repeated earlier reasoning that here it essentially reproduces the contents of Article 1 of Directive 88/361. The nomenclature in respect of 'movements of capital' annexed to that directive indicates what constitutes a capital movement for the purposes of Article 56 (1) EC.[1] The Annex sets out thirteen types of transaction and the Court has been consistent in referring back to it. On this basis, the Court has held that capital movements include the granting credit on a commercial basis,[2] reselling shares,[3] inheritance,[4] investments in real estate[5] or immovable property,[6] direct and portfolio investments;[7] the establishment of new branches or undertakings belonging solely to the capital provider, and the acquisition of undertakings.[8] Laws governing the conditions under which land, shares or other property can be bought, wills can be executed and the structure of companies will all thus fall within Article 56(1) EC. Insofar as taxation of transactions in these fields generates a large proportion of a Member State's revenue, national fiscal autonomy will be correspondingly constrained by this provision.

The second question concerning Article 56(1) EC is what constitutes a restriction on a capital movement. In *van Hilten-van der Heijden* the heirs of a Dutch national who had moved to Belgium and then Switzerland shortly before her death challenged a Dutch law which stipulated that for purposes of Dutch inheritance tax a Dutch national was to be treated as resident in the Netherlands (and therefore subject to the tax) if she died within ten years of ceasing to reside in the Netherlands. It was argued that this provided a disincentive to people to leave the Netherlands and consequently to make payments and investments abroad. The Court found that an inheritance was a capital movement and then continued.

> ## Case C-513/03 *van Hilten-van der Heijden v Inspecteur van de Belastingdienst* [2006] ECR I-1957
>
> 44. In that regard, it follows from the case-law that the measures prohibited by Article 73b(1) of the Treaty [now Article 56(1) EC], as being restrictions on the movement of capital, include those which are likely to discourage non-residents from making investments in a Member State or to discourage that Member State's residents to do so in other States or, in the case of inheritances, those whose effect is to reduce the value of the inheritance of a resident of a State other than the Member State in which the assets concerned are situated and which taxes the inheritance of those assets . . .

---

1 On this see pp. 509–11 of the main text.
2 Case C-452/04 *Fidium Finanz vBundesanstalt für Finanzdienstleistungsaufsicht* [2006] ECR I-9521.
3 Case C-265/04 *Bouanich v Skatterverket* [2006] ECR I-923.
4 Case C-513/03 *van Hilten-van der Heijden v Inspecteur van de Belastingdienst* [2006] ECR I-1957.
5 Case C-386/04 *Centro di Musicologia Walter Stauffer v Finanzamt München für Körperschaften* [2006] ECR I-8203.
6 Case C-451/05 *Elisa v Directeur général des impôts*, Judgment of 11 October 2007.
7 Joined Cases C-282/04 and C-283/04 *Commission v Netherlands* [2006] ECR I-9141. The difference between a direct and portfolio investment is that in the former one acquires shares which allow the possibility of participation in control and management of a company whereas in the latter one does not.
8 Case C-446/04 *Test Claimants in the FII Group Litigation v IRC* [2006] ECR I-11753.

45. National legislation such as that in question in the main proceedings, which provides that the estate of a national of a Member State who dies within 10 years of ceasing to reside in that Member State is to be taxed as if that national had continued to reside in that Member State, while providing for relief in respect of the taxes levied in the State to which the deceased transferred his residence, does not constitute a restriction on the movement of capital.

46. By enacting identical taxation provisions for the estates of nationals who have transferred their residence abroad and of those who have remained in the Member State concerned, such legislation cannot discourage the former from making investments in that Member State from another State nor the latter from doing so in another Member State from the Member State concerned, and, regardless of the place where the assets in question are situated, nor can it diminish the value of the estate of a national who has transferred his residence abroad. The fact that such legislation covers neither nationals resident abroad for more than 10 years nor those who have never resided in the Member State concerned is irrelevant in that regard. Since it applies only to nationals of the Member State concerned, it cannot constitute a restriction on the movement of capital of nationals of the other Member States.

47. As regards the differences in treatment between residents who are nationals of the Member State concerned and those who are nationals of other Member States resulting from national legislation such as that in question in the main proceedings, it must be observed that such distinctions, for the purposes of allocating powers of taxation, cannot be regarded as constituting discrimination prohibited by Article 73b of the Treaty. They flow, in the absence of any unifying or harmonising measures adopted in the Community context, from the Member States' power to define, by treaty or unilaterally, the criteria for allocating their powers of taxation (see to that effect, as regards Article 48 of the EC Treaty (now, after amendment, Article 39 EC) . . .

48. Moreover, the Court has already had occasion to decide that, for the purposes of the allocation of powers of taxation, it is not unreasonable for the Member States to find inspiration in international practice and, particularly, the model conventions drawn up by the Organisation for Economic Cooperation and Development (OECD) . . . As the Netherlands Government observed, the legislation in question in the main proceedings complies with the commentaries in the Model Double Taxation Convention concerning Inheritances and Gifts (Report of the Fiscal Affairs Committee of the OECD, 1982). It is clear from the commentaries on Articles 4, 7, 9A and 9B of that model that that type of legislation is justified by the concern to prevent a form of tax evasion whereby a national of a State, in contemplation of his death, transfers his residence to another State where the tax is lower. The commentaries state that double taxation is avoided by a system of tax credits and that, since prevention of tax evasion is justified only if the death occurs only a short time after the transfer of residence, the maximum permitted period is 10 years. The same commentaries state also that the scope can be extended to cover not only nationals of the State concerned but also residents who are not nationals of that State.

49. In that context, it must be observed that the mere transfer of residence from one State to another does not come within Article 73b of the Treaty. As the Advocate General pointed out in point 58 of his Opinion, such a transfer of residence does not involve, in itself, financial transactions or transfers of property and does not partake of other characteristics of a capital movement as they appear from Annex I to Directive 88/361.

50. It follows that national legislation which would discourage a national who wishes to transfer his residence to another State, and thus hinder his freedom of movement, cannot for that reason alone constitute a restriction on the movement of capital within the meaning of Article 73b of the Treaty.

The core paragraph is paragraph 44 in which it is stated that a measure will breach Article 56(1) EC if it either discourages non-residents investing in a Member State or discourages investments by residents in other Member States. Central to this is the idea that national measures should not distort investment choices between investments in one's state of residence or investments abroad. However, the matter is not as simple as looking at whether a measure differentiates between types of investment. The Court has also held that simply making an investment really unattractive will be sufficient to bring a measure within Article 56(1) EC on the grounds that such a measure will deter investment and therefore exercise significant restrictive effects on the movement of capital.

This has come up most frequently with regard to conditions attaching to the acquisition of shares. In *Commission v Germany*[9] the Commission challenged a German law which provided that, in the case of the Volkswagen motor company, no private shareholder, irrespective of the number of shares owned, could exercise more than 20 per cent of the voting rights and that the Federal and Lower Saxony authorities could appoint two members to the supervisory board of the company. The Court noted that both measures limited the possibility for other shareholders to participate effectively in control or management of the company and, thus, were liable to deter direct investors from other Member States. Consequently, they violated Article 56(1) EC. The level of deterrence is unclear, however. As the Germany authorities noted, large number of foreigners invest in Volkswagen and the supervisory board only has a general monitoring power. The basis for Article 56(1) EC is therefore ambiguous. It might be that it was the deterrent effect of the German measures which lowered the value of the asset through limiting shareholder control. Alternately, as this was not considerable, the egregious feature might have been the possibility for a national authority to intervene in an ad hoc way in the management of the asset so generating uncertainty as to its value.

The final question to be addressed is restrictions on capital between EU and non EU States. These are as prohibited by Article 56(1) EC as restrictions on capital movements between EU States. The question of whether they should be treated completely analogously was addressed in *A*.[10] This concerned a Swedish law which provided for a tax exemption on dividends received from companies established in an EEA State. This was not available for dividends received from companies established elsewhere, and therefore discouraged investment in these companies. The Court noted that the legal context for capital movements to and from non EU States is different to that within the EU. Free movement of capital there pursues different objectives to that of realising the internal market such as maintaining the credibility of the euro and EU financial centres with a world-wide dimension. In addition, there are various derogations that may be applied to such movements that may not be applied to internal

9 Case C-112/05 *Commission v Germany*, Judgment of 23 October 2007.
10 Case C-101/05 *A v Skatteverket*, Judgment of 18 December 2007.

movements of capital.[11] The Court noted, however, that the Member States had still chosen to place such movements within Article 56(1) EC. It found therefore that, insofar as the Swedish system discouraged investment outside the EEA, it fell within Article 56(1) EC. The Court indicated, however, that there may be a wider array of public interests and the proportionality principle may be interpreted differently for non-EU capital movements. In this case, it held that the Swedish measure was justified on the ground of securing the effectiveness of fiscal supervision. It accepted the argument of the Swedish authorities that the exemption could not be given as they would be unable to ascertain if it was given for the correct amount of shares. Whilst they would be able to verify this question with other tax authorities within the EU, this was not possible in the case of non EU authorities.

3. Economic and Monetary Union

Questions were raised by Jean-Claude Trichet,[12] the Head of the ECB, about whether the amendments introduced by the Lisbon Treaty sufficiently respected the independence of ECB.[13] The basis for this is the new Article 13 LTEU which places the ECB as one of the institutions of the Union who are required to 'promote its values, advance its objects'. There was a concern that this might be used to argue that the ECB could be asked to pursue more explicitly political objectives and be required to cooperate with the other EU institutions. Against this, the new specialised provisions on the ECB set out, albeit in a more truncated form, the current position on the ECB that it is to be independent and that its primary objective is to secure price stability.

> **Article 282(1) LTFEU** The European Central Bank, together with the national central banks, shall constitute the European System of Central Banks (ESCB). The European Central Bank, together with the national central banks of the Member States whose currency is the euro, which constitute the Eurosystem, shall conduct the monetary policy of the Union.
>
>   2. The ESCB shall be governed by the decision-making bodies of the European Central Bank. The primary objective of the ESCB shall be to maintain price stability. Without prejudice to that objective, it shall support the general economic policies in the Union in order to contribute to the achievement of the latter's objectives.
>
>   3. The European Central Bank shall have legal personality. It alone may authorise the issue of the euro. It shall be independent in the exercise of its powers and in the management of its finances. The institutions, bodies, offices and agencies of the Union and the governments of the Member States shall respect that independence.

The specialised provisions of the LTFEU give, from Trichet's perspective, little cause for concern whilst the general ones in the LTEU allow a hint of ambiguity. As the two

---

11 Articles 57(2) and 59 EC.
12 *Financial Times*, 'Central bank chief urges change to EU Treaty', 11 August 2007.
13 On this independence see pp. 540–51 of the main text.

Treaties are to have equal value, it is unclear as to how any clash is to be resolved, and this is regrettable whichever view is taken on the independence of the Bank. For the ambiguity is only likely to be addressed at a moment of significant crisis, and will be used by actors to justify contradictory positions with all possibilities for dysfunction entailed by that.

The second amendment put forward by the Lisbon Treaty is an amendment to the Excessive Deficit Procedure. Currently, the EC Treaty provides for the Excessive Deficit Procedure to be triggered by a Commission 'recommendation' that an excessive deficit exists in a Member State. It is now triggered by a Commission 'proposal'. This change underscores the right of initiative enjoyed by the Commission here. The Council cannot issue Recommendations to a Member State that an Excessive Deficit Procedure exists without a prior Commission proposal. Likewise, once Recommendations have been made it cannot state that these are in abeyance without a prior Commission proposal that the deficit no longer exists.[14] The consequence is that whilst the Commission cannot control the sanctions imposed under the procedure, it does act as the gatekeeper for the opening and closing of the procedure, and the consequent stigmatisation of the Member State in the financial markets.

This finely grained amendment pales compared to those introduced in 2005 to the Excessive Deficit Procedure. With five out of twelve of the euro zone Member States running an excessive budgetary deficit of more than 3 per cent of GDP, the circumstances in which it was permissible to run this and the meaning of 'excessive deficit' were redefined. A deficit of more than 3 per cent of GDP was not to be considered excessive so as to trigger the procedure if the circumstances in which it was incurred amount to a 'severe economic downturn'. Under the initial Pact, this was an annual fall in real GDP of 2 per cent – something which occurs only in a severe depression. This has now been softened so that either negative growth or even low positive growth relative to potential will be considered a 'severe economic downturn'.[15] In short, 3 per cent will only be a reference value if the Member State is running a budget deficit in excess of that in the most benign of economic circumstances.

Even, in those circumstances, 3 per cent will not automatically be a reference value. In determination of an excessive deficit, the 2005 reforms provide a more detailed list of other relevant factors of which account may be taken.[16] These include both the medium-term economic position of the Member State (e.g. its potential for growth and position in the economic cycle, level of structural reform) and its medium-term budgetary position (e.g. level of public debt, public investment, consolidation of debt). Account must also be taken of financial contributions to European policy and international solidarity of goals. Combined, these include such a wide array of

14 The amendments reinforce Case C-27/04 *Commission v Council* [2004] ECR I-4829.
15 Regulation 1467/97/EC, OJ 1997, L 209/6, article 2(2) as amended by Regulation 1056/2005/EC on speeding up and clarifying the implementation of the excessive deficit procedure, OJ 2005, L 174/5.
16 *Ibid.*, Article 2(3).

variables that the 3 per cent requirement is easily capable of being dissolved and peripheral within them.

These reforms render it unlikely that any sanctions will ever be taken under the Excessive Deficit Procedure. They not only provide considerable wiggle room for the parties to argue that there is no excessive deficit but also define away the excessive deficit as a reference point of poor budget management. Nobody knows when it now occurs or what to look at in ascertaining whether it exists. In the light of this, it is tempting to be sceptical about the prospects for EMU and about whether sufficient policy coordination can be engendered to make it a success. In this regard, the emphasis has shifted to the preventive arm of the Stability and Growth Pact, that of multilateral surveillance.

The 2005 reforms intensified the detail and commitments of the multilateral surveillance procedure significantly. It will be remembered that this procedure requires each Member State to submit for annual surveillance by ECOFIN a stability programme describing its budgetary position. Prior to 2005, the only duty on Member States was to show that their medium-term budgetary position would be close to balance or in surplus.[17] Following the 2005 reforms, the duty is far more extensive. Each must set out medium-term objectives (MTOs) for its budgetary position which are country-specific and take account of that State's current debt and potential growth. Member States must also make clear the assumptions behind their objectives.[18] The level of detail required of them is higher. They must now provide a detailed and quantitative assessment of the budgetary and economic policy measures being taken to meet the MTO, including a cost-benefit analysis of any major structural reforms. The manner of the Council evaluation is also different. The MTO will be evaluated by the Council looking at where the Member State is in the economic cycle. In making its assessment, the Council is to take as a benchmark that a Member State should be spending at least 0.5 per cent of its GDP on meeting its MTO with that figure being higher in good times and lower in bad times.

The multilateral surveillance procedure now requires extremely detailed reporting by Member States of all aspects of medium-term economic basis and a very detailed assessment of that by the EU institutions. It has been argued that this precision and labour acts as a powerful form of discipline on Member States with their being required to report on over 100 indicators.[19] Unlike the Excessive Deficit Procedure, the inter-temporal dimension also works against them as they have to justify their performance throughout the whole economic cycle measured against their place in the economic cycle. There is thus continuous scrutiny. Finally, the commitment for them

17 Regulation 1466/97 on the strengthening of the surveillance of budgetary positions and the surveillance and coordination of economic policies, OJ 1997, L 209/1, article 7(2).

18 The amendments are contained in Regulation 1055/2005 amending Regulation 1466/97 on the strengthening of the surveillance of budgetary positions and the surveillance and coordination of economic policies, OJ 2005, L 174/1.

19 W. Schelkle, 'EU fiscal governance: hard law in the shadow of soft law' (2007) 13 *CJEL* 705.

to demonstrate expenditure towards meeting their MTOs entails that the obligation is not a simple paper chasing exercise.

If multilateral surveillance is now to be considered the heart of the Stability and Growth Pact, then the third innovation introduced by Lisbon may be the most significant. It is nothing more than the formalisation and recognition of the Eurogroup through a Protocol.[20] The group has comprised the finance ministers of the States participating in the euro and meets the day before the ECOFIN Council to discuss matters of common concern, notably budgetary policy. It was an informal arrangement but was semi-formalised with the appointment of a President, the Luxembourg Prime Minister Jean-Claude Juncker, for a two-year period from 1 January 2005. The Protocol not only recognises it but requires the Commission to take part in its meetings and the ECB to be invited. The recognition is symptomatic of the Euro group's increasing importance. Its central role is not to allow members to monitor each other's budgetary policies. Instead, it is more proactive as they are there to formulate a common economic and budgetary agenda. When looked at in the context of a reinforced and more prescriptive system of multilateral surveillance, it becomes the heartbeat of a new form of European economic government. The Eurogroup will set the agenda in this government with multilateral surveillance and the Excessive Deficit Procedure enforcing the discipline. Recognition by the Treaty is desirable, as it subjects the Group to the Union disciplines of accountability and transparency.[21] Yet it also signifies that the influence of this body is likely to grow. Insofar as not all Member States are represented and the body's relationship to the rest of the Treaty framework is not clearly defined, this does generate concerns.

20 Protocol on the Euro Group.
21 U. Puetter, *The Eurogroup: How a Secretive Circle of Finance Ministers Shape European Economic Governance* (2006, Manchester University Press).

Union citizenship and non-union nationals

1. Introduction

The Lisbon Treaty is more detailed in its setting out of EU competences on non-EU nationals than is the current EC treaty. It seeks to formalise and legitimise existing institutional practices, which have moved, if not beyond, then at least to the outer edges of what was anticipated from the competences included in the EC Treaty. A similar pattern is present with regard to EU citizenship in the Lisbon Treaty, which restructures the provisions in this field. However, in the case EU citizenship, reform has not been concerned merely with the formalisation of practical developments. Two other themes have emerged. One has been to allow for the possibility of greater political engagement between EU citizens and EU institutions. The other has been to increasingly qualify the benefits available to EU citizens on the basis of some pre-existing tie (social integration) between the citizen and the Member State from which they are claiming benefits. The nature of this tie is currently ill-defined and in many ways problematic, but it does look likely to be the pivotal norm in shaping socio-economic entitlements in the future.

2. Asylum, immigration and external borders

The Lisbon Treaty systematised and detailed Union government of non-EU nationals around three policies – asylum, immigration and border control.

> **Article 67(2) LTFEU** It shall ensure the absence of internal border controls for persons and shall frame a common policy on asylum, immigration and external border control, based on solidarity between Member States, which is fair towards third-country nationals. For the purpose of this Title, stateless persons shall be treated as third-country nationals.

The central reform is that the ordinary legislative procedure (co-decision) will be applied to all these fields. Beyond that, each policy has been redrafted to reflect legislative developments that have taken place since the Treaty of Amsterdam.

On external border control, the new provision, Article 77 LTFEU contains three developments of note. First, it provides for a far more intensely managed and directed policy, speaking of common measures on external borders checks. By comparison, the current provision, Article 62(2)(a) EC, only provides for harmonisation of standards and procedures. Article 77 LTFEU, is, however, merely following legislative practice, which has established rules on the operation of border checks, the question of where border crossings can take place, on the duties entailed in border surveillance, on carrier duties as well as on biometric features of passports and, finally, on the conduct of border guards.[1] The idea that external borders are to be managed at the EU level is reinforced by the new reference in the Lisbon Treaty to the establishment of an integrated management system for external borders.[2] Second, following the judgment of *United Kingdom v Council*, it appears that this field is governed by the Schengen Protocol, meaning that only States privy to the Schengen Convention can participate in EU policy and law-making here.[3] The third development is a new proviso in Article 77(4) LTFEU that the provision shall not affect Member States' competence to define their borders in accordance with international law. Whilst the thrust of the provision is to make the establishment of borders, like nationality, a matter for State discretion, the caveat that this must comply with international law generates a certain ambiguity, suggesting that the EU could intervene where a Member State fails to respect international law.

Article 77 (1) LTFEU The Union shall develop a policy with a view to:

(a) ensuring the absence of any controls on persons, whatever their nationality, when crossing internal borders;
(b) carrying out checks on persons and efficient monitoring of the crossing of external borders;
(c) the gradual introduction of an integrated management system for external borders.

2. For the purposes of paragraph 1, the European Parliament and the Council, acting in accordance with the ordinary legislative procedure, shall adopt measures concerning:

(a) the common policy on visas and other short-stay residence permits;
(b) the checks to which persons crossing external borders are subject;

---

1 See notably Directive 2004/82/EC on the obligation of carriers to communicate passenger data, OJ 2004, L 261/24; Regulation 2252/2004/EC on standards for security features and biometrics in passports and travel documents issued by Member States, OJ 2004, L 385/1; Regulation 562/2006 establishing a Community Code on the rules governing the movement of persons across the borders (Schengen Borders Code), OJ 2006, L105/1.
2 Regulation 2007/2004/EC establishing a European Agency for the Management of Operational Cooperation at the External Borders of the Member States of the European Union, OJ 2004, L 349/1.
3 Case C-137/05 *United Kingdom v Council*, Judgment of 18 December 2007. See pp. 37–9 of the updates for a more detailed discussion of this case.

(c) the conditions under which nationals of third countries shall have the freedom to travel within the Union for a short period;

(d) any measure necessary for the gradual establishment of an integrated management system for external borders;

(e) the absence of any controls on persons, whatever their nationality, when crossing internal borders.

3. If action by the Union should prove necessary to facilitate the exercise of the right referred to in Article 20(2)(a)[the right of EU citizens to move and reside freely within the territory of the Union], and if the Treaties have not provided the necessary powers, the Council, acting in accordance with a special legislative procedure, may adopt provisions concerning passports, identity cards, residence permits or any other such document. The Council shall act unanimously after consulting the European Parliament.

4. This Article shall not affect the competence of the Member States concerning the geographical demarcation of their borders, in accordance with international law.

The provision on asylum, Article 78 LTFEU, also incorporates three important developments. First, it establishes the principle of *non-refoulement* as a Union Treaty requirement.[4] This entails not only that there can be no derogation from the principle, but that it is to be interpreted in an autonomous manner according to norms of the Union, rather than solely in relation to international law. Second, Union asylum policy is to form part of a broader policy of humanitarian protection, which includes subsidiary protection. This widens the grounds on which the Union will offer asylum to those seeking protection. As well as granting protection to those meeting the definition of a refugee, those facing a real risk of serious harm are also protected. Yet, there is a double edge to this broadening of the scope of protection, since neither temporary nor subsidiary protection offer the guarantees or entitlements attached to refugee status. There is therefore a danger that these secondary protection statuses provide an incentive for Member States to use them to supplant refugee status in order to limit their protection obligations.[5] The final innovation is an emphasis on the management of asylum policy through agreements with non-EU States. Such agreements, alongside other border control measures, are designed to impede the access of asylum seekers to the EU, and thus pose a number of dangers to the integrity and practical efficacy of the notion of international protection.[6]

4 The principle is set out in Article 33(1) of the 1951 Geneva Convention on Refugees and establishes that a refugee cannot be expelled or returned in any manner whatsoever to territories where their life or freedom would be threatened on account of their race, religion, nationality, membership of a particular social group or political opinion. See pp. 623–4 of the main text.

5 On this see Directive 2004/83/EC on minimum standards for the qualification and status of third country nationals or stateless persons as refugees or as persons who otherwise need international protection and the content of the protection granted, OJ 2004, L 304/12. See pp. 648–56 of the main text. On temporary protection see Directive 2001/55/EC on minimum standards for giving temporary protection in the event of a mass influx of displaced persons, OJ 2001, L 212/12.

6 See currently Regulation 1905/2006/EC establishing a financing instrument for development cooperation, OJ 2006, L 378/41. On the difficulties see N. El-Enany, 'Who is the new European refugee?' (2008) 33 *ELR* 313.

> **Article 78(1) LTFEU** The Union shall develop a common policy on asylum, subsidiary protection and temporary protection with a view to offering appropriate status to any third-country national requiring international protection and ensuring compliance with the principle of *non-refoulement*. This policy must be in accordance with the Geneva Convention of 28 July 1951 and the Protocol of 31 January 1967 relating to the status of refugees, and other relevant treaties.
>
> 2. For the purposes of paragraph 1, the European Parliament and the Council, acting in accordance with the ordinary legislative procedure, shall adopt measures for a common European asylum system comprising:
>
> (a) a uniform status of asylum for nationals of third countries, valid throughout the Union;
> (b) a uniform status of subsidiary protection for nationals of third countries who, without obtaining European asylum, are in need of international protection;
> (c) a common system of temporary protection for displaced persons in the event of a massive inflow;
> (d) common procedures for the granting and withdrawing of uniform asylum or subsidiary protection status;
> (e) criteria and mechanisms for determining which Member State is responsible for considering an application for asylum or subsidiary protection;
> (f) standards concerning the conditions for the reception of applicants for asylum or subsidiary protection;
> (g) partnership and cooperation with third countries for the purpose of managing inflows of people applying for asylum or subsidiary or temporary protection.
>
> 3. In the event of one or more Member States being confronted with an emergency situation characterised by a sudden inflow of nationals of third countries, the Council, on a proposal from the Commission, may adopt provisional measures for the benefit of the Member State(s) concerned. It shall act after consulting the European Parliament.

The provision on a common immigration policy, Article 79 LTFEU, includes two developments of note. First, it takes account of existing practices and provides an explicit EU competence to combat human trafficking and for the conclusion of readmission agreements with non-EU States.[7] Second, Article 79(5) LTFEU ring-fences Member States' prerogatives to protect their labour markets. On the face of it, Member States will be able to prevent non-EU nationals working or being self-employed on their territories even where they are family members of long term residents working in that territory, or where they are long term residents from another Member State. This seems to be dangerously illiberal and paradoxically at odds with the idea of a single market, in which one has the right of free circulation once one is lawfully a part of it.

---

7 An example of such a readmission agreement is Council Decision 2007/341/EC on the conclusion of the Agreement between the European Community and the Russian Federation on readmission, OJ 2007, L 129/38. On human trafficking see Framework Decision 2002/629/JHA on combating trafficking in human beings, OJ 2002, L 203/1; Directive 2004/81/EC on the residence permit issued to third-country nationals who are victims of trafficking in human beings or who have been the subject of an action to facilitate illegal immigration, who cooperate with the competent authorities, OJ 2004, L 261/19.

Article 79(1) LTFEU The Union shall develop a common immigration policy aimed at ensuring, at all stages, the efficient management of migration flows, fair treatment of third-country nationals residing legally in Member States, and the prevention of, and enhanced measures to combat, illegal immigration and trafficking in human beings.

2. For the purposes of paragraph 1, the European Parliament and the Council, acting in accordance with the ordinary legislative procedure, shall adopt measures in the following areas:

(a) the conditions of entry and residence, and standards on the issue by Member States of long-term visas and residence permits, including those for the purpose of family reunification;

(b) the definition of the rights of third-country nationals residing legally in a Member State, including the conditions governing freedom of movement and of residence in other Member States;

(c) illegal immigration and unauthorised residence, including removal and repatriation of persons residing without authorisation;

(d) combating trafficking in persons, in particular women and children.

3. The Union may conclude agreements with third countries for the readmission to their countries of origin or provenance of third-country nationals who do not or who no longer fulfil the conditions for entry, presence or residence in the territory of one of the Member States.

4. The European Parliament and the Council, acting in accordance with the ordinary legislative procedure, may establish measures to provide incentives and support for the action of Member States with a view to promoting the integration of third-country nationals residing legally in their territories, excluding any harmonisation of the laws and regulations of the Member States.

5. This Article shall not affect the right of Member States to determine volumes of admission of third-country nationals coming from third countries to their territory in order to seek work, whether employed or self-employed.

3. EU citizenship

(i) Citizenship and the Lisbon Treaty

The Lisbon Treaty seeks to systematise further Union citizenship by detailing existing citizenship rights in a single provision, with subsequent provisions setting out the rights individually and the legislative procedures to be deployed to regulate them.[8]

Article 20(1) LTFEU Citizenship of the Union is hereby established. Every person holding the nationality of a Member State shall be a citizen of the Union. Citizenship of the Union shall be additional to and not replace national citizenship.

2. Citizens of the Union shall enjoy the rights and be subject to the duties provided for in the Treaties. They shall have, *inter alia*:

---

8 Articles 21–24 LTFEU.

(a) the right to move and reside freely within the territory of the Member States;

(b) the right to vote and to stand as candidates in elections to the European Parliament and in municipal elections in their Member State of residence, under the same conditions as nationals of that State;

(c) the right to enjoy, in the territory of a third country in which the Member State of which they are nationals is not represented, the protection of the diplomatic and consular authorities of any Member State on the same conditions as the nationals of that State;

(d) the right to petition the European Parliament, to apply to the European Ombudsman, and to address the institutions and advisory bodies of the Union in any of the Treaty languages and to obtain a reply in the same language.

These rights shall be exercised in accordance with the conditions and limits defined by the Treaties and by the measures adopted there under.

Apart from the systematisation of EU citizenship, there is only one other difference of note. Currently, Article 18(2) EC provides for legislation to be adopted under the co-decision procedure to attain the objective of freedom of movement and residence for Union citizens. By virtue of Article 18(3) EC, however, it cannot apply to provisions on passports, identity cards, residence cards or other such documents, or to provisions on social security or social protection. Although these do not fall outside the remit of EC law, such measures must be adopted under Article 308 EC. The Lisbon Treaty removes the caveat in Article 18(3) EC. Instead, whilst the ordinary legislative procedure (co-decision) is generally to be applied here, the consultation procedure, with a unanimity vote in the Council, is required for measures relating to social protection and social assistance.[9]

The attempt in Article 20 LTFEU to consolidate EU citizenship rights is only partially successful because it fails to acknowledge a move made elsewhere in the Lisbon Treaty to strengthen the relationship between EU citizenship and political engagement with the EU institutions. Indeed, this idea of citizenship as political engagement could be said to be the central reform in this field brought about by Lisbon. Despite the omission in Article 20 LTFEU, the procedures governing the citizens' initiative, the right for a petition of at least one million citizens to suggest an initiative to the Commission, are set out as an integral part of citizenship in this Title.[10] More generally, the Lisbon Treaty establishes a number of principles regarding citizenship:

- **Equality**: citizens are to be treated equally by all EU institutions.
- **Accountability**: EU institutions must pay attention to EU citizens.[11]
- **Participation**: citizens have the right to participate in the democratic life of the Union.
- **Subsidiarity**: decisions are to be taken as openly and closely to the citizen as possible.[12]

9 Article 21(3) LTFEU.   10 Article 24(3) LTFEU.   11 These two principles are in Article 9 LTEU.
12 These two principles are in Article 10(3) LTEU.

- **Deliberation**: citizens should have the possibility to make known and publicly exchange their views in all areas of Union action.[13]
- **Representation**: citizens are to be represented directly by the European Parliament.[14]

It is difficult to ascertain presently whether the articulation of these principles will be little more than rhetorical. Whether they are taken up and acquire any normative of regulative force will depend upon the attitude of the EU institutions, national institutions and, above all, EU citizens. Equally interesting will be the qualitative result of the expression of these principles, that is how these principles will be interpreted and deployed. At the moment, they carry a certain ambiguity. It is not clear whether they have been 'constitutionalised' in order to merely rally support for the EU and its institutions, or whether they have the potential to prompt a more radical response whereby they are used to question and regenerate political community.

(ii)   Citizenship and mutual responsibility

A central concern of recent case law has been that EU citizenship should not be seen as a free lunch – it should not be treated as an easy source of entitlements or as an easy route to the evasion of responsibilities. This concern has manifested itself most obviously in the way in which EU citizenship provisions are invoked by Member States' own nationals. For some time now the Court has allowed their invocation by a State's own nationals, most notably in cases where an individual returns from a period of residence in another Member State to find herself discriminated against by reason of her non-residence in her home State.[15] *De Cuyper* differed from these cases by focusing on the question of whether States were in fact permitted to place such restrictions on their nationals' movement and residence rather than on their discriminatory nature. The case concerned a Belgian requirement that citizens had to be available to work in Belgium in order to claim unemployment allowance. The requirement for habitual residence in Belgium existed so that work offered could be taken up and so that the authorities could verify the availability of workers. In a raid, the authorities discovered De Cuyper had moved to France and discontinued his unemployment allowance.

Case C-406/04 De Cuyper [2006] ECR I-6947

38. According to [its] wording, the right to reside within the territory of the Member States which is conferred directly on every citizen of the Union by Article 18 EC is not unconditional.

---

13 Article 11(1) LTEU.   14 Article 10(2) LTEU.
15 Case C-224/98 *D'Hoop* [2002] ECR I-6191; Case C-224/02 *Pusa* [2004] ECR I-5763.

It is conferred subject to the limitations and conditions laid down by the Treaty and by the measures adopted to give it effect . . .

39. It is established that national legislation such as that in this case which places at a disadvantage certain of its nationals simply because they have exercised their freedom to move and to reside in another Member State is a restriction on the freedoms conferred by Article 18 EC on every citizen of the Union . . .

40. Such a restriction can be justified, with regard to Community law, only if it is based on objective considerations of public interest independent of the nationality of the persons concerned and proportionate to the legitimate objective of the national provisions.

41. In the present case, the enactment of a residence clause reflects the need to monitor the employment and family situation of unemployed persons. That clause allows ONEM inspectors to check whether the situation of a recipient of the unemployment allowance has undergone changes which may have an effect on the benefit granted. That justification is accordingly based on objective considerations of public interest independent of the nationality of the persons concerned.

42. A measure is proportionate when, while appropriate for securing the attainment of the objective pursued, it does not go beyond what is necessary in order to attain it.

43. The justification given by the Belgian authorities for the existence, in the present case, of a residence clause is the need for ONEM inspectors to monitor compliance with the legal requirements laid down for retention of entitlement to the unemployment allowance. Thus it must *inter alia* allow those inspectors to check whether the situation of a person who has declared that he is living alone and unemployed has undergone changes which may have an effect on the benefit granted.

44. So far as concerns, in the main proceedings, the possibility of less restrictive monitoring measures, such as those mentioned by Mr De Cuyper, it has not been established that they would have been capable of ensuring the attainment of the objective pursued.

45. Thus, the effectiveness of monitoring arrangements which, like those introduced in this case, are aimed at checking the family circumstances of the unemployed person concerned and the possible existence of sources of revenue which the claimant has not declared is dependent to a large extent on the fact that the monitoring is unexpected and carried out on the spot, since the competent services have to be able to check whether the information provided by the unemployed person corresponds to the true situation. In that regard it must be pointed out that the monitoring to be carried out as far as concerns unemployment allowances is of a specific nature which justifies the introduction of arrangements that are more restrictive than those imposed for monitoring in respect of other benefits.

The language of *De Cuyper* is similar to that of *Cassis de Dijon*. It is the restrictiveness of the measure which is considered to be egregious, but it will be considered lawful if it is in the public interest and proportionate. Such language exposes a variety of national measures to challenge on grounds of their restrictiveness – anti-terrorism detention orders requiring individuals to remain within an address, bail restrictions, jury service, anti-social behaviour orders containing restrictions on movement, or even restrictions on residence which are imposed to prevent tax evasion.[16] Following *De Cuyper* it would seem as though all these are susceptible to challenge. Of equal

16 In this regard see the Opinion of Advocate General Mazák in Case C-33/07 *Jipa*, Opinion of 14 February 2008.

interest is the fact that Member States are permitted to impose restrictions for public interest reasons. Whilst the formal language is that of an exception to a right to free movement, another way of looking at these cases is that they allow Member States to demand responsibilities of their citizens before they can exercise their right to free movement. These include demanding citizenship responsibilities of the individual – obeying law and order, carrying out public service and paying taxes. EU citizenship may therefore be on the verge of significantly shaping, albeit indirectly, national civic responsibilities.

The case of *Tas Hagen* is of particular interest.[17] Tas Hagen grew up in Indonesia and acquired Dutch nationality in 1961. She applied for benefits granted to Dutch civilian victims of the Second World War in the late 1980s, but was refused as her disability was not regarded as sufficiently serious to qualify her. This finding was reversed in 1999, but she was still denied the benefit as she had subsequently moved to Spain. The benefit was only available to those who were resident in the Netherlands at the time their application was submitted. Importantly, the Court of Justice recognised that a measure designed to limit the benefit to those with links to the Dutch population during and after the Second World War was justifiable for public interest reasons on the basis of solidarity between the Dutch population and those in receipt of the benefit. Eventually it held that the restriction was not proportionate as a requirement of residence at the time of the application did not relate sufficiently to the desire to ensure a link between the national population and those in receipt of the benefit. The principle set out in the judgment is, however, potentially radical. The judgment suggests an idea of social solidarity at the core of EU citizenship in whose name States can not only justify restrictions, but which can be deployed as a means of differentiating between citizens in terms of their attachment to or sacrifice for the society.

The central idea of *Tas Hagen* appears to be that a Member State can award special benefits to citizens who demonstrate extraordinary commitment to or suffering for it. A more mundane, though equally disturbing issue arose in *Morgan*. The question here was whether a Member State could deny benefits to its own nationals who had migrated to another Member State on the grounds that they no longer have a sufficiently strong social link to that society. Morgan was a German who had been an au pair in the United Kingdom for one year, after which she decided to stay in the UK to enroll on an undergraduate degree in genetics. She applied for a study grant from the German authorities who refused on the grounds that such grants were only available to finance the continuation of an education programme in which at least one year had taken place in Germany. In a similar case, Bucher, also a German national, began studying ergotherapy in the Netherlands. She continued to reside in Germany, but moved closer to the border. Whilst the German authorities awarded grants to those living in the border areas, they refused them where an individual was deemed

---

17 Case C-192/05 *Tas-Hagen and Tas v Raadskamer WUBO van de Pensioen- en Uitkeringsraad* [2006] ECR I-10451.

to have moved to the area exclusively to obtain a grant to study abroad. Bucher was denied the grant on this basis.

Joined Cases C-11/06 & C-12/06 Morgan v Bezirksregierung Köln, Judgment of 23 October 2007

24. In this respect, it should first of all be pointed out that, although, as the German, Netherlands, Austrian, Swedish and United Kingdom Governments as well as the Commission have observed, the Member States are competent, under Article 149(1) EC, as regards the content of teaching and the organisation of their respective education systems, it is none the less the case that that competence must be exercised in compliance with Community law . . .

25. Next, it should be recalled that national legislation which places certain nationals of the Member State concerned at a disadvantage simply because they have exercised their freedom to move and to reside in another Member State constitutes a restriction on the freedoms conferred by Article 18(1) EC on every citizen of the Union . . .

26. Indeed, the opportunities offered by the Treaty in relation to freedom of movement for citizens of the Union cannot be fully effective if a national of a Member State can be deterred from availing himself of them by obstacles placed in the way of his stay in another Member State by legislation of his State of origin penalising the mere fact that he has used those opportunities . . .

27. That consideration is particularly important in the field of education in view of the aims pursued by Article 3(1)(q) EC and the second indent of Article 149(2) EC, namely, inter alia, encouraging mobility of students and teachers . . .

28. Consequently, where a Member State provides for a system of education or training grants which enables students to receive such grants if they pursue studies in another Member State, it must ensure that the detailed rules for the award of those grants do not create an unjustified restriction of the right to move and reside within the territory of the Member States . . .

31. . . . . the requirement that students spend one year at an educational establishment in Germany before they are entitled to receive assistance for an education or training course attended in another Member State is liable to discourage them from moving subsequently to another Member State in order to pursue their studies. This is *a fortiori* the case where that year of study in Germany is not taken into account for the purposes of calculating the duration of studies in the other Member State.

32. Contrary to what the German Government in effect contends, the restrictive effects created by the . . . studies condition cannot be regarded as too uncertain or too insignificant, in particular for those whose financial resources are limited, to constitute a restriction on the freedom to move and reside within the territory of the Member States, as conferred by Article 18(1) EC.

33. Such a restriction can be justified in the light of Community law only if it is based on objective considerations of public interest independent of the nationality of the persons concerned and if it is proportionate to the legitimate objective pursued by the provisions of national law . . . It follows from the case-law of the Court that a measure is proportionate if, while appropriate for securing the attainment of the objective pursued, it does not go beyond what is necessary in order to attain that objective . . .

34. It is in the light of the requirements of the case-law recalled in the previous paragraph that the arguments submitted to the Court seeking to justify the first-stage studies condition should be examined . . .

42 . . . the Bezirksregierung Köln as well as the Netherlands and Austrian Governments contend, in essence, that a restriction such as that arising from the implementation of the first-stage studies condition may be justified by the interest in preventing education or training grants awarded in respect of studies pursued entirely in a Member State other than that of origin from becoming an unreasonable burden which could lead to a general reduction in study allowances granted in the Member State of origin. The Swedish Government and the Commission take the view that it is legitimate for a Member State, so far as concerns the award of training or education grants, to ensure a link between the students concerned and its society in general as well as its education system.

43. It is true that the Court has recognised that it may be legitimate for a Member State, in order to ensure that the grant of assistance to cover the maintenance costs of students from other Member States does not become an unreasonable burden which could have consequences for the overall level of assistance which may be granted by that State, to grant such assistance only to students who have demonstrated a certain degree of integration into the society of that State.

44. In principle, if a risk of such an unreasonable burden exists, similar considerations may apply as regards the award by a Member State of education or training grants to students wishing to study in other Member States.

45. However, in the main proceedings, as the referring court essentially observed, the degree of integration into its society which a Member State could legitimately require must, in any event, be regarded as satisfied by the fact that the applicants in the main proceedings were raised in Germany and completed their schooling there.

46. In those circumstances, it is apparent that the first-stage studies condition, in accordance with which higher education studies of at least one year must have been undertaken beforehand in the Member State of origin, is too general and exclusive in this respect. It unduly favours an element which is not necessarily representative of the degree of integration into the society of that Member State at the time the application for assistance is made. It thus goes beyond what is necessary to attain the objective pursued and cannot therefore be regarded as proportionate . . .

The tone of the ruling suggests it is intended to curry favour with national governments. The Court indicates that both the cost and degree of integration into its society can determine the level of entitlements it grants to other Member State nationals. The measurement of integration is likely to be a pernicious process. It has the potential to include consideration not only of the duration of residence, but, *inter alia*, the amount of tax paid, benefits claimed, knowledge of the host State language and commitment to the host State. It is worrying that these factors may be used to determine the distribution of entitlements. Equally disturbing is the opportunity this offers for Member States to police the integration of EU citizens resident on their territories. Integration can now be claimed to be a matter of public concern which the State has the right to monitor and scrutinise.

The freedom to pursue an occupational activity and freedom to provide services

1. Introduction

Developments in this field have pulled in two directions. One direction is provided by the case law of the Court emphasising the synergies between Article 43 EC (Article 49 LTFEU after Lisbon), and Article 39 EC, (Article 45 LTFEU) which conceives the central mission of these provisions on the freedom of establishment and the free movement of workers as the development of a right to pursue an occupational activity in another Member State and their common reference point as the economic integration of an EU citizen in another Member State. The other direction has been provided by Directive 2006/123/EC on services in the internal market.[1] In providing common principles for the exercise of establishment and the right to provide service, the Directive emphasises the link between services and establishment whose common reference point lies in the economic activity not being under the control of another party. Unless both lines of reasoning are interpreted in similar ways, there is a danger of competing logics. The matter is further complicated by Directive 2006/123/EC acknowledging that the diversity of the services economy is such that a single set of principles cannot apply. It therefore establishes three sub-regimes: one whose

---

1 Directive 2006/123/EC on services in the internal market, OJ 2006, L 376/36, Article 1(1). The directive has to be transposed into national law by 28 December 2009, Article 44(1).

activities are governed by sectoral EC legislation; one whose activities are governed by Directive 2006/123/EC; and one whose activities are governed by Articles 43 EC and 49 (Article 57 LTFEU after Lisbon). The outlook for this field is therefore complexity, specialisation and increasing internal tensions.

2. Occupational activity and citizenship

The right to pursue an occupational activity in another Member State has continued to be used to set out the limits and aims of Articles 39 and 43 EC as well as organising and coordinating their interpretation. In *Commission v Portugal*, the Commission challenged a Portuguese law, 10(5) of the CIRS, the Personal Income Tax Code, which stated that one of the conditions for gains made from the sale of an immovable property to be exempt from tax is that these be reinvested in a Portuguese property.

Case C-345/05 Commission v Portugal [2006] ECR I-10633

13. Article 18 EC, which sets out in general terms the right of every citizen of the Union to move and reside freely within the territory of the Member States, finds specific expression in Article 43 EC with regard to freedom of establishment . . . and in Article 39 EC with regard to freedom of movement for workers.

14. It is therefore necessary to consider, firstly, whether Articles 39 EC and 43 EC preclude national legislation such as Article 10(5) of the CIRS which makes entitlement to exemption from capital gains tax arising on the transfer for valuable consideration of real property intended for the taxable person's own and permanent residence or for that of a member of his family subject to the condition that the gains realised should be reinvested in the purchase of real property situated in Portuguese territory.

15. The provisions of the EC Treaty on freedom of movement for persons are intended to facilitate the pursuit by Community citizens of occupational activities of all kinds throughout the Community, and preclude measures which might place Community citizens at a disadvantage when they wish to pursue an economic activity in the territory of another Member State . . .

16. Provisions which preclude or deter a national of a Member State from leaving his country of origin in order to exercise his right to freedom of movement therefore constitute an obstacle to that freedom even if they apply without regard to the nationality of the workers concerned . . .

17. It is clear from the case-law of the Court that, even if, according to their wording, the rules on freedom of movement for workers are directed, in particular, at ensuring that foreign nationals and companies are treated in the host Member State in the same way as nationals of that State, they also preclude the State of origin from obstructing the freedom of one of its nationals to accept and pursue employment in another Member State . . .

18. The same applies to the provisions relating to freedom of establishment. According to the same case-law, even though, according to their wording, those provisions are directed at ensuring that foreign nationals and companies are treated in the host Member State in the same way as nationals of that State, they also prohibit the State of origin from hindering the establishment in another Member State of one of its nationals or of a company incorporated under its legislation . . .

20 . . . Even if Article 10(5) of the CIRS does not prevent a person liable to income tax in Portugal from pursuing employment in another Member State or generally exercising his right of establishment, that provision is none the less likely to restrict the exercise of those rights by having, at the very least, a deterrent effect on taxable persons wishing to sell their real property in order to settle in a Member State other than the Portuguese Republic.

21. It is clear that a taxable person who decides to sell property that he owns in Portugal and uses as his own residence in order to transfer his residence to another Member State and to purchase a new property there for the purposes of his accommodation is, in the context of the exercise of the rights conferred by Articles 39 EC and 43 EC, subject to more unfavourable tax treatment than that enjoyed by a person who maintains his residence in Portugal.

22. That difference in treatment in relation to the taxation of capital gains may affect the estate of a taxable person who wishes to transfer his residence outside Portugal and, as a consequence, is likely to deter him from proceeding with such a transfer . . .

36. As it has not been established that the national legislation in question, namely Article 10(5) of the CIRS, is justified by overriding reasons of public interest, it must be concluded that such legislation is inconsistent with Articles 39 EC and 43 EC.

37. Lastly, with regard to persons who are not economically active, the same conclusion applies, for the same reasons, to the complaint relating to Article 18 EC.

This right to pursue an occupational activity has two main pillars. The first is that EU citizens should not be deterred or restricted by either their home or host State from the pursuit of activities which enable their integration into the economy of another Member State. The second is that excessive regulatory restrictions should not be placed on the economic activity carried out in that other Member State.[2] Embedding this principle within the institution of EU citizenship emphasises its fundamental nature. There has thus been reiteration of the reasoning in subsequent case law.[3] It also guides the interpretation of both Article 39 EC and 43 EC suggesting that these provide a number of common entitlements and outlaw a number of national restrictions, irrespective of the thrust of Community secondary legislation.

3. Policy differentiation in establishment and services

Notwithstanding its commitment to set out a unitary regime, the central feature of Directive 2006/123/EC is its recognition that the sheer range of activities falling under the umbrella of the services economy makes a single set of principles unviable. Instead, the Directive establishes three types of regime in the fields of establishment and services.[4]

---

2 See pp. 730–4 of the main text.
3 Case C-152/03 *Ritter-Coulais* [2006] ECR I-1711; Case C-104/06 *Commission v Sweden* [2007] ECR I-671; Case C-152/05 *Commission v Germany*, Judgment of 17 January 2008.
4 Relatively little is written on Directive 2006/123/EC. See, however, G. Davies, 'The services directive: extending the country of origin principle and reforming public administration' (2007) 32 *ELR* 232; U. Neergaard, R. Nielsen and L. Roseberry (eds.) *The Services Directive – Consequences for the Welfare State and the European Social Model* (2008, Djøf, Copenhagen).

(i)   Services governed by sectoral legislation

Fields governed by specific EU sectoral legislation continue to be governed by that legislation which will regulate both the conditions of economic activity and permissible forms of regulation.

> **Article 3(1)** If the provisions of this Directive conflict with a provision of another Community act governing specific aspects of access to or exercise of a service activity in specific sectors or for specific professions, the provision of the other Community act shall prevail and shall apply to those specific sectors or professions.

The Directive provides some examples of this[5] but there is a particular challenge as many sectors are governed only partially by sectoral legislation. In such circumstances, a dual regime will apply where some elements are governed by the Directive and others by the sectoral legislation in question. This is anticipated in some fields in which there is significant sectoral legislation. The Directive therefore provides that financial services, electronic communications, transport, temporary work agencies and audiovisual services are not governed by the Directive.[6] In addition, a number of other activities partially regulated by EU secondary legislation are not governed by the Directive's central provisions on freedom to provide and receive services but are governed by the Directive's other provisions. These include postal, electricity, gas, water, posted workers and treatment and movement of waste, data protection, copyright, professional qualifications, and administrative formalities concerning the free movement of EU citizens.[7]

(ii)   Activities not governed by the Directive but continuing to be governed by Articles 43 and 49 EC

The Directive also does not apply to a large number of activities in which there is very limited or no EC legislation. These activities are still governed by Articles 43 and 49 EC. This is not simply because the Directive, as a piece of secondary legislation, cannot derogate from EC Treaty obligations but also because it stipulates this to be the case:

> **Article 3(3)** Member States shall apply the provisions of this Directive in compliance with the rules of the Treaty on the right of establishment and the free movement of services.

The activities falling under this umbrella are numerous and include:

• some public sector economic activities, namely what are services of general economic interest, privatisation and the abolition of monopolies;[8]

---

5 Supra n.1, Article 3(1)(a)–(d).   6 *Ibid.*, Article 2(2)(b)–(g).   7 *Ibid.*, Article 17.
8 *Ibid.*, Article 1(2) and (3).

- some cultural activities, namely laws on cultural or linguistic diversity, media plu-ralism[9] and gambling;[10]
- labour law[11] and many activities concerning the welfare state, notably social security, health care, non-economic services of a general interest and social services relating to child care, family support or social housing;[12]
- some law and order activities, private security services and services provided by notaries and bailiffs, as well as services connected with the exercise of official author-ity.[13]

All the above are discrete activities which will only be governed by the economic freedoms. In addition, there are a number of cross-cutting matters which arise in all fields of service activity and which will not be regulated by the Directive. These are criminal law,[14] taxation[15] and the exercise of fundamental rights.[16]

Furthermore, the same distinction arises in these fields as in the one above, namely that some activities are not governed by the Directive's central provisions on freedom to provide and receive services but are covered by its provisions on establishment. The most important are matters of private international law,[17] and visa and residence requirements for non EU nationals moving from one Member State to another.[18]

(iii)   Activities governed by the Directive

All other activities are to be governed by Directive 2006/123/EC, which acts as a residual category. Yet the two previous categories are so large, it begs the question what types of activity are regulated by Directive 2006/123/EC. The answer is a large number of mid-range activities. Paragraph 33 of Preamble sets out a non-exhaustive list.

> The services covered by this Directive concern a wide variety of ever-changing activities, including business services such as management consultancy, cer-tification and testing; facilities management, including office maintenance; advertising; recruitment services; and the services of commercial agents. The services covered are also services provided both to businesses and to consumers, such as legal or fiscal advice; real estate services such as estate agencies; con-struction, including the services of architects; distributive trades; the organisa-tion of trade fairs; car rental; and travel agencies. Consumer services are also covered, such as those in the field of tourism, including tour guides; leisure services, sports centres and amusement parks; and, to the extent that they are not excluded from the scope of application of the Directive, household support services, such as help for the elderly.

---

9 *Ibid.*, Article 1(4).   10 *Ibid.*, Article 2(2)(h).
11 *Ibid.*, Article 1(6).   12 *Ibid.*, Article 2(2)(f) and 2(2)(j). See also Article 3(1)(b).
13 *Ibid.*, Article 2(2) (i)(k)(l).   14 *Ibid.*, Article 1(5).   15 *Ibid.*, Article 2(3).
16 *Ibid.*, Article 1(7).   17 *Ibid.*, Article 17(15).   18 *Ibid.*, Article 17(9).

Whilst the allocation of particular activities to individual headings was a matter of political negotiation, and it would be fruitless looking for the presence of a universal logic, there appear to be two dominant ethos at work. The first is that the Directive should not disrupt existing legal integration. This is, after all, the logic of article 3(1), which establishes this *lex specialis* rule. The presence of three distinct sub-regimes will, however, inevitably bring some disruption. There will be arguments about when an activity falls under one heading and not the other. Even more crucially many activities will cut across the different headings. It is possible, therefore, for an activity partially regulated by sectoral legislation to be governed by that legislation, by Directive 2006/123/EC for the activities not regulated by that legislation and by Articles 43 or 49 EC insofar as the activity raises questions of fundamental rights, criminal law or tax law. This will be fiendishly difficult to navigate, and it is questionable whether the Directive actually makes life easier for traders or regulators in this regard.

The other dominant ethos of the Directive is that it should not govern particularly sensitive activities. This is, after all, the rationale for the distinction between the second and third category. This balances rests, however, on an assumption about the innocuousness of Articles 43 and 49 EC, namely that these cannot be deployed to challenge aggressively national measures in the excluded activities. *Laval* illustrated the dangers of such an assumption. One of its central actors was Bygnnads, the main Swedish trade union in the building sector with 87 per cent of workers in the sector belonging to it, which has a collective agreement with Swedish employers. Under this rates are determined locally but there is a fall back rate equivalent to €12/hour. In addition, employers must pay 1.5 per cent of total gross wages to part of it for purposes of the pay review it carries out and a further 6.7 per cent in various insurance charges to FORA, a central insurance company. Laval, a Latvian company was constructed to work on a school site in Vaxholm in Sweden. It had a collective agreement with Latvian workers. It entered into negotiations with Bygnnads where it offered to pay its workers €1500 per month (€8.5/hour). Bygnnads asked it to apply the Stockholm rate of €16/hour. When negotiations broke down and Laval began work at Vaxholm, Bygnnads organised a blockade of theVaxholm site and a boycott of Laval throughout Sweden. All parties agreed this effectively prevented Laval carrying out business in Sweden. Laval argued, inter alia, that the blockage violated Article 49 EC. The Swedish trade unions argued that industrial action fell outside Article 49 EC and, if it did not, it was, in any case, justified by the need to protect workers.

Case C-341/05 *Laval v Svenska Byggnadsarbetareförbundet*, Judgment of 18 December 2007

89. According to the observations of the Danish and Swedish Governments, the right to take collective action constitutes a fundamental right which, as such, falls outside the scope of Article 49 EC . . .

90. In that regard, it must be recalled that the right to take collective action is recognised both by various international instruments which the Member States have signed or cooperated

in, such as the European Social Charter, signed at Turin on 18 October 1961 – to which, moreover, express reference is made in Article 136 EC – and Convention No 87 of the International Labour Organisation concerning Freedom of Association and Protection of the Right to Organise of 9 July 1948 – and by instruments developed by those Member States at Community level or in the context of the European Union, such as the Community Charter of the Fundamental Social Rights of Workers adopted at the meeting of the European Council held in Strasbourg on 9 December 1989, which is also referred to in Article 136 EC, and the Charter of Fundamental Rights of the European Union proclaimed in Nice on 7 December 2000.

91. Although the right to take collective action must therefore be recognised as a fundamental right which forms an integral part of the general principles of Community law the observance of which the Court ensures, the exercise of that right may none the less be subject to certain restrictions. As is reaffirmed by Article 28 of the Charter of Fundamental Rights of the European Union, it is to be protected in accordance with Community law and national law and practices.

92. Although it is true, as the Swedish Government points out, that the right to take collective action enjoys constitutional protection in Sweden, as in other Member States, nevertheless as is clear from paragraph 10 of this judgment, under the Swedish constitution, that right – which, in that Member State, covers the blockading of worksites – may be exercised unless otherwise provided by law or agreement.

93. In that regard, the Court has already held that the protection of fundamental rights is a legitimate interest which, in principle, justifies a restriction of the obligations imposed by Community law, even under a fundamental freedom guaranteed by the Treaty, such as the free movement of goods . . .

94. As the Court held, in *Schmidberger* and *Omega*, the exercise of the fundamental rights at issue, that is, freedom of expression and freedom of assembly and respect for human dignity, respectively, does not fall outside the scope of the provisions of the Treaty. Such exercise must be reconciled with the requirements relating to rights protected under the Treaty and in accordance with the principle of proportionality . . .

95. It follows from the foregoing that the fundamental nature of the right to take collective action is not such as to render Community law inapplicable to such action, taken against an undertaking established in another Member State which posts workers in the framework of the transnational provision of services.

96. It must therefore be examined whether the fact that a Member State's trade unions may take collective action in the circumstances described above constitutes a restriction on the freedom to provide services, and, if so, whether it can be justified . . .

102. The Swedish Government and the defendant trade unions in the main proceedings submit that the restrictions in question are justified, since they are necessary to ensure the protection of a fundamental right recognised by Community law and have as their objective the protection of workers, which constitutes an overriding reason of public interest.

103. In that regard, it must be pointed out that the right to take collective action for the protection of the workers of the host State against possible social dumping may constitute an overriding reason of public interest within the meaning of the case-law of the Court which, in principle, justifies a restriction of one of the fundamental freedoms guaranteed by the Treaty . . .

104. It should be added that, according to Article 3(1)(c) and (j) EC, the activities of the Community are to include not only an 'internal market characterised by the abolition, as between Member States, of obstacles to the free movement of goods, persons, services and capital', but also 'a policy in the social sphere'. Article 2 EC states that the Community

is to have as its task, inter alia, the promotion of 'a harmonious, balanced and sustainable development of economic activities' and 'a high level of employment and of social protection'.

105. Since the Community has thus not only an economic but also a social purpose, the rights under the provisions of the EC Treaty on the free movement of goods, persons, services and capital must be balanced against the objectives pursued by social policy, which include, as is clear from the first paragraph of Article 136 EC, inter alia, improved living and working conditions, so as to make possible their harmonisation while improvement is being maintained, proper social protection and dialogue between management and labour.

106. In the case in the main proceedings, Byggnads and Byggettan contend that the objective of the blockade carried out against Laval was the protection of workers.

107. In that regard, it must be observed that, in principle, blockading action by a trade union of the host Member State which is aimed at ensuring that workers posted in the framework of a transnational provision of services have their terms and conditions of employment fixed at a certain level, falls within the objective of protecting workers.

108. However, as regards the specific obligations, linked to signature of the collective agreement for the building sector, which the trade unions seek to impose on undertakings established in other Member States by way of collective action such as that at issue in the case in the main proceedings, the obstacle which that collective action forms cannot be justified with regard to such an objective . . . with regard to workers posted in the framework of a transnational provision of services, their employer is required . . . to observe a nucleus of mandatory rules for minimum protection in the host Member State.

109. Finally, as regards the negotiations on pay which the trade unions seek to impose, by way of collective action such as that at issue in the main proceedings, on undertakings, established in another Member State which post workers temporarily to their territory, it must be emphasised that Community law certainly does not prohibit Member States from requiring such undertakings to comply with their rules on minimum pay by appropriate means.

110. However, collective action such as that at issue in the main proceedings cannot be justified in the light of the public interest objective referred to in paragraph 102 of the present judgment, where the negotiations on pay, which that action seeks to require an undertaking established in another Member State to enter into, form part of a national context characterised by a lack of provisions, of any kind, which are sufficiently precise and accessible that they do not render it impossible or excessively difficult in practice for such an undertaking to determine the obligations with which it is required to comply as regards minimum pay . . .

Laval raises at least two important points of note.[19] The first is whether there is any case for exceptionalism with regard to the economic freedoms. The thrust of Directive 2006/123/EC is for some differentiation but we have seen how the Court has refused this on ethical issues or matters concerning the welfare state.[20] *Laval* continues this trend. Whilst the Court frames the matter in terms of the right to strike, this is treated as an exception to the single market and therefore must be interpreted in light of the proportionality principle. The alternative is not adopted – namely that realisation of the single market be treated as a limited exception to the right to strike, and therefore

19 A similar judgment was given in relation to collective action by the International Transport Workers' Federation against a vessel that was operating under an Estonian flag of convenience. Case C-438/05 *International Transport Workers' Federation et al v Viking Line*, Judgment of 11 December 2007.

20 See pp. 760–70 of the main text.

be interpreted accordingly in the light of proportionality principle. This language of norm and exception creates a subtle hierarchy of norms in which strikes have to be justified whereas the reasons for trade do not.

The second point of interest concerns the application of the proportionality principle to private organisations such as trade unions. The Court indicated that the trade unions could not strike to secure minimum pay where the national context was sufficiently imprecise that it was excessively difficult for undertakings to determine the obligations they must meet to comply with this. This is a little confusing. Insofar as there are national laws governing this, these are not the responsibilities of the trade unions and it would seem bizarre to deny their right to strike because national laws are unclear. Insofar as the statement of the Court relates to the claims and practice of the union itself, it establishes a false analogy between the latter and public authorities. For public authorities it can be argued that they must set out their laws clearly so that traders can see how to comply and that the least restrictive measures are taken. The equivalent for trade unions is not clear. Is it saying that they must set out an a priori position before negotiating a collective agreement or that they must have a national framework to which an employer must subscribe? Neither would seem a duty of prevailing industrial practice. Trade unions' duty is to represent the interests of their members and secure the best deal for them and this can be done in some cases through local negotiations so there is no national norm.

4. Freedom of establishment and the Services Directive

In relation to freedom of establishment, Directive 2006/123 has three missions.

First, it sets out the circumstances and conditions under which a Member State may make access to a service activity subject to an authorisation. The central provision is Article 9(1).

> **Article 9(1)** Member States shall not make access to a service activity or the exercise thereof subject to an authorisation scheme unless the following conditions are satisfied:
>
> (a) the authorisation scheme does not discriminate against the provider in question;
> (b) the need for an authorisation scheme is justified by an overriding reason relating to the public interest;
> (c) the objective pursued cannot be attained by means of a less restrictive measure, in particular because an a posteriori inspection would take place too late to be genuinely effective

This provision catches more restrictions than Article 43 EC which has never been successfully invoked to challenge the requirement of prior authorisation per se.[21] It differs from Article 49 EC as the former usually relies on a system of controls imposed

---

21 For a comparison with Article 49 EC see Case C-465/05 *Commission v Italy*, Judgment of 13 December 2007.

by the home State of the service provider, and is merely indicating that these controls rather than those of the host State should apply. It is arguably the most deregulatory feature of the Directive as it is simply an injunction to do away with controls unless they can be justified. Many trades currently regulated could now be liberalised. In addition, the prohibition is wide-ranging. Planning laws and licenses for pubs and nightclubs would all seem to be caught by the Directive.

The conditions attached to authorisations are also to be tightly policed. These must be non-discriminatory; justified by an overriding reason relating to the public interest; proportionate to that public interest objective; clear and unambiguous; objective; made public in advance; and transparent and accessible.[22] In like vein the procedures and formalities attached to the grant of authorisations must be made public in advance, accessible and not unduly complicated, and provide guarantees of impartiality and of as quick process as possible.[23] Authorisations may also not be given for a limited period except where this can be justified either generally or individually by an overriding requirement relating to the public interest or authorisation is subject to continued fulfilment of requirements.[24]

Secondly, the Directive outlaws completely certain restrictions on the access to or exercise of service activity within a member State's territory. These include:

> direct and indirect discrimination on grounds of nationality or place of registered office; prohibitions on having an establishment, or being registered or professionally enrolled in more than one Member State; requirements for a service provider to have their principal establishment in the territory; conditions of reciprocity with another Member State; involvement of competitors with an authorisation procedure or subjecting authorisation to a test of economic need; being pre-registered for a given period in the territory or having to take out or participate in a financial guarantee from a provider in that territory.[25]

All these would be currently caught by Article 43 EC. Yet the difference with the Directive is that those caught by the Directive can never be justified under any circumstances.

Thirdly, the Directive sets out a series of restrictions which are only to be allowed if they are in the public interest, proportionate, necessary and non-discriminatory. In this, it extends to a number of restrictions, some of which would be clearly within Article 43 EC whilst others would only arguably fall within that provision. These include:

> quantitative or territorial restrictions on the activity; obligations on the provider to take a legal form; restrictions which relate to the shareholding of the company or minimum number of employees; obligations to supply other services; fixed minimum or maximum tariffs; a ban on more than one establishment in the

22 Supra n.1, Article 10(2).   23 *Ibid.*, Article 13(1) and (2).   24 Supra n. 1, Article 11(1).
25 *Ibid.*, Article 14.

Member State; requirements other than professional qualifications covered by Directive 2005/36[26] which reserve access to the activity by virtue of the specific nature of the activity.[27]

Although these provisions seem to extend the ambit of freedom of establishment by covering a number of restrictions which fall into a sort of grey zone, this provision is in some ways the least dramatic of the three. The restrictions mentioned are discrete in nature, and can, if necessary, be justified by Member States. Moreover, most are the kind of restriction which few Member State would defend. Insofar as they limit activity it makes sense to get rid of them. The economic consequences are not likely to be large, however. More significantly, the list of restrictions caught by the Directive may now be used as a reference point for the interpretation of Article 43 EC, as it would be odd if certain measures are deemed restrictive purely by dint of whether the activity falls within the remit of the Directive or not. Whilst this would formalise and give coherence and legal certainty to the ambit of the freedom of establishment, a cost would be the restrictiveness on judicial creativity and adaptability imposed.

5. Freedom to provide services and the Services Directive

The central provision on the right to provide services is Article 16.

> **Article 16(1)** Member States shall respect the right of providers to provide services in a Member State other than that in which they are established.
> The Member State in which the service is provided shall ensure free access to and free exercise of a service activity within its territory.
> Member States shall not make access to or exercise of a service activity in their territory subject to compliance with any requirements which do not respect the following principles:
>
> (a) non-discrimination: the requirement may be neither directly nor indirectly discriminatory with regard to nationality or, in the case of legal persons, with regard to the Member State in which they are established;
> (b) necessity: the requirement must be justified for reasons of public policy, public security, public health or the protection of the environment;
> (c) proportionality: the requirement must be suitable for attaining the objective pursued, and must not go beyond what is necessary to attain that objective. . . .
>
> 3. The Member State to which the provider moves shall not be prevented from imposing requirements with regard to the provision of a service activity, where they are justified for reasons of public policy, public security, public health or the protection of the environment and in accordance with paragraph 1. Nor shall that Member State be prevented from applying, in accordance with Community law, its rules on employment conditions, including those laid down in collective agreements.

26 See pp. 719–22 of the main text.   27 Supra n.1, Article 15(2).

Article 16 applies a different test for trade liberalisation to that in Article 49 EC. The latter catches any measure 'liable to prohibit or otherwise impede the activities of a provider of services established in another Member State'.[28] Article 16(1) instead talks of ensuring 'free access to and free exercise of a service activity' within its territory. It remains to be seen which test is broader or whether they will be interpreted in parallel.

More significantly, Article 16 contains a number of restrictions which suggest it will be very rare for any measure caught by Article 16 to be found to be lawful. First, it narrows the public interest grounds on which restrictions can be placed to four – public security, protection of the environment, public health and public policy. In general, these would not seem particularly relevant to the types of activities caught by the Directive. It is difficult to see how management consultants or estate agents, for example, could threaten public security, the environment or public health. Secondly, Article 16 outlaws all forms of discriminatory restriction. Under Article 49 EC, these measures can be justified if they do not arbitrarily discriminate against foreign service providers. No such leeway is provided by Article 16(1)(a). Discrimination is outlawed, per se. Finally, a strict proportionality test is set out in Article 16(1)(c). Latitude does not appear to be given to the measures falling within Article 16 that is sometimes given to those falling under Article 49 EC.

Alongside this, a number of types of restrictions are not merely held to be caught by the Directive but to be fully outlawed. These include requirements to have an establishment in the territory; to obtain an authorisation or be registered with the authorities; restrictions, except those necessary for health and safety at work, which affect the use of equipment and material which are an integral part of the service provided;[29] Discrimination based on the nationality or place of residence of the recipient of the service is also to be prohibited.[30] Finally, requirements can never be imposed on a recipient requiring her to get authorisation before using a service from another Member State or limiting financial assistance to her by reason of her using these services.[31]

Concern about the deregulatory effects of Article 16 led to the establishment of an exceptional procedure derogating from it. The conditions under which this derogation can be used are set out in Article 18.

Article 18 (1) By way of derogation from Article 16, and in exceptional circumstances only, a Member State may, in respect of a provider established in another Member State, take measures relating to the safety of services.

2. The measures provided for in paragraph 1 may be taken only if the mutual assistance procedure laid down in Article 35 is complied with and the following conditions are fulfilled:

(a) the national provisions in accordance with which the measure is taken have not been subject to Community harmonization in the field of the safety of services;

---

28 Case C-76/90 *Säger v Dennemeyer* [1991] ECR I-4221.
29 *Ibid.*, Article 16(2).   30 *Ibid.*, Article 20.   31 *Ibid.*, Article 19.

(b) the measures provide for a higher level of protection of the recipient than would be the case in a measure taken by the Member State of establishment in accordance with its national provisions;
(c) the Member State of establishment has not taken any measures or has taken measures which are insufficient as compared with those referred to in Article 35(2);
(d) the measures are proportionate.

The procedure referred to in article 35 is a three stage one.[32] In the first stage, set out in article 35(2), the host Member State must ask the Member State of establishment to take measures against the service provider after providing it with information on the service in question and the circumstances of the case. The Member State of establishment must check the service provider is acting lawfully, then must either take measures or inform the requesting State within the shortest period why it has not taken measures. The second stage involves the Member State notifying the Commission and the Member State of establishment of the reasons why it believes the latter's actions are inadequate and the measures it intends to take and why these fulfill Article 18.[33] The third stage involves the Commission taking a decision within the shortest period of time on whether these measures meet Article 18.[34] Meanwhile, the measures may not be taken until fifteen working days after notification of the Commission.[35] If the Commission authorises the measures, they may be taken. Otherwise they may not.

The cumbersome nature of the procedure and its only being available in exceptional circumstances concerning public safety suggest it to be very much an institution of last resort. However, the procedure set out in Articles 18 and 35 embodies the ethos of Directive 2006/123/EC with regard to services. The Directive is based on the principle of home State control. It is only where this goes awry or for the limited grounds set out in Article 16(1)(b) that the host State can intervene. For this reason the host State must contact the home State to find out if its legal procedures have been applied correctly and to give it the opportunity to be a regulator of first resort. It is only where the latter does not play this game that it can intervene and only in circumstances which are heavily policed by the Commission. Such a regime relies heavily on mutual trust. In a Union as complex and multifarious as the European Union, it is not clear whether that trust is present or that the first value of regulators should be faith in other regulators rather than commitment to their citizens.

---

32 In urgent cases, the three stage procedure can be dispensed with and there can be simple notification of the Commission and authorisation by it. *Ibid.*, Article 35(6).
33 *Ibid.*, Article 35(3).   34 *Ibid.*, Article 35(5).   35 *Ibid.*, Article 35(4).

Discrimination law

1. Legislative and policy developments

(i) The Treaty of Lisbon

The European Union remains committed to 'combat discrimination' and 'promote equality between women and men',[1] but the Treaty of Lisbon does not make major changes to the EU's equality policy. There is a minor amendment to Article 13 EC (renumbered Article 19 LTFEU). Now, the Council must, acting unanimously in accordance with a special legislative procedure,[2] secure the *consent* of the European Parliament (by simple majority), which goes beyond *consulting* the EP as provided under Article 13 EC. Greater involvement of the EP is to be welcomed, but the requirement of Council unanimity (retained because of the significant impact of Community equality legislation in the Member States) will continue to prevent bold legislative action. There is no amendment to Article 141 EC (renumbered Art 157 LTFEU) which may be regretted given the difficulties with ensuring that Member States' affirmative action initiatives fall within the exception of Article 141(4) EC. The most significant amendment is that mainstreaming is given a more prominent role for all protected groups.

---

1 Article 3 LTEU (ex Art 2 TEU).   2 Defined in Article 289 LTFEU.

Article 8 LTFEU (ex Article 3(2) LEC)
In all its activities, the Union shall aim to eliminate inequalities, and to promote equality, between men and women.
Article 10 LTFEU
In defining and implementing its policies and activities, the Union shall aim to combat discrimination based on sex, racial or ethnic origin, religion or belief, disability, age or sexual orientation.

The separate reference to mainstreaming gender policy probably has to do with lobbying by the European Women's Group for a separate provision on gender equality.[3] A declaration attached to Article 8 LTFEU also provides that 'the Union will aim in its different policies to combat all kinds of domestic violence. The Member States should take all necessary measures to prevent and punish these criminal acts and to support and protect the victims'. This may impact the measures adopted under Title V LTFEU (Area of Freedom, Security and Justice).

(ii)   Policy developments

The Equal Treatment Directive was recast in 2006.[4] Recasting is not a means to amend Community Law substantially but allows the legislator to consolidate in one legislative text a number of disparate directives addressing gender equality, and to make minor amendments to clarify the law.[5] The most significant impact of the recast is that by consolidating the provisions on equal pay and equal treatment in one directive, the same definitions of direct and indirect discrimination apply to both forms of discrimination. Recasting is not a process for amending the law to overturn unpopular Court judgments, so while the Commission had considered overruling the principle established in *Allonby* (that to determine what work of equal value is, the pay must come from a single source so that the plaintiff cannot compare herself to the work of equal value done in another workplace),[6] the Commission was persuaded to drop the amendment and to allow the ECJ to develop the case law.[7]

Two new bodies have been established in 2007: a European Institute for Gender Equality (whose objective is to strengthen the promotion of gender equality and whose tasks include gathering and comparing information about gender equality issues, set up and coordinate a European Network on Gender, develop dialogue with NGOs, and

---

3 M. Bell 'Equality and the European Constitution' (2004) 33 *Industrial Law Journal* 242, 257–8.
4 Directive 2006/54 of the European Parliament and the Council of 5 July 2006 on the implementation of the principle of equal opportunities and equal treatment of men and women in matters of employment and occupation (recast) [2006] OJ L204/23.
5 N. Burrows and M. Robinson 'An assessment of the recast of Community equality laws' (2006) 13 *ELJ* 186.
6 Case C-256/01 *Allonby v Accrington and Rossendale College* [2004] ECR I-873.
7 J. Shaw, J. Hunt and C. Wallace, *Economic and Social Law of the European Union* (Basingstoke, Palgrave Macmillan: 2007), pp. 372–3.

disseminate information),[8] and the EU Fundamental Rights Agency, which replaces the EU Monitoring Centre for Racism and Xenophobia, and has similar information gathering/dissemination tasks.[9] These bodies have no enforcement powers, which remain exclusively in the hands of national equality bodies.

Commentators have suggested that there is a general move towards a substantive concept of equality: in the legislation and also in a range of policy initiatives, for example mainstreaming, employment guidelines, and several initiatives to raise public awareness of the benefits of a more inclusive society.[10] This is confirmed by a range of policy initiatives: in March 2006 the Commission published *A Roadmap for Equality Between Women and Men*, identifying priority actions for the next four years;[11] 2007 was declared the European Year of Equal Opportunities for All with a budget of 15 million euros allocated to a range of awareness raising projects;[12] perhaps more significantly the EU's employment and social solidarity programme, PROGRESS, was launched in 2007. It is designed to promote mainstreaming of the principle of non-discrimination and to promote gender equality by commissioning studies on the effect of current legislation, supporting the implementation of EC discrimination law and raising awareness of the key policy issues.[13] However, there are also concerns that the scope of some of the recent legislative initiatives is not sufficiently ambitious,[14] and that in spite of the promises of mainstreaming, tangible results are difficult to identify.[15] Finally, it should be noted that in spite of the vast number of initiatives in particular addressing gender discrimination, women's employment remains lower than men in spite of better educational qualifications, women's presence in management positions stands at 33 per cent, and women's pay is 15 per cent less than that of men.[16]

2. The case law of the Court

The Court has rendered a spate of judgments interpreting the framework directive (Directive 2000/78) and the race directive (Directive 2000/43). Each enables

---

8 Articles 2 and 3 Regulation 1922/2006 on establishing a European Institute for Gender Equality (2006) OJ L43/9

9 Regulation 168/2007 establishing a European Union Agency for Fundamental Rights [2007] OJ L53/1. See further pp. 65–8 of the update.

10 E. Howard, 'The European Year of Equal Opportunities for All 2007: Is the EU moving away from a formal idea of equality?' (2008) 14 *ELJ* 168.

11 COM(2006) 92. The six areas are: equal economic independence for women and men; reconciliation of private and professional life; equal representation in decision-making; eradication of all forms of gender-based violence; elimination of gender stereotypes; promotion of gender equality in external and development policies.

12 Decision 771/2006 establishing the European Year of Equal Opportunities for All (2007) – towards a just society (2006) OJ L14/1.

13 Articles 2, 7 and 8 Decision 1672/2006 establishing a Community Programme for Employment and Social Solidarity [2006] OJ L315/1.

14 E.g. E. Caracciolo di Torella, 'The principle of gender equality, the goods and services directive and insurance: a conceptual analysis' (2006) 13 *Maastricht Journal of European and Comparative Law* 3.

15 See generally F. Beveridge 'Building against the past: the impact of mainstreaming on EU gender law and policy' (2007) 32 *ELR* 193.

16 EC Commission *Equality Between Women and Men* 2008 COM(2008)10.

the Court to explore the outer boundaries of the legislation. No distinctive pattern can be discerned yet, but the judgments indicate a tension between members of the judiciary who wish for an expansive interpretation of the principles of non-discrimination, and those who favour a more restrictive view. The cases are classified below according to the ground of discrimination, but as the directives are worded similarly, it means that some of the principles established apply to all grounds of discrimination.

(i)   Age discrimination as a general principle of Community law

It is helpful to begin with age discrimination because of the important *Mangold v Helm* judgment,[17] which Professor Schiek said 'constitutes a first step in what will hopefully lead towards judicial development of a coherent framework for equal treatment of persons from a less than satisfactory legislative package'.[18] Mangold (56 years old) entered into a fixed-term employment contract with Helm. The terms of the contract specified that the duration was fixed in accordance with German law at the time which was designed to make it easier to enter into fixed-term contracts with older workers, while restricting the freedom to enter into fixed-term contracts with younger workers. In 2002 (after Directive 2000/78 was agreed, but before it was implemented in Germany) the German law was amended to lower the age at which fixed-term contracts could be entered into freely from 58 to 52. However, Mangold argued that this agreement, which he entered into after 2002, was in breach of Directive 2000/78 and constituted discrimination based on his age. The Court's response that the discriminatory measure was not justified by Article 6(1) of Directive 2000/78 is based on two significant moves: first, that the Directive applied even though it had not yet been transposed into German law, and even if Germany had secured an extension of time to implement the Directive, because 'the principle of non-discrimination on grounds of age must . . . be regarded as a general principle of Community law'.[19] Second, having placed the Directive within this general principle, it felt empowered to apply Article 6(1) to test whether discrimination was justified. It found that the legislation was based on a legitimate objective: 'to promote the vocational integration of unemployed older workers, in so far as they encounter considerable difficulties in finding work'.[20] But it was ruled that the law went beyond what was necessary to achieve that aim by taking into consideration only age and not the personal circumstances of the individual or the conditions in the labour market.[21] This suggests that the Court adopts a strict standard of review when Member States seek to depart from the general obligation not to discriminate. The judgment in *Palacios de la Villa* offers a helpful contrast.[22] The employer terminated the employee's contract pursuant to a collective

17 Case C-144/04 *Werner Mangold v Rüdiger Helm* [2005] ECR I-9981.
18 D. Schieck 'The ECJ decision in Mangold: a further twist on effects of Directives and Constitutional relevance of Community equality legislation' (2006) 35 *Industrial Law Journal* 329.
19 Above n. 17 para. 75.   20 Above n. 17 para. 59.   21 Above n. 17 paras 64–65.
22 Case C-411/05 *Félix Palacios de la Villa v Cortefiel Servicios SA*, judgment of 17 October 2007.

agreement which governed the relationship between the parties which established a compulsory retirement age of 65 unless an employee had not worked enough years to qualify for a pension. Rejecting the advice of the Advocate General (whose conservative opinion led him to find that laws fixing the retirement age fell outside the scope of the Directive), the Court found that the Spanish law which facilitated this agreement pursued a legitimate objective (viz. promoting employment), and that the measure was proportionate for two reasons: first the legislation took into account that the person receives a pension upon termination, and the scheme was entered into by a collective agreement 'so that due account may be taken not only of the overall situation in the labour market concerned, but also of the specific features of the jobs in question'.[23] Thus the circumstances allowed for the right balance to be struck between the fundamental right not to be discriminated against because of age and Spanish employment policy.

But it is the first ground of the *Mangold* judgment that is arguably its most significant and controversial. By finding the obligation not to discriminate on age a general principle of Community Law, it means that, irrespective of the specific obligations in Directive 2000/78 Member States have a general obligation not to discriminate even in spheres not covered by the Directive. So, for example, legislation that offers discriminatory access to health services based on age may be challenged as contrary to Community law even if Directive 2000/78 only applies to employment relations. It remains to be seen whether the obligation not to discriminate on other grounds (e.g. race or disability) also qualifies as a general principle, but as we explain below the judgment has not been unanimously welcomed by commentators and in subsequent cases.[24] Moreover, the door is open for this general principle to have horizontal effect and regulate private parties,[25] or even to apply as a ground to review Community legislation should it fall foul of this general principle.

(ii)   Disability discrimination – a retreat from Mangold

In *Chacón Navas* an employee was certified as unfit for work on grounds of sickness and while she was on leave from work the employer terminated her contract because of her illness. The question arose whether sickness was a kind of disability so that the employee's termination was discriminatory. The Court's view is that disability for the purposes of Directive 2000/78 means 'a limitation which results in particular from physical, mental or psychological impairments and which hinders the participation

---

23 *Ibid.* Para. 74.
24 Editorial 'Out with the old . . .' (2006) 31 *ELR* 1. See also the very sceptical opinion of AG Mazák in *Palacios de la Villa*, ibid.
25 See the critical reflections in E. Muir 'Enhancing the effects of Community law on national employment policies: the Mangold case' (2006) 31 *ELR* 879.

of the person concerned in professional life'.[26] The legislature specifically chose to focus on disability, not sickness so the two terms were not equivalent and a dismissal based on sickness did not give the employee protection under EC Law. The most disappointing feature of the judgment is that the Court was given insufficient detail about the nature of the employee's illness. It must surely be the case that certain forms of sickness would contribute to disability (e.g. chronic fatigue syndrome), while some forms of disability might perhaps not count (e.g. an employee who suffers injury on holiday and is on crutches for six months), so the Court cannot be taken to mean that all forms of 'sickness' are not forms of disability.[27] Second, it has been argued that the Court narrowed the scope of the concept of disability by giving a 'medical' as opposed to a 'social' definition of the term that focuses on discrimination based on stereotypes; the latter would give protection to a wider range of persons (e.g. those who have had a mental illness, those who have a condition that shows no symptoms).[28] The result is that the Court has opted for a very narrow definition of disability at EC level, which on a practical level means that there will be variations on the protection individuals receive as some Member States may opt for the Community minimal level and some afford protection to a wider range of persons. Against this criticism one might find persuasive the rationale offered by AG Geelhoed: that the legislative intention is for a narrow interpretation of Article 13 EC (upon which the directive is based); that the potentially significant financial and economic consequences of non discrimination obligations lead legislatures to define the scope of discrimination laws precisely and narrowly; that Member States retain 'core powers' in fields like employment policy, social policy, health and education and one therefore cannot read Article 13 as 'an Archimedean position, from which the prohibitions of discrimination defined in Article 13 EC can be used as a lever to correct, without the intervention of the authors of the Treaty or the Community legislature, the decisions made by the Member States in the exercise of the powers which they – still – retain'.[29] The Advocate General was keen to distance himself from the approach the Court had taken in *Mangold*, favouring a focus on the precise text of the Directives.

(iii)   Discrimination 'on the grounds of' disability

In *Coleman* the ECJ has an opportunity to decide whether a person who is not disabled and is the victim of discrimination because she is the carer of a disabled son is entitled to the protection offered by Directive 2000/78. Advocate General Maduro has recommended an affirmative answer.

---

26 Case C-13/05 *Sonia Chacón Navas v Eurest Colectividades SA* [2006] ECR I-6467, para. 43.
27 To a degree this is recognised in the Advocate General's Opinion, ibid., paragraphs 77–80.
28 D. L. Hosking 'A high bar for EU disability rights' (2007) 36 *Industrial Law Journal* 228.
29 Above n. 26.

Case C-303/06 *S. Coleman v Attridge Law and Steve Law*, Opinion of Advocate General Maduro 31 January 2008

8. Article 13 EC is an expression of the commitment of the Community legal order to the principle of equal treatment and non-discrimination. Thus, any interpretation of both that article and any directive adopted under this legal basis must be undertaken against the background of the Court's case-law on these principles. The Directive itself states in Article 1 that its purpose is 'to lay down a general framework for combating discrimination . . . *with a view to putting into effect in the Member States the principle of equal treatment*' (my emphasis). The Court's case-law is clear as regards the role of equal treatment and non-discrimination in the Community legal order. Equality is not merely a political ideal and aspiration but one of the fundamental principles of Community law. As the Court held in Mangold the Directive constitutes a practical aspect of the principle of equality. In order to determine what equality requires in any given case it is useful to recall the values underlying equality. These are human dignity and personal autonomy.

12. Yet, directly targeting a person who has a particular characteristic is not the only way of discriminating against him or her; there are also other, more subtle and less obvious ways of doing so. One way of undermining the dignity and autonomy of people who belong to a certain group is to target not them, but third persons who are closely associated with them and do not themselves belong to the group. A robust conception of equality entails that these subtler forms of discrimination should also be caught by anti-discrimination legislation, as they, too, affect the persons belonging to suspect classifications. [a term used in US law to refer to those protected by discrimination law].

13. Indeed, the dignity of the person with a suspect characteristic is affected as much by being directly discriminated against as it is by seeing someone else suffer discrimination merely by virtue of being associated with him. In this way, the person who is the immediate victim of discrimination not only suffers a wrong himself, but also becomes the means through which the dignity of the person belonging to a suspect classification is undermined.

14. Furthermore, this subtler form of discrimination undermines the ability of persons who have a suspect characteristic to exercise their autonomy. For instance, the autonomy of members of a religious group may be affected (for example, as to whom to marry or where to live) if they know that the person they will marry is likely to suffer discrimination because of the religious affiliation of his spouse. The same can happen, albeit to a lesser extent, with individuals who are disabled. People belonging to certain groups are often more vulnerable than the average person, so they have come to rely on individuals with whom they are closely associated for help in their effort to lead a life according to the fundamental choices they have made. When the discriminator deprives an individual of valuable options in areas which are of fundamental importance to our lives because that individual is associated with a person having a suspect characteristic then it also deprives that person of valuable options and prevents him from exercising his autonomy. Put differently, the person who belongs to the suspect classification is excluded from a range of possibilities that would otherwise have been open to him.

This philosophical argument is strengthened by a literal reading of the Directive, which prohibits discrimination 'on the grounds of' disability, and does not say on grounds of the *claimant's* disability.[30] It is hoped the Court will follow this advice,

---

30 *Ibid.* para. 23.

in particular as the Court can apply a literal interpretation of the directive to achieve protection so it does not have to rely on the wider approach suggested by the Advocate General. If the Court does so, one issue that will need clarification is how close the bond between the victim of discrimination and the person who he is associated with must be. In this case the family bond and the fact that the victim was the disabled child's primary carer sufficed, but what if a white person is discriminated against because he has friends of Asian origin?

(iv)   Sexual orientation and registered partnerships

Readers will recall the Court's reluctance to recognise same sex partnerships, and afford such couples protection under the sex discrimination legislation.[31] In *Tadao Maruko*, however, the Court recognised that under the Framework Directive, same sex couples were entitled to protection. The claimant was in a same sex registered partnership (a 'life partnership' under German law) and was denied a widower's pension on his partner's death because the rules of the association managing that pension made no provision for same sex partners. After finding that the pension constituted 'pay' so that the dispute fell within the Framework Directive, the Court noted that the conditions for life partnerships were increasingly aligned with those of marriage. It followed that if the national court should decide that surviving spouses and surviving life partners are in a comparable situation, then the denial of a widower's pension to the latter would constitute direct discrimination.[32] It appeared crucial that German law gave life partners increasingly similar rights to married couples, so the national court was able to compare the registered partnership to marriage as a way of finding direct discrimination. It follows that not all registered partnerships will necessarily benefit from this ruling when the rights of registered partners are not similar to those of married couples. In the latter instance, a more difficult case based on indirect discrimination appears necessary.

(v)   Race Discrimination – speech acts

The *Centre for Equal Opportunities and Opposition to Racism*, a body charged with the promotion of equal treatment in Belgium, took action against an employer who had stated publicly that he was not going to recruit persons of certain races, seeking a declaration that these statements breached the Belgian Laws implementing the race directive. Significantly there was no evidence that the employer had in fact rejected a job applicant on the basis of race or ethnicity, so the question arose whether on the facts the defendant had acted illegally. Advocate General Maduro is of the view

31 Joined Cases C-122/99 P and C-125/99 P *D v Council* [2001] ECR I-4319.
32 Case C-267/06 *Tadao Maruko v Versorgungsanstalt der deutschen Bühnen*, judgment of 1 April 2007, para. 72.

that the race directive extends to this scenario, first because of the 'humiliating and demoralising impact on persons of that origin who want to participate in the labour market and, in particular, on those who would have been interested in working for the employer at issue'[33] so that the employer is committing a 'speech act'.[34] Second, 'it would defeat the very purpose of the Directive if public statements made by an employer in the context of a recruitment drive, to the effect that applications from persons of a certain ethnic origin would be turned down, were held to fall outside the concept of direct discrimination'.[35] Turning to remedies, the Advocate General advised that it was for the national court to determine what was appropriate to ensure the effectiveness of the directive, and suggested that a declaration of illegality might be insufficient and a prohibitory injunction would be more apt.

In a significant prefatory paragraph laying down his interpretative stance AG Maduro said:

> when a directive is adopted on the basis of Article 13 EC, it must be interpreted in the light of the broader values underlying that provision. Admittedly, the Directive lays down minimum measures, but that is no reason to construe its scope more narrowly than a reading in the light of those values would warrant. A minimum standard of protection is not the same as a *minimal* standard of protection. Community rules for protection against discrimination may leave a margin for the Member States to ensure even greater protection, but from that we cannot conclude that the level of protection offered by the Community rules is the lowest conceivable.[36]

This is diametrically opposed to the position in *Chacón Navas*. While the ECJ in that case was conscious of the economic impact of discrimination law, and of the reluctance of some Member States for expansive regulation, AG Maduro frames his construction on a rights-based approach. The tension between these two visions of equality law seems set to cause unpredictable judgments from the Court until a consensus is reached.

---

33 Case C–54/07 *Centrum voor Gelijkheid van Kansen en voor Racismebestrijding v Firma Feryn NV* Opinion of 12 March 2008 para. 15.
34 *Ibid.* para. 16, quoting J. Searle *Speech Acts* (Cambridge: Cambridge University Press, 1969); J. L. Austin *How to Do Things With Words* (Oxford: Clarendon Press, 1962).
35 *Ibid.* para. 17.   36 *Ibid.* para. 14.

21

EC competition law: function and enforcement

CONTENTS

1. The Treaty of Lisbon and competition law

No reform of competition law was sought when the Treaty Establishing a Constitution for Europe was negotiated,[1] nor in drafting the Treaty of Lisbon.[2] But at the last minute in June 2007, the newly elected French President insisted on an amendment to one of the foundational Treaty articles to remove the word 'competition'. We first explain the amendment and then examine its motivation and potential significance.

In the EC Treaty two foundational articles refer to competition. Article 3(1)(g) EC states that one of the Community's activities is to establish a system ensuring that competition in the internal market is not distorted. Article 4(1) EC refers to the activities of the Member States and the Community which include the adoption of an economic policy 'conducted in accordance with the principle of an open market economy with free competition'.

The Treaty of Lisbon retains Article 3(1)(g) EC: Article 3 EC as a whole has been replaced by a list of exclusive and non exclusive competences of the Union, and Article 3(1)(b) LTFEU provides that the Union has exclusive legislative competence in 'the establishing of the competition rules necessary for the functioning of the internal market'. The word competition was deleted from what was Article I-3 of the Constitutional Treaty (which replaced Article 4 EC). Both provisions listed the Union's

1 (2004) Cm6429.
2 [2007] OJ C306/1. A consolidated version is available at: http://europa.eu/lisbon_treaty/index_en.htm.

objectives, among which the Union shall offer its citizens 'an internal market where competition is free and undistorted'. When this was revisited in the Intergovernmental Conference in the summer of 2007, President Sarkozy of France was successful in demanding the deletion of the word competition from this article, which should be read together with an accompanying protocol.

Article 3(3) LTEU

The Union shall establish an internal market. It shall work for the sustainable development of Europe based on balanced economic growth and price stability, a highly competitive social market economy, aiming at full employment and social progress, and a high level of protection and improvement of the quality of the environment. It shall promote scientific and technological advance.

Protocol on the Internal Market and Competition

The High Contracting Parties, considering that the internal market as set out in Article 2 of the Treaty on European Union includes a system ensuring that competition is not distorted, have agreed that:
to this end, the Union shall, if necessary, take action under the provisions of the Treaties, including under Article 308 of the Treaty on the Functioning of the European Union.

The protocol is the compromise that the Member States accepted, which is designed for two purposes: first to keep the focus on competition policy as a key part of the Union, and second to ensure that the Union has legislative competence to use Article 308 EC (renumbered Article 352 LTFEU) to enact legislation in the field of competition (this article was used, for example, to give a legal basis to the EC Merger Regulation).[3]

When this amendment was announced the press and some commentators reacted with fear that competition as a key principle had been lost, and the competition commissioner responded with anger suggesting that in her view the amendments are insignificant.[4] Both exaggerated responses are unwarranted. It is highly unlikely that the Commission's powers in enforcing Articles 81 and 82 EC (renumbered Articles 101 and 102 LTFEU) or the merger rules will be affected in any significant way. Nevertheless while the Lisbon Treaty continues to grant the Union legislative competence over competition law, the Union's role in using competition policy as a principle underpinning its initiatives is undermined. It is likely that the main objective that the French had in mind in securing this amendment is to slow down the liberalisation of utilities, in particular in the energy sector. It remains to be seen how far progress in this field is affected.[5] Another, related, field where this amendment could have significance

---

3 Regulation 139/2004 on the control of concentrations between undertakings [2004] OJ L24/22, based on Articles 83 and 308.

4 Statement by European Commissioner for Competition Neelie Kroes on results of 21–22 June European Council – Protocol on Internal Market and Competition, Memo 07/250 27 June 2007.

5 The current legislative package is under discussion and Member States are resisting the Commission's pressure on certain aspects of the reform. See N. Kroes 'Structural Reforms to the Energy Market' Speech of 27 February 2008.

is in the application of competition to services of general interest, where the emphasis according to some Member States (including France and The Netherlands) should be on the provision of public services to all citizens rather than on providing these services through competitive markets. It is also possible that in individual decisions some Commissioners might feel emboldened to exempt agreements or authorise mergers that contribute to creating 'European champions' given Article 3(3)'s reference to a high level of competitiveness, however, this already happens under the existing rules.[6]

The European Courts might be affected in two ways: first, it is well known that teleological reasoning forms a key part of its interpretative techniques and this has been used to develop competition law.[7] Perhaps the Court will not feel so bold in the future seeing that the legislative intention is to give less priority to competition law. A second, related effect is that the Court might be more willing to exclude the application of competition law from certain practices when it judges there are valid reasons to do this. An example of this is the *Meca-Medina* judgment which we discuss in chapter 22 of this update.

Whatever the practical significance that this amendment will have, it shows that there is some controversy among Member States as to the role of competition law in regulating markets. One of the main reasons why the Constitutional Treaty was not accepted in some Member States is said to be the concern that it favoured an Anglo-Saxon conception of capitalism, and in this light the amendment can be said to be a change to assuage certain Member States that the Union's markets are not going to be transformed radically as a result of the new Treaty.

2. Cartel enforcement

In the past two years the principal development has been the Commission's increased interest in enforcing Article 81 against cartels. This is reflected both in the significant increase in the number of cases and in the revision of its notices on fines and leniency to improve enforcement.[8] Between 2003 and 11 March 2008 the Commission has imposed fines under Article 81 that total over €6 billion,[9] the highest fines to date were imposed in February 2007 to undertakings that took part in a cartel in the markets for the installation and maintenance of lifts and escalators, amounting to a total of €992 million.[10]

---

6 G. Monti, 'Merger defences' in G. Amato and C-D Ehlermann (eds.) *EC Competition Law – A Critical Assessment* (Oxford: Hart Publishing, 2007).

7 Most notably in Case 6/72 *Europemballage Corp and Continental Can Co Inc v Commission* [1972] ECR 215.

8 See generally W. P. J. Wils, *Efficiency and Justice in European Antitrust Enforcement* (Hart Publishing: Oxford, 2008).

9 The precise figure is €6,725,392,000 (see http://ec.europa.eu/comm/competition/cartels/statistics/statistics.pdf). This figure however does not take into account whether the fines have been increased or reduced by the European Courts.

10 Commission fines members of lifts and escalators cartels over €990 million, Press Release IP/07/209 (27 February 2007).

(i) Fines

New guidelines on the method of setting fines were published in 2006, which replace the 1998 guidelines.[11] The guidelines try and reflect the Commission's practice and take into account the rulings of the Court of Justice.[12] The key aim was to provide for tougher fines for cartel members. This is achieved in three ways:

(a) The way the fine is calculated changes. The 1998 guidelines provided that a basic amount was set by considering the gravity of the infringement and an *addition* was made depending on the duration of the agreement. So a 'very serious infringement' would invite a basic amount of at least 20 million, and if it lasted for three years there would be an increase of 50 per cent, a total fine of 30 million. The new system provides that the basic amount is calculated by reference to the value of sales during the last year of the cartel (up to 30 per cent of the value), depending on the gravity of the infringement, *multiplied* by the number of years.[13] So in a very serious cartel one would take perhaps 25 per cent of the sales (e.g. 20 million) if it lasts for three years, the basic amount would be 60 million. Thus, duration becomes a much more significant variable.

(b) An 'entry fee' is added to the basic amount (of between 15 and 25 per cent of the value of sales) to cartels that involve price-fixing, market-sharing or output limitation, irrespective of duration.[14]

(c) It is an aggravating circumstance for an undertaking to have repeated the same or a similar infringement, such that the basic amount will be increased by 100 per cent for each prior infringement.[15]

Two themes can be detected in the Notice – deterrence features most prominently, and, a second, the Notice imposes a more accurate fine on each member of the cartel by focusing on sales as a proxy for how much each member stood to gain from the cartel. It can thus be said to lead to fairer fines as between cartel members.

(ii) Leniency

A new leniency notice was published in 2006.[16] This makes marginal amendments to the 2002 Notice, specifically in three respects: first it clarifies what evidence is necessary to gain immunity and what the conditions for securing immunity are. There is some concern that the new conditions for getting immunity are more difficult to

---

11 Guidelines on the method of setting fines imposed pursuant to Article 23(2)(a) of Regulation 1/2003 [2006] OJ C210/2.

12 See further: P. Manzini, 'European Antitrust in Search of the Perfect Fine' (2008) 31(1) *World Competition* 3 C. Veljanovski 'Cartel Fines in Europe: Law, Practice and Deterrence' (2007) 30(1) *World Competition* 65

13 Above n. 11 para. 19.   14 Above n. 11 para. 25.   15 Above n. 11 para. 28.

16 Notice on Immunity from Fines and Reduction of Fines in Cartel Cases [2006] OJ C298/17.

satisfy than under the 2002 Notice.[17] Second, it implements a 'marker system'. That is, a party wishing to ask for leniency can provide partial information to secure its place at the front of the queue of parties who confess, and supply fuller information at a later date; third, the statements made to the Commission when applying for leniency are protected from discovery in civil actions for damages. This may hamper private enforcement but the Commission justifies it because otherwise parties who do not confess are at an advantage in private litigation. However, given that once the Commission begins an investigation the best strategy for claimants will be to wait until a final decision and then follow on with an action for damages, the lack of evidence may not be as problematic as it seems.

(iii)   Settlements

A final enforcement mechanism being proposed by the Commission is to allow parties to settle a claim. Essentially the Commission would approach parties after having concluded an investigation and invite them to settle, avoiding the lengthy procedures in exchange for a discount on the fine. The aim is not deterrence but saving in administrative costs, allowing the Commission to use its limited resources to tackle more infringements. At the time of writing the Commission is consulting on draft legislation and a draft settlement notice. Of particular interest are the comments of the American Bar Association given the US experience with settlements. In their view a sound settlement system relies upon four key principles: transparency (so that the defendant knows what the benefits are); generosity (the reduction in fine should be substantial); legal certainty (the person settling should be clear that his offer to settle will be accepted); confidentiality (preventing disclosure of the settlement which might expose the applicant to claims in other jurisdictions). The claim is that absent these features there is a risk that parties have no incentives to settle, and that the current proposal is weak when judged against these benchmarks.[18] It must be borne in mind that settlements in cartel cases are not currently possible, even under Article 9 of Regulation 1/2003, which is limited to less serious infringements and which require consultation of interested parties.[19]

3. Private enforcement

The ECJ has confirmed its earlier ruling in *Courage* that individuals have a Community right to damages when they suffer harm as a result of infringements of competition

---

17 A. Jones and B. Sufrin, *EC Competition Law: Text, Cases and Materials* 3rd ed (Oxford: Oxford University Press, 2007).
18 The proposals and comments are available at: http://ec.europa.eu/comm/competition/cartels/legislation/leniency_legislation.html
19 Recital 13 Regulation 1/2003, [2003] OJ L1/1.

law.[20] In *Manfredi*, the ECJ was confronted with an action by Italian consumers who had purchased liability insurance for motor vehicles at inflated prices after insurers had colluded. This was a follow-on claim after the Italian competition authority had found an infringement of Italian competition law (whose wording is very close to Article 81). However, the plaintiff claimed damages based on Article 81, for two reasons: first, because a claim for damages for breaches of Italian competition law rests with the Court of Appeal, while a claim under Article 81 can be taken to a small claims court, which is less formal and probably cheaper and also quicker at delivering judgment. Second, because Italian law at the time provided that consumers were not entitled to sue for damages (on this point the law has now changed). The ECJ agreed that it was plausible to find that the cartel affected trade between Member States, allowing the application of Article 81, and then gave some anodyne guidance on the role of national courts, suggesting that in the absence of Community rules on matters such as the jurisdiction of national courts, limitation periods and the measure of damages, it was up to Member States to ensure that plaintiffs received adequate safeguards 'provided that such rules are not less favourable than those governing similar domestic actions (principle of equivalence) and that they do not render practically impossible or excessively difficult the exercise of rights conferred by Community law (principle of effectiveness)'.[21] The Court elaborated somewhat on the measure of damages.

> ### Joined Cases C-295/04 to C-298/04 *Vincenzo Manfredi et al. v. Lloyd Adriatico Assicurazioni SpA et al.*, [2006] ECR I-6619
>
> 93. . . . in accordance with the principle of equivalence, it must be possible to award particular damages, such as exemplary or punitive damages, pursuant to actions founded on the Community competition rules, if such damages may be awarded pursuant to similar actions founded on domestic law.
>
> 94. However, it is settled case-law that Community law does not prevent national courts from taking steps to ensure that the protection of the rights guaranteed by Community law does not entail the unjust enrichment of those who enjoy them.
>
> 95. Secondly, it follows from the principle of effectiveness and the right of any individual to seek compensation for loss caused by a contract or by conduct liable to restrict or distort competition that injured persons must be able to seek compensation not only for actual loss (damnum emergens) but also for loss of profit (lucrum cessans) plus interest.
>
> 96. Total exclusion of loss of profit as a head of damage for which compensation may be awarded cannot be accepted in the case of a breach of Community law since, especially in the context of economic or commercial litigation, such a total exclusion of loss of profit would be such as to make reparation of damage practically impossible.

The relevant Italian court has now rendered a judgment that among other matters awards the claimant 'double damages' as a means of giving effect to the ECJ judgment,

---

20 Case C-453/99 *Courage v Crehan* [2001] ECR I-6297.
21 Joined Cases C-295/04 to C-298/04 *Vincenzo Manfredi et al. v. Lloyd Adriatico Assicurazioni SpA et al.* [2006] ECR I-6619 para. 62.

but it has been suggested that this is not what the ECJ intended.[22] Further guidance is probably needed on the quantum of damages, and it is significant that the ECJ suggests that claimants have a right to seek damages for loss of profit as well, although the difficulties in showing a causal link between an infringement of competition law and the loss of a chance to make profit seem insurmountable, and it is likely that most claimants will settle for a claim of actual loss (i.e. the overcharge caused by the cartel).[23]

On 2 April 2008 the Commission published a *White Paper on Damages Actions for Breach of the EC Antitrust Rules*.[24] It begins by recalling the findings of the 2005 Green Paper that the dearth of private litigation is caused by 'legal and procedural hurdles' in Member States and that the primary objective of the White Paper is to lower these hurdles, guided by three principles: full compensation (inherently this leads to greater deterrence);[25] that the legal framework should be based on a genuinely European approach, so the proposals are 'balanced measures that are rooted in European legal culture and traditions';[26] and to preserve strong public enforcement so that damages actions complement public enforcement. A brief comment on these three principles is warranted before considering the proposals. The first one confirms the views of some scholars that the action for damage is premised primarily upon the principle of corrective justice and not on optimal deterrence. This means that preference is given to allow as many claims as possible rather than restricting claims to those plaintiffs whose lawsuits are most likely to deter future anticompetitive conduct.[27] The second is designed to allay fears of a US-style approach so there are no proposals for punitive damages, class actions, contingency fees or other procedures that would jar with established civil law cultures. The third is a recognition that too much private enforcement can undermine the Commission's leniency programme: if a firm applies for leniency but is then liable to pay considerable sums in damages, it may decide to keep its involvement in cartels secret.

Turning to the detail, the White Paper addresses the following issues:

• Indirect purchasers have standing to seek damages because this is now part of the *acquis communautaire*.[28] It means that, for example, in a cartel in the cement market where a building company buys from the cartel and passes some of the price

---

22 P. Nebbia, 'So what happened to Manfredi?' [2007] ECLR 591 for a strong critique of the Italian court's decision.

23 For example, *Devenish Nutrition Ltd (and others) v. Sanofi (and others)* [2007] EWHC 2394 (Ch).

24 COM (2008) 165. It is accompanied by a more detailed Commission Staff Working Paper on Damages Actions for Breach of the EC Antitrust Rules SEC (2008) 404 and an Impact Assessment Report SEC(2008) 405. All three documents are available at: http://ec.europa.eu/comm/competition/antitrust/actionsdamages/documents.html).

25 COM (2008) 165 pp. 1–2.   26 *Ibid.* p. 2.

27 W. M. Landes and R. A. Posner, 'Should indirect purchasers have standing to sue under the antitrust laws? An Economic analysis of the Rule in Illinois Brick' (1979) 46 *University of Chicago Law Review* 602 (banning indirect purchaser suits enhances deterrence).

28 *Manfredi* above n. 21.

increase to the buyer of the buildings, the latter as an indirect purchaser is entitled to damages. No legislative measure on this point seems to be envisaged.

- Collective redress should be facilitated because often the harm is diffuse (as in *Manfredi*, several hundred people are victims of a cartel but each loss is relatively small). Two mechanisms are proposed: (i) representative actions brought by qualified entities (e.g. consumer associations) and (ii) opt-in collective actions whereby plaintiffs can decide to combine their claims in one single action.
- To facilitate access to evidence national courts should be empowered to order the defendant to disclose certain evidence (only when specific conditions are met, e.g. the inability to secure the evidence by other means, that specific categories of evidence are identified and that the disclosure is relevant to the case, necessary and proportionate). This should be coupled with penalties if the defendant refuses to comply, including the option to draw adverse inferences from the refusal.
- National courts should be bound by findings of any national competition authority in the European Competition Network. This would allow a follow-on claim, for example, in a Slovenian court after the UK competition authority reached a final decision.
- A defendant should be liable for damages unless he proves that the breach was caused by a 'genuinely excusable error'. An error is excusable if 'a reasonable person applying a high standard of care could not have been aware that the conduct restricted competition'. This is designed to harmonise different approaches in Member States as to the presence of a fault requirement and is said to be in line with the principle of effectiveness.
- Codification of the scope of damages is recommended, to clarify that damages can be claimed for: (i) actual loss, and (ii) loss of profits resulting from any reduction in sales. Further, a soft law instrument is proposed with 'pragmatic guidance' to quantify damages with simplified rules on estimating loss.
- In claims by direct purchasers, the defendant should benefit from the passing-on defence so that a claimant who has bought goods from a cartel at a higher price but has mitigated this loss by passing the excess price to downstream buyers would see his damages claim reduced, otherwise he would be unjustly enriched. (So, for example, if the cartel causes the price to rise by €2 and the claimant resells the goods to the indirect purchaser at a price that is €1 higher than before the cartel, he has passed on half of the overcharge, so damages would be €1, not €2.). But the burden of proof is on the defendant to show that the claimant has passed on (some of) the overcharge, which seems a tricky burden to satisfy.
- To facilitate claims by indirect purchasers, these 'should be able to rely on a rebuttable presumption that the illegal overcharge was passed on to them in their entirety'.[29] On the example above therefore the indirect purchaser is entitled to make a claim of €2 even if only a €1 overcharge was passed on to it. This is justified by

---

29 COM (2008) 165 p. 8.

indicating that indirect purchasers would otherwise find it too hard to prove the existence and extent of the passing on, but it is not particularly fair to ask the defendant to show how much of the higher costs were absorbed by the direct purchaser, so this proposal seems to lead to over compensation of indirect purchasers.

- There are two proposals on limitation periods. The most significant is that in cases where anticompetitive activity is subject to public enforcement, a new limitation period of at least two years starts once the competition authority's infringement decision becomes final. The second is that a limitation period in other instances should not begin to run before the day on which the infringement ceases (even in cases of continuous or repeated infringement) and not before the victim can reasonably be expected to have knowledge of the infringement and of the harm it caused. The duration of this limitation period is not harmonised.
- Member States should reconsider their cost allocation rules to ensure that these do not put off meritorious cases, settlements should be considered, as well as limits on court fees, and cost orders that do not always make the losing party bear all the costs of the winning party.
- To safeguard the attraction of leniency programmes, the Commission considers that those who receive immunity should only face claims from direct and indirect contractual partners, so that by reducing the financial impact of damages claims leniency applications continue to be made. This qualifies the ECJ case law giving anyone a right to damages in all cases, as the defendant who benefits from this provision is not held jointly and severally liable for the losses suffered by those who did not buy goods from it.

It will have become apparent that the White Paper is not a blueprint for a single legislative instrument: some of the proposals are recommendations for Member State action (on costs), some are suggestions for soft law instruments (on calculating damages) and some for discrete legislative tools whether directives (on representative actions) or Regulations (on the function of the passing on defence and the fault requirement).[30] The legal base for any legislative measure is not yet determined, and according to A. P. Komninos, two are possible: Article 65 (allowing for legislative measures in the field of judicial cooperation necessary for the proper functioning of the internal market), although this seems to be more focused on matters that have cross border implications, which is not necessarily the case with all private antitrust claims, or Article 83 which allows the Council to implement regulations or directives to give effect to the principles of Articles 81 and 82.[31]

The Commissioner for competition, Neelie Kroes said that '[t]he suggestions in this White Paper are about justice for consumers and businesses, who lose billions of euros each and every year as a result of companies breaking EU antitrust rules. These

---

30 A. P. Kmoninos 'Enter the White Paper for damages actions: a first selective appraisal' (4 April 2008) available at www.globalcompetitionpolicy.org
31 *Ibid.*

people have a right to compensation through an effective system that complements public enforcement, whilst avoiding the potential excesses of the US system'.[32] While the proposals seem well designed to achieve this, from the perspective of tort law, seeing rules designed to facilitate claims by victims of economic losses over other tort victims cannot be justified so easily (e.g. the difficulties faced by victims of asbestos exposure). What makes antitrust victims so deserving? The Commission's justification seems to be that the estimated cost to antitrust victims ranges between €25 to €69 billion,[33] and that 'EU-wide infringements are becoming more and more frequent'.[34] However, this second finding is troubling: given that Regulation 1/2003 was designed to strengthen antitrust enforcement, has there been a failure of public enforcement? And if so might resources not be best allocated at that end?

32 Press Release IP/08/515 (3 April 2008).   33 Impact assessment above n. 24 paras 42–43.
34 Above n. 24 para. 32.

22

Restrictive practices

CONTENTS

1. Reconceptualising Article 81?

The most significant development in the interpretation of Article 81 is the CFI's judgment in *GlaxoSmithKline* (*GSK*).[1] The dispute arose when GSK, a producer of pharmaceuticals, inserted a clause in its contracts with Spanish wholesalers (the General Sales Conditions) to ensure that they did not export the medicines to other Member States. The commercial rationale for GSK's practice is that medicines are bought by national health authorities and these buy medicines at different prices: in some, like Spain, the price is low because the government wants to guarantee availability of medicines, while in the UK the price is higher because the government wishes to reward pharmaceutical firms and encourage future innovation. Given low transport costs, there is a clear incentive for wholesalers in Spain to export to the UK, and an obvious interest in GSK to prevent these exports because they harm profits in the UK market. The Commission found the agreement had as its object the restriction of competition, a result which was to be expected given that the agreement served to partition the internal market.[2] The CFI held that this was insufficient to find an anticompetitive object.

---

1 Case T-186/01 *GlaxoSmithKline Services Unlimited v Commission*, judgment of 27 September 2006.
2 *Glaxo Wellcome* [2001] OJ L302/1.

Case T-186/01 *GlaxoSmithKline Services Unlimited v Commission*, judgment of 27 September 2006

118. In effect, the objective assigned to Article 81(1) EC, which constitutes a fundamental provision indispensable for the achievement of the missions entrusted to the Community, in particular for the functioning of the internal market, is to prevent undertakings, by restricting competition between themselves or with third parties, from reducing the welfare of the final consumer of the products in question. At the hearing, in fact, the Commission emphasised on a number of occasions that it was from that perspective that it had carried out its examination in the present case, initially concluding that the General Sales Conditions clearly restricted the welfare of consumers, then considering whether that restriction would be offset by increased efficiency which would itself benefit consumers.

119. Consequently, the application of Article 81(1) EC to the present case cannot depend solely on the fact that the agreement in question is intended to limit parallel trade in medicines or to partition the common market, which leads to the conclusion that it affects trade between Member States, but also requires an analysis designed to determine whether it has as its object or effect the prevention, restriction or distortion of competition on the relevant market, to the detriment of the final consumer. . . . [T]hat analysis, which may be abridged when the clauses of the agreement reveal in themselves the existence of an alteration of competition, as the Commission observed at the hearing, must, on the other hand, be supplemented, depending on the requirements of the case, where that is not so.

121. While it has been accepted since then that parallel trade must be given a certain protection, it is therefore not as such but, as the Court of Justice held, in so far as it favours the development of trade, on the one hand, and the strengthening of competition, on the other hand, that is to say, in this second respect, in so far as it gives final consumers the advantages of effective competition in terms of supply or price. Consequently, while it is accepted that an agreement intended to limit parallel trade must in principle be considered to have as its object the restriction of competition, that applies in so far as the agreement may be presumed to deprive final consumers of those advantages.

Applied to the facts of this case, the CFI found that final consumers would not get an immediate benefit from parallel trade as the price of medicines does not fall if there are parallel imports, so the financial benefit is only to the wholesaler. These passages are remarkable for two reasons: first, because they make the category of 'object' cases close to that of 'effect' cases by requiring the Commission to carry out some assessment of the foreseeable effects of a restriction; second, because the CFI, for the first time so clearly, explains that the function of Article 81(1) is to protect the final consumer. This tallies with the policy that the Commission has sought to embrace in recent years.

However, this part of the judgment is difficult to reconcile with the next section where the CFI examined whether the agreement had anticompetitive effects. It found that two groups of buyers suffered: first, the national sickness insurance schemes (which it held also constituted a final consumer) who reimbursed retailers because if there was intra brand competition between wholesalers the retailers would pay a lower price thus requiring lower levels of compensation from the national insurance schemes; second, since a small part of the price was paid by the patient, it is perhaps possible that the price could be lower with parallel trade.[3] The problem with this part of the judgment is twofold: first, it widens the class of final consumers compared to the analysis under the 'object' category, second, it is not clear why these foreseeable anticompetitive effects should not have allowed the Commission to hold that the agreement was restrictive by object.

2. Justified restrictions of competition

(i)   The scope of application of Article 81

The Court returned to consider the scope of application of competition law in a dispute that arose between two swimmers on the one hand and the International Olympic Committee (IOC) and international swimming federation (FINA) on the other. The swimmers were given a two-year ban because a drugs test revealed that they had taken a banned substance, Nandrolone. The practice of the sporting association and their laboratories was that since the body could produce Nandrolone innocently, the presence of that substance is defined as doping only if it exceeds a limit of 2 nanogrammes per millilitre of urine. The parties considered that these anti-doping rules were too strict, that they did not take into account that the body could innocently contain more Nendrolone, and that the ban was anticompetitive because it restricted their ability to participate in sport. The Court of First Instance had referred to its case law on the internal market and found that purely sporting rules were not subject to Articles 39 and 49 EC, and *mutatis mutandis* those rules were not subject to Articles 81 and 82 EC.[4] However, the Court of Justice disagreed with this reasoning and ruled that the analysis of the anti-doping regulations under the competition rules must be assessed by considering 'the specific requirements of Articles 81 EC and 82 EC'.[5] The rules in question were a 'decision' of an association of undertakings, the IOC, so the key question was whether they restricted competition.

> ### Case C-519/04 P *Meca-Medina and Majcen v Commission* judgment of 18 July 2006
>
> 42. . . . [T]he compatibility of rules with the Community rules on competition cannot be assessed in the abstract. Not every agreement between undertakings or every decision of an association of undertakings which restricts the freedom of action of the parties or of one of them necessarily falls within the prohibition laid down in Article 81(1) EC. For the purposes of application of that provision to a particular case, account must first of all be taken of the overall context in which the decision of the association of undertakings was taken or produces its effects and, more specifically, of its objectives. It has then to be considered whether the

---

3 Above n. 1 paras 182–90.   4 Case T-313/02 *Meca-Medina and Majcen v Commission* [2004] ECR II-3291.
5 Case C-519/04 P *Meca-Medina and Majcen v Commission* judgment of 18 July 2006 paragraph 33.

consequential effects restrictive of competition are inherent in the pursuit of those objectives and are proportionate to them.

43. As regards the overall context in which the rules at issue were adopted, the Commission could rightly take the view that the general objective of the rules was, as none of the parties disputes, to combat doping in order for competitive sport to be conducted fairly and that it included the need to safeguard equal chances for athletes, athletes' health, the integrity and objectivity of competitive sport and ethical values in sport.

44. In addition, given that penalties are necessary to ensure enforcement of the doping ban, their effect on athletes' freedom of action must be considered to be, in principle, inherent itself in the anti-doping rules.

45. Therefore, even if the anti-doping rules at issue are to be regarded as a decision of an association of undertakings limiting the appellants' freedom of action, they do not, for all that, necessarily constitute a restriction of competition incompatible with the common market, within the meaning of Article 81 EC, since they are justified by a legitimate objective. Such a limitation is inherent in the organisation and proper conduct of competitive sport and its very purpose is to ensure healthy rivalry between athletes.

47. It must be acknowledged that the penal nature of the anti-doping rules at issue and the magnitude of the penalties applicable if they are breached are capable of producing adverse effects on competition because they could, if penalties were ultimately to prove unjustified, result in an athlete's unwarranted exclusion from sporting events, and thus in impairment of the conditions under which the activity at issue is engaged in. It follows that, in order not to be covered by the prohibition laid down in Article 81(1) EC, the restrictions thus imposed by those rules must be limited to what is necessary to ensure the proper conduct of competitive sport.

48. Rules of that kind could indeed prove excessive by virtue of, first, the conditions laid down for establishing the dividing line between circumstances which amount to doping in respect of which penalties may be imposed and those which do not, and second, the severity of those penalties.

Applying this standard the Court concluded that banning Nandrolone was justified and that banning athletes whose tests reveal a Nandrolone content higher than 2 nanogrammes per millilitre of urine was a practice that did not go beyond that which was necessary to ensure that sporting events take place and function properly. The parties had not contested that the penalty was disproportionate so the second limb of the test set out above was not considered. This judgment is an extension of the principle that the Court of Justice had set out in *Wouters* where, it will be recalled, a ban on multi-disciplinary practices of lawyers and accountants in The Netherlands was said to be justified to ensure the proper practice of the legal profession.[6] Here the anti-doping rules are deemed necessary to safeguard a variety of public policy interests, listed in paragraph 43 above. Professor Weatherill has taken the view that the judgment means that 'sports bodies cannot keep out of court simply by asserting that sport is special'.[7] This is on the basis that the Court requires that sporting

6 Case C-309/99 *Wouters v Algemene Raad van de Nederlandse Orde van Advocaten* [2002] ECR I-1577.
7 S. Weatherill, 'Anti-doping revisited – the demise of the rule of "purely sporting interest"' [2006] *ECLR* 645, 652.

regulations are not automatically excluded from the scope of competition law but are tested for compatibility with competition law: sports bodies must justify their rules. However, another view is that the Court (and the Commission in the original decision) failed to tackle some fairly basic questions, most significantly how the ban restricted competition. Rather than addressing this question the Court jumps immediately to consider whether there is a justification for the rule. This seems to betray the Court's view that in applying competition law to sport one should consider the specific requirements of Article 81. The rule excludes two athletes from the market (they lose what fees they might earn from competing, and can potentially lose lucrative sponsorship deals) but it is not clear how this restricts competition as defined in GSK – where is the consumer harm?[8] Even assuming that there is damage to consumer welfare (arguably spectators may suffer if athletes are wrongly excluded, so the race is less exciting to watch), the Court offers a wide range of legitimate interests that can excuse a restriction of competition so that applying this case to subsequent disputes is highly uncertain – the Court makes reference to the integrity of the sport (not perhaps dissimilar to the integrity of the legal profession) but also to the health and safety of athletes, so one is left to wonder what else can justify a restriction of competition. This uncertainty is particularly problematic in light of the modernisation of Article 81(3) in which the Commission tried to suggest that anticompetitive agreements can only be justified upon a showing of efficiency. This judgment suggests that parties who wish to justify their anticompetitive agreement on non-economic grounds may find the Court willing to take these into consideration in deciding that there is no infringement of Article 81(1), so consider the following examples: bars agree to cut down 'happy hours' when drinks are cheaper and justify this as contributing to the health of drinkers, or supermarkets phasing out cheap beer on the same grounds; or an association of fashion houses refuses to use models who are too thin because they think very slim models contribute to anorexia in young women. Is competition law really an appropriate place to adjudicate upon the achievement of these non economic objectives?

(ii)   Article 81(3) exemptions

The GSK judgment discussed in section 1 above also contains a significant analysis on the application of Article 81(3). GSK's argument that its restrictions on parallel trade merited an exemption was based on considerations of dynamic efficiencies: an increase in parallel trade would reduce GSK's profits and as a direct result its capacity to innovate would be dented given the high costs of research and development.

---

8 A good example of how sporting regulations can be analysed to determine a restriction of competition is found in a decision of the New Zealand commerce commission, Decsion 580 New Zealand Rugby Football Union Incorporated (2 July 2006) available at: http://www.comcom.govt.nz. For comment, see R. Adhar 'Professional rugby, competitive balance and competition law' [2007] *ECLR* 36.

The CFI explained that when an undertaking pleads that its agreement merits an exemption in a notification, the Commission must examine the submissions to test if the conditions for the application of Article 81(3) are made out.[9] The Commission has a margin of discretion in weighing up the advantages expected from the implementation of the agreement and the disadvantages that result. According to the Court this balancing exercise is to be carried out 'in the light of the general interest appraised at Community level'.[10] Unfortunately this obscure reference to the general interest is not developed further, but the CFI concludes that in this case the decision was 'vitiated by failing to carry out a proper examination' of the efficiency claims that GSK raised.[11] The final resolution of this dispute will be significant for two reasons: first, because the Commission has long been concerned about the lack of market integration and now has to determine whether consumers are better off with an integrated market or whether stifling market integration yields more benefits to consumers in the long run. There is significant difference of opinion on this point, not least two Advocate Generals have given diametrically opposed views on this issue.[12] Second, the Commission's approach will set a more general precedent over how dynamic efficiency claims are handled in exemption decisions.

Another judgment of the ECJ offers a provocative interpretation of Article 81(3): *Asnef-Equifax v. Ausbanc*.[13] Spanish banks agreed to set up an electronic register of credit information that would disclose the credit history of potential customers. The effect is that each bank is aware of each potential client's credit history and takes this into account when negotiating further loans. The Court held that it was unlikely that this agreement would restrict competition, but also added some reflections on how one might go about analysing the consumer benefit test in Article 81(3). It suggested that two groups of consumers benefit: those who get loans on better terms, and those who do not get loans because of their bad credit scores, and this is a benefit because it avoids over indebtedness. That persons who are unable to obtain a service as a result of an anticompetitive agreement can be seen as deriving a benefit requires further reflection – would one, for example, say that a cartel to fix the prices of cigarettes benefits smokers who therefore smoke less?

3. Agreements and concerted practices

As noted in the update to chapter 21, the Commission pursues an aggressive anti cartel policy. One temptation for the Commission is to extend the reach of Article 81

---

9 Above n. 1 para. 236. This point is relevant to the application of Regulation 17/62, it is not relevant under Regulation 1/2003 which places the burden of proof on the defendant when Article 81(3) is pleaded.
10 Above n. 1 para. 244.   11 Above n. 1 para. 303.
12 Case C-53/03 *Syfait* [2003] ECR I-4609 (AG Jacobs) and Joined Cases C-468/06 to C-478/06 *Sot. Lélos kai Sia E.E and others* Opinion of AG Colomer 1 April 2008.
13 Case C-238/05, judgment of 26 November 2006.

so as to ensure it is able to catch as many cartels as possible. This has led to disputes over the meaning of the concepts of agreement and concerted practice. In the *BASF* case the Court of First Instance had an opportunity to give guidance on a new concept that the Commission has been utilising: that of a single, continuous infringement. The facts will help explain the concept and its utility: in 1999 the Commission was made aware (thanks to a leniency application) of a cartel in the market for chlorine chloride. The evidence found a global cartel to fix prices and allocate territories between 1992 and 1994, and then a European cartel designed to continue the global cartel between 1994 and 1998. The Commission's decision treated the two parts of the cartel as a single infringement because if the two were separate agreements then the global cartel would not be caught as it had ended five years before the investigation started and was protected by the limitation period and the parties' fines would be reduced as a result. On appeal the parties questioned the Commission's characterisation of the two agreements as a single infringement.

Joined Cases T-101/05 and T-111/05 *BASF AG and UCB SA v Commission* judgment of 12 December 2007

179. However, it does not automatically follow from the application of that case-law to the present case that the arrangements at the global and European levels, taken together, form a single and continuous infringement. It appears that, in the cases which the case-law envisages, the existence of a common objective consisting in distorting the normal development of prices provides a ground for characterising the various agreements and concerted practices as the constituent elements of a single infringement. In that regard, it cannot be overlooked that those actions were complementary in nature, since each of them was intended to deal with one or more consequences of the normal pattern of competition and, by interacting, contributed to the realisation of the set of anti-competitive effects intended by those responsible, within the framework of a global plan having a single objective.

180. In that connection, it must be made clear that the concept of single objective cannot be determined by a general reference to the distortion of competition in the choline chloride market, since an impact on competition, whether it is the object or the effect of the conduct in question, constitutes a consubstantial element of any conduct covered by Article 81(1) EC. Such a definition of the concept of a single objective is likely to deprive the concept of a single and continuous infringement of a part of its meaning, since it would have the consequence that different types of conduct which relate to a particular economic sector and are prohibited by Article 81(1) EC would have to be systematically characterised as constituent elements of a single infringement.

The Court must therefore ascertain whether the two sets of agreements and concerted practices penalised by the Commission in the Decision as a single and continuous infringement are complementary in the way described at paragraph 179 above. The Commission itself bases its theory on the fact that the global and European arrangements were 'closely linked'. In that regard, it will be necessary to take into account any circumstance capable of establishing or casting doubt on that link, such as the period of application, the content (including the methods used) and, correlatively, the objective of the various agreements and concerted practices in question.

Applying these standards the CFI found that while the global agreement involved North American manufacturers and was designed to divide the American and European markets, the European agreement did not involve the North American firms and was designed to divide the European market. Nor was there any evidence that the effect of the global agreement continued beyond the date when it had formally ceased.

> 208. In the present case, the Commission has not established that in participating in the global arrangements the applicants had a longer-term objective of allocating the EEA market as was done in the framework of the European arrangements. Nor has it demonstrated a connection between the methods and practices used in each set of arrangements.
> 209. In light of the consequences drawn from the absence of any temporal overlap between the implementation of the global and European arrangements (see paragraphs 182 to 191 above), from the fact that the mutual withdrawal from the European and North American markets and the sharing of the EEA market by the allocation of customers constitute different objectives implemented by dissimilar methods (see paragraphs 192 to 202 above) and, last, from the absence of evidence that the European producers intended to adhere to the global arrangements in order to divide the EEA market (see paragraph 203 above), it must be concluded that the European producers committed two separate infringements of Article 81(1) EC and not a single and continuous infringement.

While this conclusion served to reduce the fine, it was a pyrrhic victory as BASF also saw its fine increase: the CFI found that its application for leniency was based on providing evidence of the global cartel and as the Commission could not use this evidence in a meaningful way, the reduction of the fine by 10 per cent which the Commission had awarded was removed. Overall BASF saw its fine rise from €34.97 million to €35.024 million. It must be queried whether appeals against cartel decisions are worthwhile. Admittedly the Court is able to restrain the more audacious interpretations of Article 81 by the Commission, but this seems to come at a significant cost to the appellants.

23

Abuse of a dominant position

CONTENTS

1. Introduction

In late 2005 DG Competition published a Discussion Paper on Exclusionary Abuse which indicated that it sought to redirect its policy by using a more economics-oriented framework.[1] This stimulated a lively debate.[2] So far the Commission has not yet issued any further document; in part this is because a number of significant cases were pending before the European Courts. Now that these have been decided, we may see further initiatives from the Commission, probably in the form of draft guidelines. The three principal Article 82 cases that have been decided are *Microsoft* (tying and refusals to deal), *France Télécom* (predatory pricing) and *British Airways* (rebates).[3] A review of these three decisions allows us to explore the state of play in Article 82. In brief, the main message that can be gathered from these judgments is that the Court continues to support the existing policy on abuse of dominance, and this may place limits on the Commission's efforts to push for a less aggressive approach. At the same time, there are some hints that the courts are willing to support a change of direction.

---

1 Discussion Paper on the Application of Article 82 of the Treaty to Exclusionary Abuses (December 2005) (available at: http://ec.europa.eu/comm/competition/antitrust/art82/index.html).
2 See, for example, the 2006 special issue of the European Competition Journal; C-D. Ehlermann and I. Atanasiu (eds.) *European Competition Law Annual 2003: What is an Abuse of a Dominant Position?* (Oxford: Hart Publishing, 2004); C-D. Ehlermann and M. Marquis (eds.) *European Competition Law Annual 2007: A Reformed Approach to Article 82 EC* (Oxford: Hart Publishing, 2008 forthcoming); R. O'Donoghue and A. J. Padilla *The Law and Economics of Article 82 EC* (Oxford: Hart Publishing, 2006).
3 See also Case T–271/03 *Deutsche Telekon v Commission*, judgment of 10 April 2008.

2. The function of Article 82

A good starting place to assess the recent case law is *British Airways*, where the Commission had condemned BA's strategy of offering travel agents extra commissions when they promoted BA tickets on the basis that this was discriminatory, designed to induce loyalty, and served to exclude competing airlines.[4]

Case C-95/04 P *British Airways plc. v Commission* judgment of 15 March 2007

Criteria for assessing exclusionary effects

68. It follows that in determining whether, on the part of an undertaking in a dominant position, a system of discounts or bonuses which constitute neither quantity discounts or bonuses nor fidelity discounts or bonuses within the meaning of the judgment in *Hoffmann-La Roche* constitutes an abuse, it first has to be determined whether those discounts or bonuses can produce an exclusionary effect, that is to say whether they are capable, first, of making market entry very difficult or impossible for competitors of the undertaking in a dominant position and, secondly, of making it more difficult or impossible for its co-contractors to choose between various sources of supply or commercial partners.

69. It then needs to be examined whether there is an objective economic justification for the discounts and bonuses granted. In accordance with the analysis carried out by the Court of First Instance . . . an undertaking is at liberty to demonstrate that its bonus system producing an exclusionary effect is economically justified.

70. With regard to the first aspect, the case-law gives indications as to the cases in which discount or bonus schemes of an undertaking in a dominant position are not merely the expression of a particularly favourable offer on the market, but give rise to an exclusionary effect.

71. First, an exclusionary effect may arise from goal-related discounts or bonuses, that is to say those the granting of which is linked to the attainment of sales objectives defined individually.

73. It is also apparent from the case-law that the commitment of co-contractors towards the undertaking in a dominant position and the pressure exerted upon them may be particularly strong where a discount or bonus does not relate solely to the growth in turnover in relation to purchases or sales of products of that undertaking made by those co-contractors during the period under consideration, but extends also to the whole of the turnover relating to those purchases or sales. In that way, relatively modest variations – whether upwards or downwards – in the turnover figures relating to the products of the dominant undertaking have disproportionate effects on co-contractors.

75. Finally, the Court took the view that the pressure exerted on resellers by an undertaking in a dominant position which granted bonuses with those characteristics is further strengthened where that undertaking holds a very much larger market share than its competitors. It held that, in those circumstances, it is particularly difficult for competitors of that undertaking to outbid it in the face of discounts or bonuses based on overall sales volume. By reason of its

---

4 *Virgin/British Airways* [2000] OJ L30/1; affirmed by the CFI Case T-219/99 *British Airways v Commission* [2003] ECR II-5917. See further: G. Monti *EC Competition Law* (Cambridge: Cambridge University Press, 2007) pp. 162–72 and O. Odudu 'Case Note on BA v Commission' [2007] 44 *CMLR* 1781.

significantly higher market share, the undertaking in a dominant position generally constitutes an unavoidable business partner in the market. Most often, discounts or bonuses granted by such an undertaking on the basis of overall turnover largely take precedence in absolute terms, even over more generous offers of its competitors. In order to attract the co-contractors of the undertaking in a dominant position, or to receive a sufficient volume of orders from them, those competitors would have to offer them significantly higher rates of discount or bonus.

Objective economic justification

86. Assessment of the economic justification for a system of discounts or bonuses established by an undertaking in a dominant position is to be made on the basis of the whole of the circumstances of the case. It has to be determined whether the exclusionary effect arising from such a system, which is disadvantageous for competition, may be counterbalanced, or outweighed, by advantages in terms of efficiency which also benefit the consumer. If the exclusionary effect of that system bears no relation to advantages for the market and consumers, or if it goes beyond what is necessary in order to attain those advantages, that system must be regarded as an abuse.

Applying these standards to the facts of the case, the ECJ confirmed that BA had abused its dominant position: the bonuses were drawn up individually for each travel agent; they were based upon the total number of tickets sold, and not on those sold over a given level, so selling a few extra BA tickets meant a significant increase in bonus payments, so that it was often more worthwhile selling a few extra BA tickets over selling some other airlines' tickets; BA's size was such that other competitors lacked 'a sufficiently broad financial base to allow them effectively to establish a reward scheme similar to BA's'.[5] It may be argued that this is insufficient to sustain a finding of abuse, for instance there was no evidence that BA's scheme meant that its prices were below cost, in which case BA was simply more efficient than its rivals, or at least lucky to have been the first on the market and benefited from a statutory monopoly for several years giving it a significant advantage over new entrants.

The Court's approach to objective justification is quite close to that articulated by the Commission in its discussion paper: efficiencies must outweigh the anticompetitive effects, but there must be a benefit to consumers and the restriction of competition must be proportionate. While the willingness to consider efficiencies is to be welcomed, it must be noted that no dominant firm has yet to succeed in showing that its behaviour is justified once it has been shown that the rebate scheme has exclusionary effects.[6]

It is also worth noting an important passage from AG Kokott's Opinion in *British Airways*, written in the context of whether a finding of abuse requires an adverse effect:

5 Case C-95/04 P *British Airways plc. v Commission* judgment of 15 March 2007 para. 76.
6 E. Rousseva 'Abuse of dominant position defences' in G. Amato and C-D. Ehlermann (eds.) *EC Competition Law – A Critical Assessment* (Oxford: Hart Publishing, 2007).

> 68. The starting-point here must be the protective purpose of Article 82 EC. The provision forms part of a system designed to protect competition within the internal market from distortions (Article 3(1)(g) EC). Accordingly, Article 82 EC, like the other competition rules of the Treaty, is not designed only or primarily to protect the immediate interests of individual competitors or consumers, but to protect the structure of the market and thus competition as such (*as an institution*), which has already been weakened by the presence of the dominant undertaking on the market. In this way, consumers are also indirectly protected. Because where competition as such is damaged, disadvantages for consumers are also to be feared.
>
> 69. The conduct of a dominant undertaking is not, therefore, to be regarded as abusive within the meaning of Article 82 EC only once it has concrete effects on individual market participants, be they competitors or consumers. Rather, a line of conduct of a dominant undertaking is abusive as soon as it runs counter to the purpose of protecting competition in the internal market from distortions (Article 3(1)(g) EC). That is because, as already mentioned, a dominant undertaking bears a particular responsibility to ensure that effective and undistorted competition in the common market is not undermined by its conduct.

This passage runs counter to the tenor of the CFI's judgment in *GSK* noted in the update to chapter 22, where the focus was placed squarely on consumer welfare. The Advocate General instead prefers a more structural based approach to competition, whereby the presence of competitors is necessary for a competitive market. This does little to reduce the criticisms that EC competition law protects competitors, and not competition.[7]

3. Conservatism on predatory pricing

France Télécom is an appeal against the Commission's decision finding that WIN (*Wanadoo Interactive* which, following a merger was now a part of France Télécom) set prices for its ADSL services at prices that did not cover its variable costs between March and August 2001 and at prices below total cost from August 2001 until October 2002, 'as part of a plan to pre-empt the market in high-speed internet access during a key phase in its development'.[8] The CFI confirmed that high speed internet access is in a separate market; from low speed access (because some downloads are impossible with low speed connection, the telephone line remains available when connecting with high speed access, consumers migrate from low to high speed access but only a negligible proportion migrate from high speed back to low speed access, and 80 per cent of high speed access subscribers would retain their subscription even with a 5–10 per cent price increase), and that the undertaking was dominant with market shares above 50 per cent and even though it was a growing market, the undertaking retained a leading position with eight times the amount of subscribers as its nearest rival. Turning to the abuse, the appellant raised three arguments that tested the limits

---

7 But see H. Schweitzer 'Parallels and differences in the attitudes towards and rules regarding market power: What are the reasons?' in Ehlermann and Marquis (eds.) above n. 1.
8 Case COMP/38.233, *Wanadoo Interactive*, decision of 16 July 2003, Article 1.

of Article 82: that it had a right to align its prices to those of its competitors, that there was no predatory plan, and that the Commission would have to show that the predator is able to recover its costs post predation to establish a finding of predatory pricing. All were rejected by the CFI.

Case T 340/03 *France Télécom SA v Commission* judgment of 30 January 2007

WIN's right to align its prices on its competitors' prices

185. It should be recalled that, according to established case-law, although the fact that an undertaking is in a dominant position cannot deprive it of the right to protect its own commercial interests if they are attacked and such an undertaking must be allowed the right to take such reasonable steps as it deems appropriate to protect those interests, such behaviour cannot be countenanced if its actual purpose is to strengthen this dominant position and abuse it.

186. The specific obligations imposed on undertakings in a dominant position have been confirmed by the case-law on a number of occasions. . . . [I]t follows from the nature of the obligations imposed by Article 82 EC that, in specific circumstances, undertakings in a dominant position may be deprived of the right to adopt a course of conduct or take measures which are not in themselves abuses and which would even be unobjectionable if adopted or taken by non-dominant undertakings.

187. WIN cannot therefore rely on an absolute right to align its prices on those of its competitors in order to justify its conduct. Even if alignment of prices by a dominant under-taking on those of its competitors is not in itself abusive or objectionable, it might become so where it is aimed not only at protecting its interests but also at strengthening and abusing its dominant position.

Absence of a plan of predation and reduction in competition

195. As regards the conditions for the application of Article 82 EC and the distinction between the object and effect of the abuse, it should be pointed out that, for the purposes of applying that article, showing an anti-competitive object and an anti-competitive effect may, in some cases, be one and the same thing. If it is shown that the object pursued by the conduct of an undertaking in a dominant position is to restrict competition, that conduct will also be liable to have such an effect. Thus, with regard to the practices concerning prices, the Court of Justice held in *AKZO v Commission* that prices below average variable costs applied by an undertaking in a dominant position are regarded as abusive in themselves because the only interest which the undertaking may have in applying such prices is that of eliminating competitors, and that prices below average total costs but above average variable costs are abusive if they are determined as part of a plan for eliminating a competitor. In that case, the Court did not require any demonstration of the actual effects of the practices in question.

196. Furthermore, it should be added that, where an undertaking in a dominant position actually implements a practice whose object is to oust a competitor, the fact that the result hoped for is not achieved is not sufficient to prevent that being an abuse of a dominant position within the meaning of Article 82 EC.

199. In recital 110, the decision refers to a number of documents, relating to the whole period at issue, which attest to the existence of WIN's strategy of 'pre-emption' for the high-speed market [. . .]

200. In addition, WIN's documents prove that it was seeking to acquire and then hold onto very significant market shares. The framework letter for 2001 states, for example, that '70 per cent . . . 80 per cent of the ADSL market should accrue to [WIN]'. A presentation by the CEO of WIN to the board of France Télécom dated June 2001 refers to a market share of 80 per cent over the entire period 2001 to 2004 in the segment of '"dissociated" offers, like Wanadoo ADSL' and a market share increasing by an average of 50 per cent in 2001 to 72 per cent in 2004 in the segment of '"packaged" offers, like eXtense'.

201. It is true that WIN disputed the scope of those documents and, in particular, the significance of the term 'pre-emption' which they contain. According to WIN, such informal and spontaneous, even unconsidered words, are merely a reflection of the dialectics of the decision-making process. They bind only their authors and not the undertaking.

202. It should be pointed out, however, that those words come from management-level staff within the undertaking and that some of them were expressed in the context of formal presentations for the purpose of taking a decision or of a very detailed framework letter. Their spontaneous and unconsidered nature thus appears to be questionable.

Recoupment of losses

227. In line with Community case-law, the Commission was therefore able to regard as abusive prices below average variable costs. In that case, the eliminatory nature of such pricing is presumed. In relation to full costs, the Commission had also to provide evidence that WIN's predatory pricing formed part of a plan to 'pre-empt' the market. In the two situations, it was not necessary to establish in addition proof that WIN had a realistic chance of recouping its losses.

228. The Commission was therefore right to take the view that proof of recoupment of losses was not a precondition to making a finding of predatory pricing.

There are three unconvincing aspects of the judgment. The first is that predatory pricing is defined as an abuse by 'object'. This lowers the burden of proof on the Commission because there is no need to show effects, in fact even an ineffective abuse is punishable. It is also problematic because unlike Article 81, Article 82 does not draw a distinction between object and effect. Second, the exclusive use of statements of intention to establish a predatory plan, and the absence of other objective evidence to confirm this further lowers the Commission evidentiary burden. Third, the Court limits the ability of dominant firms to defend themselves; paragraph 186 seems to suggest that even behaviour which is not an abuse can be forbidden when it is intended to strengthen one's dominance. This must be erroneous because it would make intent sufficient to find an abuse, no matter what form the conduct takes.

4. Refusals to supply – competition versus innovation

While it is easy to explain why rebates and predatory pricing strategies by dominant firms should be condemned, it is more controversial to impose a duty on a dominant firm to supply rivals and subsidise competition to itself. This is why the Court has been cautious and restricted the circumstances when a refusal to supply should be an abuse. In the *Microsoft* decision the Commission found that the company was dominant in the market for client PC operating systems (with a market share of over 90 per cent) and had refused to supply 'interoperability information' to its competitors in the market for work group servers operating systems (software that connects networks of computers allowing e.g. file sharing, access to resources on the network) where Microsoft was present with a market share of 60 per cent. The information would have allowed competitors to sell work group servers to users of Microsoft's operating system, but the refusal excluded them and allowed Microsoft to strengthen its position in the work group server market.[9] In addition to a fine, Microsoft was ordered to supply interoperability information and a monitoring trustee was appointed to oversee the implementation of the remedy. The Commission grounded its finding on two alternatives: first, that the criteria established in *Magill* were met: (1) the refusal concerns a product or service which is indispensable for rivals; (2) the refusal prevents the appearance of a new product for which there is consumer demand; (3) there is no objective justification; (4) the dominant firm, by its refusal reserves for itself a secondary market by excluding competition.[10] Second, even if these requirements were not met, the Commission took the view that *Magill* merely provided an example of the exceptional circumstances when a refusal to licence an intellectual property right constituted an abuse, and the facts of this case presented good reasons for finding the refusal abusive. The CFI agreed that the criteria in *Magill* had been fulfilled. Of particular interest in the lengthy judgment are the CFI's views on the anticompetitive effects of the abuse, its wide interpretation of the 'new product' requirement, and its clarification of the burden of proof when examining the defence of objective justification.[11]

Case T-201/04 Microsoft Corp. v Commission judgment of 17 September 2007

Elimination of competition

560. In the contested decision, the Commission considered whether the refusal at issue gave rise to a 'risk' of the elimination of competition on the work group server operating systems market. Microsoft contends that that criterion is not sufficiently strict, since according to the case-law on the exercise of an intellectual property right the Commission must demonstrate that the refusal to license an intellectual property right to a third party is 'likely to eliminate all competition', or, in other words, that there is a 'high probability' that the conduct in question will have such a result.

---

9 [2007] OJ L32/23. For completeness, the Commission's decision also related to a second abuse: Microsoft's tying its Windows Media Player (WMP) to the Windows operating system. The effect was that other makers of media player software found it harder to penetrate the market. The Commission found an abuse and ordered Microsoft to supply both a version of Windows without WMP and one with WMP.
10 Joined Cases C 241/91 P and C 242/91 P *RTE and ITP v Commission* [1995] ECR I 743.
11 For further discussion, see H. First 'Strong spine, weak underbelly: The CFI Microsoft decision' www.antitrustinstitute.org/archives/files/First_Strong%20Spine_100220071356.pdf

561. The Court finds that Microsoft's complaint is purely one of terminology and is wholly irrelevant. The expressions 'risk of elimination of competition' and 'likely to eliminate competition' are used without distinction by the Community judicature to reflect the same idea, namely that Article 82 EC does not apply only from the time when there is no more, or practically no more, competition on the market. If the Commission were required to wait until competitors were eliminated from the market, or until their elimination was sufficiently imminent, before being able to take action under Article 82 EC, that would clearly run counter to the objective of that provision, which is to maintain undistorted competition in the common market and, in particular, to safeguard the competition that still exists on the relevant market.

562. In this case, the Commission had all the more reason to apply Article 82 EC before the elimination of competition on the work group server operating systems market had become a reality because that market is characterised by significant network effects and because the elimination of competition would therefore be difficult to reverse.

563. Nor is it necessary to demonstrate that all competition on the market would be eliminated. What matters, for the purpose of establishing an infringement of Article 82 EC, is that the refusal at issue is liable to, or is likely to, eliminate all effective competition on the market. It must be made clear that the fact that the competitors of the dominant undertaking retain a marginal presence in certain niches on the market cannot suffice to substantiate the existence of such competition.

New product

643. It must be emphasised that the fact that the applicant's conduct prevents the appearance of a new product on the market falls to be considered under Article 82(b) EC, which prohibits abusive practices which consist in 'limiting production, markets or technical developments to the . . . prejudice of consumers'.

647. The circumstance relating to the appearance of a new product, as envisaged in *Magill* and *IMS Health*, cannot be the only parameter which determines whether a refusal to license an intellectual property right is capable of causing prejudice to consumers within the meaning of Article 82(b) EC. As that provision states, such prejudice may arise where there is a limitation not only of production or markets, but also of technical development.

648. It was on that last hypothesis that the Commission based its finding in the contested decision. Thus, the Commission considered that Microsoft's refusal to supply the relevant information limited technical development to the prejudice of consumers within the meaning of Article 82(b) EC and it rejected Microsoft's assertion that it had not been demonstrated that its refusal caused prejudice to consumers.

656. Thus, the contested decision rests on the concept that, once the obstacle represented for Microsoft's competitors by the insufficient degree of interoperability with the Windows domain architecture has been removed, those competitors will be able to offer work group server operating systems which, far from merely reproducing the Windows systems already on the market, will be distinguished from those systems with respect to parameters which consumers consider important (see, to that effect, recital 699 to the contested decision).

664. Last, it must be borne in mind that it is settled case-law that Article 82 EC covers not only practices which may prejudice consumers directly but also those which indirectly prejudice them by impairing an effective competitive structure. In this case, Microsoft impaired the effective competitive structure on the work group server operating systems market by acquiring a significant market share on that market.

665. The Court concludes from all of the foregoing considerations that the Commission's finding to the effect that Microsoft's refusal limits technical development to the prejudice of

consumers within the meaning of Article 82(b) EC is not manifestly incorrect. The Court therefore finds that the circumstance relating to the appearance of a new product is present in this case.

Objective Justification

688. The Court notes, as a preliminary point, that although the burden of proof of the existence of the circumstances that constitute an infringement of Article 82 EC is borne by the Commission, it is for the dominant undertaking concerned, and not for the Commission, before the end of the administrative procedure, to raise any plea of objective justification and to support it with arguments and evidence. It then falls to the Commission, where it proposes to make a finding of an abuse of a dominant position, to show that the arguments and evidence relied on by the undertaking cannot prevail and, accordingly, that the justification put forward cannot be accepted.

697. The Court finds that, as the Commission correctly submits, Microsoft, which bore the initial burden of proof, did not sufficiently establish that if it were required to disclose the interoperability information that would have a significant negative impact on its incentives to innovate.

The judgment has been criticised for being overly aggressive, focusing on the impact on market structure and competitors and not on consumer welfare and for failing to take into consideration that the network effects normally lead to monopoly firms that benefit consumers.[12] Accordingly there is a risk that competitors will free ride on the innovations of the dominant firm.[13] It also widens the scope of the *Magill* test which is in conflict with the position that refusals to licence intellectual property rights should be seen as abusive only exceptionally. However, the CFI also brings certain welcome clarifications to the nature of Article 82. First, it is a tool for pre-empting market failure; that is an action may be brought when there is a risk that the competitive process would be disrupted. This accounts for the criticisms above – with hindsight it may be that imposing liability is unnecessary but the inherent nature of Article 82 is to prevent the possibility of harm. This tallies with the ECJ's views in *British Airways*. Second, the CFI explains clearly how the burden of proof is allocated when it comes to defences, and Microsoft's failure to substantiate its claims on innovation incentives also undermines the criticisms above.

12 D. Howarth and K. McMahon 'Microsoft has performed an illegal operation' [2008] *ECLR* 117.
13 D. Waelbroeck 'The Microsoft judgment: Article 82 revisited?' (2008), available at www. globalcompetitionpolicy.org

Merger policy

CONTENTS

1. Introduction

The Commission's merger policy has not changed significantly since 2005; as is illustrated below there has been some incremental development in some recent Commission decisions but no major change. Before looking at these developments, two trends should be noted.

First, the courts have continued to consider appeals against Commission decisions closely, placing increased pressure on the decision-making process.[1] Moreover, a first successful claim for damages against the Commission (based on Article 288 EC) has been made, in *Schneider v Commission*.[2] The CFI had earlier annulled a decision blocking the merger between Schneider and Legrand,[3] and subsequently the acquirer, Schneider, sought damages on two grounds: first, the factual errors that the CFI found in the Commission's decision and second, that the Commission had denied Schneider its right of defence by failing to give sufficient information about some of the competitive concerns in the statement of objections. Schneider failed in proving that the Commission's failure in its substantive analysis warranted an award of damages (for lack of causation: the errors that the Commission made only related

---

1 E.g. Case T-464/04 *Impala v Commission* [2006] ECR II-2289 (quashing a decision to clear a merger).

2 Case T-351/03 *Schneider SA v Commission* judgment of 11 July 2007. See pp. 87–90 of this update for further analysis.

3 Case T-310/01 *Schneider v Commission* [2002] ECR II-4071.

to certain aspects of the merger, and even without those findings the Commission would have blocked the merger),[4] but won in establishing the denial of its procedural rights.[5] However, the court refused to find that this breach caused all the losses that Schneider claimed. Exceptionally in this case Schneider had bought Legrand before the Commission decision and was then forced to sell Legrand once the merger was blocked. Its claim for damages based on the difference between the price Schneider paid to buy Legrand and the price at which it sold it was denied because it was not established that the breach of a procedural right caused this loss: the merger might have been blocked anyway. The court only found a causal link between the breach by the Commission and two losses: (i) the legal costs incurred by the plaintiff from the date of the CFI's quashing of the Commission decision and (ii) the reduced price at which Schneider sold Legrand because it chose to delay the sale pending its appeal against the Commission decision.[6] Damages under the second heading were reduced by one third because the CFI held that Schneider took a real risk that the merger would be blocked.[7] Perhaps of greater significance than the detailed application of the law to this dispute is the way the CFI responded to the Commission's argument that imposing liability would have an adverse effect on its capacity to function as a regulator.

Case T-351/03 *Schneider SA v Commission* judgment of 11 July 2007

122. It must be conceded that such an effect, contrary to the general Community interest, might arise if the concept of a serious breach of Community law were construed as comprising all errors or mistakes which, even if of some gravity, are not by their nature or extent alien to the normal conduct of an institution entrusted with the task of overseeing the application of competition rules, which are complex, delicate and subject to a considerable degree of discretion.

123. Therefore, a sufficiently serious breach of Community law, for the purposes of establishing the non-contractual liability of the Community, cannot be constituted by failure to fulfil a legal obligation, which, regrettable though it may be, can be explained by the objective constraints to which the institution and its officials are subject as a result of the provisions governing the control of concentrations.

124. On the other hand, the right to compensation for damage resulting from the conduct of the institution becomes available where such conduct takes the form of action manifestly contrary to the rule of law and seriously detrimental to the interests of persons outside the institution and cannot be justified or accounted for by the particular constraints to which the staff of the institution, operating normally, is objectively subject.

125. Such a definition of the threshold for the establishment of non-contractual liability of the Community is conducive to protection of the room for manoeuvre and freedom of assessment which must, in the general interest, be enjoyed by the Community regulator of competition, both in its discretionary decisions and in its interpretation and application of the relevant provisions of primary and secondary Community law, without thereby leaving third parties to bear the consequences of flagrant and inexcusable misconduct.

Thus the rules on liability are balanced so that while on the one hand the principle of corrective justice is undermined because some plaintiffs are unable to recover

---

4 Above n. 2 paras 129–39.   5 *Ibid*. paras 145–59.   6 *Ibid*. paras 288–325.   7 *Ibid*. paras 332–4.

for non-serious breaches, on the other hand, the Commission is not deterred from developing new theories of anticompetitive effect. The position taken by the CFI is consistent with that taken generally when courts are faced with tort claims against public authorities. Accordingly it is unlikely that as a result of this judgment the Commission is more likely to clear mergers to avoid liability (after all it may also be subjected to lawsuits by competitors aggrieved that a merger has been cleared), or that it will develop the law less adventurously in future cases. Moreover, unless the court finds an error in the substantive assessment of a merger such that the entirety of the decision is tainted by a sufficiently serious breach, the quantum of damages is unlikely to be significant enough to place a significant dent in the Community budget (e.g. in this case Schneider had sought damages of €1.66 billion, but is likely to receive much less).[8] Nonetheless, damages claims provide an added incentives for parties who believe that the Commission acted wrongly in allowing or blocking a merger to demand judicial review, thus increasing oversight in the merger process.[9] In light of the case law discussed further below, this potential effect is to be welcomed.

The second trend is an increase in protectionism by Member States, which has manifested itself in interventions to block takeovers of national champions by foreign firms.[10] When a merger has an EC dimension, national laws are inapplicable and yet some Member States have insisted upon legislating to prevent foreign takeovers. The Commission, supported by the ECJ, has taken a strong stance against these strategies.[11] For example the Court of Justice has ruled that the Spanish energy regulator was in breach of EC Law when it imposed a number of conditions upon E.On's bid for Endesa after the merger had already been cleared by the Commission.[12] In spite of the hard line taken, this protectionist trend will continue, in particular as the liberalisation of utilities opens formerly state owned undertakings to takeover bids by foreign firms. However, the EC's own merger rules have not escaped criticism for protectionism either: a recent article suggests that the Commission treats foreign acquirers more strictly than mergers involving a European buyer.[13]

2. Horizontal mergers

The major plank of the 2004 reform of the EC Merger Regulation was the amendment of the substantive test, whereby a merger may be blocked even if it does not create or strengthen a dominant position provided that one can establish a substantial impediment of effective competition. There is some uncertainty over the application

---

8 More clarity may emerge on the measure of damages in a pending claim Case T-212/03 *MyTravel v Commission* [2003] OJ C200/28.

9 For further analysis see D. Bailey 'Damages actions under the EC merger regulation' (2007) 44 *CMLR* 101.

10 Galloway 'The pursuit of national champions: the intersection of competition law and industrial policy' (2007) *ECLR* 172.

11 E.g. N. Kroes 'Introductory remarks on mergers in the Internal Market' Speech 15 March 2006.

12 Case C-196/07 *Commission v Spain* judgment of 6 March 2008.

13 N. Aktas, E. de Bodt and R. Roll 'Is European M&A regulation protectionist?' (2007) 115 *Economic Journal* 1096.

of the new test, but a few recent cases help explain how the Commission's thinking is developing.[14] A distinction can be drawn between two types of merger: those involving homogeneous goods and those involving differentiated products.

(i) Homogeneous goods

In *Linde/BOC* the Commission feared anticompetitive effects in the helium wholesale market.[15] Measured by future capacity, the market shares of the players were forecast to be as follows: Linde would have 0–10 per cent of the market and BOC 20–30 per cent. There would be three other competitors with market shares between 20 and 30 per cent each. Thus at first blush the merger would not create a dominant player, however the Commission based its findings on unilateral effects. Its concern was that in the years before the merger Linde had been a keen competitor, and that post-merger this incentive to grow its market share would be dented. Two rationales were deployed to explain this: first, that pre-merger Linde would have wished to 'invest' by setting lower prices so as to gain market share, but post-merger that investment was less likely because a price decrease over a considerably larger number of units sold is less profitable; second, post-merger the entity would be able to reduce output and this would be profitable because of high entry barriers caused by capacity constraints in that there are very few natural gas fields from which helium can be made.[16] One further aspect should have been considered by the Commission (its omission is probably explained by the fact that this is a Phase 1 case where the analysis is not set out completely): this is the ability of the other firms in the market to increase their output should the merged entity choose to reduce its production. This factor is essential because no unilateral effects are plausible if the reduced output does not lead to a price rise caused by a shortage. For completeness it should be mentioned that the Commission also expressed concerns that the market was prone to coordinated effects given the degree of concentration, product homogeneity, transparency to allow for retaliation, and the fact that the merger removed a 'maverick' firm that had been aggressive in the market, suggesting that the merger would cause a price alignment.[17] It seems that this is a more plausible explanation of the anticompetitive effects than trying to suggest that the merged entity would raise prices unilaterally.

(ii) Differentiated products

A clearer case where a merger was tackled using the new test is *T-Mobile Austria/ Tele.ring*. Here the Commission applied a new theory, considering that a merger in a differentiated product market that eliminates the most important competitive force is

---

14 For more detail see G. Monti 'The new substantive test in the EC Merger Regulation – bridging the gap between economics and law?' (LSE working paper, available at www.lse.ac.uk/collections/law/wps/wps.htm).

15 Case COMP/M.4141 *Linde/BOC* (6 June 2006).   16 *Ibid.* paras 160–79.   17 *Ibid.* paras 180–92.

anticompetitive even if no dominant firm results, and even if there is no tacit collusion (although in a belt-and-braces approach the Commission does examine the risk of coordinated effects as well).[18] The competition concerns occurred in the market for mobile telecommunications services, where the market shares in 2005, measured by customers were as follows:

T-Mobile	Tele.ring	Mobilkom	ONE	H3G
[20–30%]	[10–20%]	[35–45%]	[15–25%]	[<5%]

The merged entity would not become dominant, but the Commission noted several features which suggested that unilateral effects would occur. First, that Tele.ring had almost doubled its market share in the last three years, while Mobilkom and T-Mobile have lost market shares in that period. Second, ONE was developing a different commercial strategy, selling higher value services and H3G faced an uncertain future given the regulatory framework. Third, Tele.ring was the main reason why Mobilkom and T-Mobile were cutting prices, and its elimination as a market player would reduce the incentive on the two larger firms to reduce prices. Significantly, the Commission did not say that post-merger prices would rise, merely that they would not fall as fast as before the merger.

> **Case No COMP/M.3916 *T-Mobile Austria/Tele.ring***
> **(decision of 26 April 2006)**
>
> 125. In the light of the preceding analysis, and especially with the elimination of the maverick in the market and the simultaneous creation of a market structure with two leading, symmetrical network operators, it is likely that the planned transaction will produce non-coordinated effects and significantly impede effective competition in a substantial part of the common market. It is therefore probable that the proposed merger will have a tangible effect on prices in the Austrian end-customer market for mobile telephony services. Even if prices do not rise in the short term, the eakening of competitive pressure as a result of tele.ring's elimination from the market makes it unlikely that prices will continue to fall significantly as in the past65.
>
> 126. This conclusion is consistent with the Horizontal Guidelines. These state that some firms have more of an influence on the competitive process than their market shares would suggest. A merger involving such a firm could change the competitive dynamics in a significant anti-competitive way, in particular when the market is already concentrated. This is precisely the case here . . . the Austrian market for mobile telecommunications for end customers is highly concentrated. As has also been indicated, tele.ring, as a maverick, has a much greater influence on the competitive process in this market than its market share would suggest.

In spite of the risk to competition, the Commission cleared the merger subject to commitments that facilitated H3G's expansion in the near future, in the expectation that it would become the new maverick player in the Austrian market.

---

18 Case M.3916 *T.Mobile Austria/tele.ring* 26 April 2006.

The following comments about this reasoning may be made: first, the decision seems to use the acquired firm's disruptive presence on the market as the key indicator of anticompetitive harm,[19] but it is unclear what combination of factors in addition to it will lead the Commission to reach the same conclusion, nor what sort of evidence suffices to describe a target firm as a maverick.[20] Second, while ONE had deployed a different commercial strategy pre-merger, the Commission should probably have considered more fully that firm's ability to reposition itself to become a direct competitor of the merged entity.[21] Third, given the passage quoted above it is not clear why the merger should *substantially* impede effective competition given that prices would have continued to fall. Fourth, the remedy prescribed suggests that the problems in the mobile telecommunications market in Austria had more to do with a defective regulatory regime than with the merger, so the Commission stepped in to regulate a market, not to prevent anticompetitive harm. In sum, this first decision where the Commission felt the dominance test would have prevented the application of the ECMR is one where the Commission appears to stretch its powers significantly. It follows that judicial scrutiny of the Commission's application of the new standard is necessary to rein in the Commission's discretion.

In other decisions the Commission appears to run the dominance test and the substantial impediment of competition test in parallel. An example is in *Adidas/Reebok*.[22] It noted that the merger would have led to a firm with a market share of 50–60 per cent in some shoe types (e.g. tennis shoes) in some Member States. This suggested dominance but then the Commission verified this finding by looking more closely as to whether there would be a substantial lessening of competition and it found that another market player (Nike) was likely to retain a strong position and compete aggressively against the merged entity; that Adidas and Reebok were positioned differently in the market (Adidas focused on professional sports and had European roots, while Reebok focused on the leisure industry and on US sports); that Reebok was a weaker brand than Adidas and Nike and was not a must stock item for retailers. Therefore the high market shares did not tell the whole story: the merger was unlikely to substantially impede effective competition.

3. Non-horizontal mergers

The Commission issued guidelines on non-horizontal mergers after a period of consultation.[23] This document arrives in the aftermath of criticism over the Commission's

---

19 A similar theory of harm was explored in Case M.4523 *Travelport/Worldspan* (21 August 2007) paras 106–28 but found that the target was not a maverick because (i) target was not charging lower prices (ii) target had been losing market share; (iii) the target and acquirer were not each other's closest competitors.

20 J. Killick and A. Schulz 'Horizontal and vertical mergers' in Amato and Ehlermann above n. 5 p. 467.

21 This is a consideration that is noted in the Horizontal Merger Guidelines at para. 30.

22 Case M.3942 *Adidas/Reebok* (2006).

23 Guidelines on the assessment of non-horizontal mergers under the Council Regulation on the control of concentrations between undertakings (available at http://ec.europa.eu/comm/competition/mergers/legislation/notices_on_substance.html).

handling of conglomerate mergers, where its approach is seen as overly aggressive.[24] This document begins in an encouraging manner in noting that non-horizontal mergers are less likely to result in anticompetitive effects because there is no loss of direct competition and there is a substantial scope for efficiencies. However, this is not followed up with a detailed analysis of efficiencies, instead the same efficiency test set out in the horizontal merger guidelines is applied. This is unfortunate because the standard set out in those guidelines is very strict and there is little evidence that it can be successfully applied, so the pro-competitive effects of these mergers are likely to be undermined by regulatory intervention. The main contribution of the guidelines is in clarifying the method of analysis that the Commission will follow in examining if the merger is likely to have anticompetitive effects, whether through foreclosure or by enhancing coordinated effects. The major risk is foreclosure, so we focus on this part of the guidelines. The approach is similar for vertical and conglomerate mergers, consisting of a three stage test: (i) the ability to foreclose; (ii) the incentive to foreclose; (iii) the likely effects of foreclosure. Of particular significance is the third limb of the test. In the aftermath of *GE/Honeywell* the Commission had been criticised for protecting weaker firms that would suffer as a result of the merger and had failed to convince critics that its aim was to safeguard consumer welfare. The third limb is designed to rectify this.

> ### Guidelines on the assessment of non-horizontal mergers under the Council Regulation on the control of concentrations between undertakings (2007)
>
> 113. It is only when a sufficiently large fraction of market output is affected by foreclosure resulting from the merger that the merger may significantly impede effective competition. If there remain effective single-product players in either market, competition is unlikely to deteriorate following a conglomerate merger. The same holds when few single-product rivals remain, but these have the ability and incentive to expand output.

4. Efficiencies

The analysis of efficiencies in mergers remains problematic because the Commission remains unwilling to use efficiencies as a sole basis for allowing a merger.[25] The result is that the efficiencies seem to be used merely as supporting evidence that a merger should be cleared but only when other factors point in the same direction. For example in *Korsnäs/AD Cartonboard* the merger was cleared because it did not create a dominant firm, nor were there risks of unilateral effects, plus there was

---

24 Burnley 'Conglomerate mergers' in G. Amato and C-D. Ehlermann (eds.) *EC Competition Law – A Critical Assessment* (Oxford: Hart Publishing, 2007).
25 See generally G. Monti 'Merger defences' in G. Amato and C-D. Ehlermann (eds.) *EC Competition Law – A Critical Assessment* (Oxford: Hart Publishing, 2007).

buyer power and low entry barriers.[26] These findings suffice to clear a merger, so the Commission's detailed assessment of efficiencies seems redundant. This is confirmed by the reasoning in *Inco/Falconbridge* where efficiencies came to nothing because the merged entity's market power led the Commission to fear that the efficiencies would not be passed on to consumers, nor was the Commission convinced that a merger was the least restrictive way of obtaining efficiencies.[27] Perhaps the Commission's aversion to efficiency claims (much criticised by many) finds some justification in some studies that reveal that many mergers fail and that these failures impose costs to society.[28]

26 Case M.4057 *Korsnäs/Assidomän Cartonboard* decision of 12 May 2006.
27 Case M.4000 *Inco/Falconbridge* decision of 4 July 2006.
28 H. Schenk 'Mergers and concentration policy' in P. Bianchi and S. Laborey *International Handbook on Industrial Policy* (Cheltenham: Edward Elgar, 2006).

State regulation and EC competition law

CONTENTS	
1. The Lisbon Treaty and services of general interest	188
2. The case law of the Court	189
3. Liberalisation of network industries	192

1. The Lisbon Treaty and services of general interest

Article 16 EC on services of general interest, inserted in the Amsterdam Treaty, has proven to be a damp squib: the courts have not relied upon it in any meaningful way to loosen the application of competition law to services of general economic interest; nor has the Commission reduced its efforts to increase competition and to stimulate the delivery of services of general economic interests through competitive markets in spite of paying lip-service to the concept through several exploratory documents.[1] At the request of Member States eager to safeguard public services, the Lisbon Treaty tries to strengthen the position of services of general interest.

- Article 14 LTFEU (ex Art 16 EC) is amended in two ways: first, the duty on the Union and Member States to take care that such services operate on the basis of principles and conditions enabling them to fulfil their mission, is rendered more specific by noting the importance of *economic and financial conditions* of service providers. Second, the Union gains legislative competence: '[t]he European Parliament and the Council, acting by means of regulations in accordance with the ordinary legislative procedure, shall establish these principles and set these conditions without prejudice to the competence of Member States, in compliance with the Treaties, to provide, to commission and to fund such services'.
- Protocol 26 on services of general interest contains two declarations. Article 1, regarding services of general *economic* interest (e.g. provision of electricity,

---

1 These can be found at: http://ec.europa.eu/services_general_interest/interest_en.htm.

telecommunications, water), notes 'the essential role and the wide discretion of national, regional and local authorities in providing, commissioning and organising services of general economic interest as closely as possible to the needs of the users; the diversity between various services of general economic interest and the differences in the needs and preferences of users that may result from different geographical, social or cultural situations; a high level of quality, safety and affordability, equal treatment and the promotion of universal access and of user rights'. Article 2 regarding *non-economic* services of general interest (e.g. police, social security benefits), declares that the Treaty does not affect the 'competence of Member States to provide, commission and organise' such services.

These reforms pull in opposite directions: on the one hand, they indicate that the Union has a role to play in regulating services of general interest, while the protocol tries to strengthen the hand of Member States, and seems an attempt to rein in the Commission and the Court, demanding greater latitude for Member States. In particular the reference to the economic and financial conditions of service providers seems a direct plea for a more lenient application of state aid rules when governments subsidise providers of services of general interest. These amendments pit the Commission's liberalisation drive, which it believes is compatible with the delivery of public services, against a policy premised upon the reduction in the scope of competition law to ensure the Union and Member States fulfil their duties to the citizens. A clash between these two visions on how to deliver public services is likely as the Commission's communication in November 2007, reflecting on the Treaty amendments, suggests that it is satisfied with the present rules and its plans are merely to inform parties what the rules are, to ensure that the liberalisation of utilities continues, and to monitor the effects of liberalisation.[2] Member States and the European Parliament are likely to want a different focus.[3]

2. The case law of the Court

The case law indicates that anticompetitive legislation enacted by Member States may be challenged on two main grounds: first, when the State confers an exclusive or special right that leads an undertaking to infringe competition law (based on Article 86(1) read jointly with Article 81 or 82 EC), and second, when State law ratifies or encourages anticompetitive agreements (based on a combined reading of Articles 3(1)(g), 10 and 81 EC). The obligation on Member States set out in Article 10 EC has now been moved to Article 4 LTEU, where paragraph 3 provides that Member

---

2 EC Commission *Services of general interest, including social services of general interest: a new European commitment* COM (2007) 725 final.

3 See generally M. G. Ross 'Promoting solidarity: from public services to a European model of competition?' (2007) 44 *Common Market Law Review* 1057; N. Boeger 'Solidarity and EC competition law' (2007) 32 *ELR* 319.

States shall 'refrain from any measure which could jeopardise the attainment of the Union's objectives'. And Article 3 EC has been replaced by a list of competences, the Union having exclusive competence on competition (Art 3(1)(b) LTFEU), so this legal basis for challenging anticompetitive state regulation remains. However, it might be argued that the removal of competition as one of the aims of the Union as listed in Article 3 LTEU is intended to render the Court's case law inapplicable. It is unlikely that a Court would be persuaded by this suggestion, and in any way the significance of the case law based on a combined reading of Articles 10 and 81 is marginal given that most anticompetitive legislation is likely to be regulated under the rules on the internal market.[4]

The case law has been sparse and has not led to major developments;[5] but of note is the *Cipolla* judgment,[6] which casts some doubts over the Commission's wish to inject more competition in markets of professional services.[7] At issue was the way lawyer's fees were fixed in Italy. The procedure for fixing fees begins with a recommendation from the national lawyers' council, which is sent to the Minister of Justice who considers the recommendations in consultation with the Council of State and an inter-ministerial committee on prices before issuing a law fixing the fees. The claimants, who had been the recipients of legal services, challenged this manner of fixing fees as contrary to EC Law.[8] The argument based on Articles 10 and 81, that Italy had delegated price fixing to an association of undertakings (the national lawyer's council), was rejected because even though the association might not set fees taking the public interest into account, its fee scale was only a recommendation which the State considered closely and could vary, and moreover the courts could, in individual cases, depart from the scales set. Accordingly the State had not facilitated a cartel among lawyers.[9] In reaching this conclusion the Court rejected the Commission's argument that this approach, based on *Arduino*, should no longer be followed.[10] However, the Court found that the State law itself was contrary to EC Law, on the basis of Article 49 EC in that it restricted the freedom of foreign lawyers to provide services in Italy by offering more competitive prices than Italian lawyers. Even so, the Court felt that it should allow Italy to justify this if it could show that it served an overriding requirement relating to the public interest.

---

4 See J. Baquero Cruz 'The state action doctrine' in G. Amato and C-D. Ehlermann (eds.) *EC Competition Law – A Critical Assessment* (Oxford: Hart Publishing, 2007) for a review of the case law.
5 Case C-446/05 *Doulamis* judgment of 13 March 2008; Case C-49/07 *MOTOE* Opinion of AG Kokott 6 March 2008.
6 Joined Cases C-94/04 and C-202/04 *Federico Cipolla and Others v Rosaria Fazari, née Portolese, and Roberto Meloni* judgment of 6 December 2006.
7 *Report on Competition in Professional Services*, COM (2004) 83 final; *Professional Services – Scope for more reform – Follow-up to the Report on Competition in Professional Services*, COM (2005) 405 final.
8 M. Illmer 'Lawyer's fees and access to justice' (2007) 26 *Civil Justice Quarterly* 301.
9 Above n. 6, paras 47–52.
10 Case C-35/99 *Arduino* [2002] ECR I-1529.

Joined Cases C-94/04 and C-202/04 *Federico Cipolla and Others v Rosaria Fazari, née Portolese, and Roberto Meloni* judgment of 6 December 2006

62. In order to justify the restriction on freedom to provide services which stems from the prohibition at issue, the Italian Government submits that excessive competition between lawyers might lead to price competition which would result in a deterioration in the quality of the services provided to the detriment of consumers, in particular as individuals in need of quality advice in court proceedings.

63. According to the Commission, no causal link has been established between the setting of minimum levels of fees and a high qualitative standard of professional services provided by lawyers. In actual fact, quasi-legislative measures such as, inter alia, rules on access to the legal profession, disciplinary rules serving to ensure compliance with professional ethics and rules on civil liability have, by maintaining a high qualitative standard for the services provided by such professionals which those measures guarantee, a direct relationship of cause and effect with the protection of lawyers' clients and the proper working of the administration of justice.

64. In that respect, it must be pointed out that, first, the protection of consumers, in particular recipients of the legal services provided by persons concerned in the administration of justice and, secondly, the safeguarding of the proper administration of justice, are objectives to be included among those which may be regarded as overriding requirements relating to the public interest capable of justifying a restriction on freedom to provide services, on condition, first, that the national measure at issue in the main proceedings is suitable for securing the attainment of the objective pursued and, secondly, it does not go beyond what is necessary in order to attain that objective.

65. It is a matter for the national court to decide whether, in the main proceedings, the restriction on freedom to provide services introduced by that national legislation fulfils those conditions. For that purpose, it is for that court to take account of the factors set out in the following paragraphs.

66. Thus, it must be determined, in particular, whether there is a correlation between the level of fees and the quality of the services provided by lawyers and whether, in particular, the setting of such minimum fees constitutes an appropriate measure for attaining the objectives pursued, namely the protection of consumers and the proper administration of justice.

67. Although it is true that a scale imposing minimum fees cannot prevent members of the profession from offering services of mediocre quality, it is conceivable that such a scale does serve to prevent lawyers, in a context such as that of the Italian market which, as indicated in the decision making the reference, is characterised by an extremely large number of lawyers who are enrolled and practising, from being encouraged to compete against each other by possibly offering services at a discount, with the risk of deterioration in the quality of the services provided.

68. Account must also be taken of the specific features both of the market in question, as noted in the preceding paragraph, and the services in question and, in particular, of the fact that, in the field of lawyers' services, there is usually an asymmetry of information between 'client-consumers' and lawyers. Lawyers display a high level of technical knowledge which consumers may not have and the latter therefore find it difficult to judge the quality of the services provided to them.

69. However, the national court will have to determine whether professional rules in respect of lawyers, in particular rules relating to organisation, qualifications, professional ethics, supervision and liability, suffice in themselves to attain the objectives of the protection of consumers and the proper administration of justice.

This judgment hampers the Commission's policy in two ways: first, by restricting the scope of state responsibility under Article 10 to cases where the state delegates decision-making power or ratifies or encourages a cartel, it confirms that Article 10 is not engaged every time national law has anticompetitive effects. Second, by allowing governments to justify restrictions on the free movement of services on the basis that the quality of legal services, and access to justice, might be better with restrictions of competition, it runs directly against the Commission's policy to open these markets to competition, a policy that some economists have questioned.[11] On the other hand, the judgment did not prevent Italy from reversing its policy and abandoning the system of fixed fees.[12]

3. Liberalisation of network industries

The Commission has continued to press for further liberalisation of utilities, proposing bold legislative packages in the telecommunications and energy markets,[13] pressing ahead even when, in particular in the context of energy markets, the enthusiasm of Member States for liberalisation is uneven.[14]

In the field of postal services, a Directive 'with regard to the full accomplishment of the internal market of Community postal services' was enacted on 20 February 2008, that sees the removal of all special and exclusive rights by 31 December 2010 for most Member States and by 2012 for the others (mostly those who joined the EU in 2004),[15] rendering the market fully open to competition.[16] This is a controversial move, not least because the rationale behind the grant of exclusive rights in the current Directive is designed to allow the holder to use the revenue generated in that segment of the market to finance the provision of universal postal services.[17] In justifying this radical proposal, the Commission notes first that the current system gives the incumbent monopolies a reserved area which overcompensates them for carrying out universal services obligations. This has two adverse effects: incumbents have no incentive to rationalise their business or develop new products, and entry is discouraged. Second, today's postal operators are complex, multi-product firms

---

11 R. van den Bergh and I. Montaigne 'Competition in professional services markets: are Latin notaries different?' (2006) 2 *Journal of Competition Law and Economics* 189.

12 Decree Law n. 223, 4 July 2006.

13 See details of the two legislative packages at: http://ec.europa.eu/information_society/policy/ecomm/ tomorrow/index_en.htm; and http://ec.europa.eu/energy/electricity/package_2007/index_en.htm.

14 Progress in creating the internal gas and electricity market COM (2008) 192 final.

15 Articles 2 and 3 Directive 2008/6/ of 20 February 2008 amending Directive 97/67/EC with regard to the full accomplishment of the internal market of Community postal services [2008] OJ L52/3.

16 See also: Proposal for a Directive of the European Parliament and Council amending Directive 97/67/EC concerning the full accomplishment of the internal market of Community postal services COM (2006) 594 final.

17 It is based on the *Corbeau* judgment discussed at p. 1140 of the main text.

offering a range of services, and 87.5 per cent of all mail originates from business.[18] Accordingly entry of more competitors is required to satisfy demand and to overcome the remaining inefficiencies in the marketplace. The Commission maintains that competitive pressure will lead to universal service providers to adapt by becoming more efficient, diversifying their business and reducing costs. In addition, the efficient provision of universal services can be ensured by empowering National Regulatory Authorities to monitor the performance of operators, to grant new entrants access to the incumbent's delivery network in high cost areas (so injecting competition in the provision of universal services), to use licenses imposing certain obligations, price caps to protect consumers from excessive charges, and possibly removing the obligations to set uniform tariffs so that prices are based on cost. If competition and regulation are insufficient to ensure that the provider of universal services have the resources to deliver, then EU Law provides 'a set of alternative options to the reserved area . . . to provide for compensation (state aid, sector fees or compensation fund) or to find alternative ways to provide the service (public tendering, imposing universal service obligations on other operators)'.[19] The removal of the reserved area and details of these alternative means of finance are provided in Article 7 of the Directive.

Article 7 Directive 2008/6/ of 20 February 2008 amending Directive 97/67/EC with regard to the full accomplishment of the internal market of Community postal services [2008] OJ L52/3

1. Member States shall not grant or maintain in force exclusive or special rights for the establishment and provision of postal services. Member States may finance the provision of universal services in accordance with one or more of the means provided for in paragraphs 2, 3 and 4, or in accordance with any other means compatible with the Treaty.

2. Member States may ensure the provision of universal services by procuring such services in accordance with applicable public procurement rules and regulations, including, as provided for in Directive 2004/17/EC of the European Parliament and of the Council of 31 March 2004 coordinating the procurement procedures of entities operating in the water, energy, transport and postal services, competitive dialogue or negotiated procedures with or without publication of a contract notice.

3. Where a Member State determines that the universal service obligations, as provided for in this Directive, entail a net cost, calculated taking into account Annex I, and represent an unfair financial burden on the universal service provider(s), it may introduce:

(a) a mechanism to compensate the undertaking(s) concerned from public funds; or
(b) a mechanism for the sharing of the net cost of the universal service obligations between providers of services and/or users.

4. Where the net cost is shared in accordance with paragraph 3(b), Member States may establish a compensation fund which may be funded by service providers and/or users' fees,

---

18 EC Commission *Prospective study on the impact on universal service of the full accomplishment of the postal internal market in 2009* COM (2006) 596 final pp. 3–4.
19 EC Commission *Prospective study on the impact on universal service of the full accomplishment of the postal internal market in 2009* COM (2006) 596 final p. 9.

and is administered for this purpose by a body independent of the beneficiary or beneficiaries. Member States may make the granting of authorisations to service providers under Article 9(2) subject to an obligation to make a financial contribution to that fund or to comply with universal service obligations. The universal service obligations of the universal service provider(s) set out in Article 3 may be financed in this manner.

5. Member States shall ensure that the principles of transparency, non-discrimination and proportionality are respected in establishing the compensation fund and when fixing the level of the financial contributions referred to in paragraphs 3 and 4. Decisions taken in accordance with paragraphs 3 and 4 shall be based on objective and verifiable criteria and be made public.

The choice to delay the timing of liberalisation,[20] is designed to afford Member States the time to alleviate the social impact that liberalisation will bring, but the Council has agreed the competition-based scheme proposed by the Commission. Two brief comments can be offered at this early stage. First, whether opening the letter market will cause new entry. In Sweden and the UK where the market is already liberalised the incumbent has retained over 90 per cent of the letter market,[21] so removing the reserved area need not inject those competitive pressures that are said to be necessary to create incentives to invest and reduce costs. It means that Member States will likely have to resort to the means of finance provided in Article 7. Second, the view that universal services can be provided through competitive markets and subjected to public regulation and consumer redress seems to leave little scope for developing an alternative approach to universal services that the draftsman of the Lisbon Treaty envisaged. Instead, more attention has been paid to improving the competitiveness of the postal sector, to achieve the goals of the Lisbon competitiveness agenda.[22] The tension between the EU's role in strengthening the economy on the one hand and ensuring its citizens access to universal services remains.

20 Common Position adopted by the Council on 8 November 2007 with a view to the adoption of a Directive of the European Parliament and of the Council amending Directive 97/67/EC with regard to the full accomplishment of the internal market of Community postal services 8 November 2007 (available at http://register.consilium.europa.eu/pdf/en/07/st13/st13593-re06.en07.pdf)
21 Study on the Evolution of the Regulatory Model for Postal Services (WIK Consult July 2005).
22 The Commission welcomes the adoption of the EU Postal Directive. Market Opening brings clear benefits for postal users Press Release IP/08/163.

INDEX

Schengen Acquis Integrated into the
Framework of the European Union,
Amsterdam Protocol on
Case C-77/05 *United Kingdom v Council*
37–8
enhanced cooperation (LTEU 20) and 36–9
'Schengen acquis' 36
Schengen Conventions (1985 and 1990), *see
also* AFSJ (Area of Freedom, Security
and Justice); asylum, immigration,
visas and other policies related to the
free movement of persons (61–69
TEC); Prüm Convention on
Cross-Border Cooperation (Schengen
III)
Amsterdam Treaty and 17
incorporation into EU and 17
legitimacy of law deriving from 17
parties to 17
scope 17
variable geometry and 17
security agency (Prüm Convention) 17
Services Directive (Directive 2006/123/EC)
133–43
activities covered by, examples (preamble
33) 135
activities governed by TEC Articles 43
(establishment) and 49 (services),
exclusion (Art. 3(3)) 134–5
examples 334–5
exceptionalism in respect of economic
freedoms and 138–9
freedom of establishment and (Art. 9(1))
139–41
authorisations, control of conditions 140
justifiable restrictions 140–1
restrictions subject to absolute bar 140
TEC 43 distinguished 139–41
text 139
freedom to provide services (Art. 16) and
141–3
derogation from (Art. 18 and 35), text
(Art. 18) 142–3
derogation from (Arts. 18 and 35) 142–3:
complexity 143; public safety,
limitation to 143
justifiable restrictions, requirements 142
restrictions subject to absolute bar 142
TEC 49 distinguished 141–2
text 141
home State control as basis 143

ITWF v Viking Line 138 n 19
Laval 136–9
legal integration and 136
as residual category 135–9
sectoral legislation, primacy (Art. 3(1)) 134
dual regime 134
sensitive activities, exclusion 136
services, freedom to provide (49–55
TEC/56–61 LTFEU)
applicability, legal services 190–2
non-discriminatory restrictions,
justification/requirements
Cipolla 190–2
public interest 190–2
Seville European Council
Council configurations 26
Council meetings 26
sexual discrimination, prohibition, as core
Community objective (3(2) TEC)
(mainstreaming): *see* gender
mainstreaming (3(2) TEC/8 LTFEU)
sexual orientation, prohibition of
discrimination
Framework Directive (2000/78/EC) and 151
Tadao Maruko 151
marry, right to 151
SGEIs (services of general economic interest),
derogation (16 and 86 TEC/14 and 106
LTFEU), *see also* postal sector,
liberalisation; public undertakings,
applicability of competition law (86
[90] TEC)
allocation of competences 10, 188–9
as balance between competition and
provision of public services 189
fulfilment of functions, obligation to ensure
(16 TEC/14 LTFEU) 188
economic and financial conditions of
providers and 188, 189
as means of protecting national public
services 9
legislative competence 188
LTFEU changes 188–9
non-economic services of general interest 189
Protocol on SGEIs (LTFEU Protocol 26) 10
protection of public services and 9
single market, *see also* competition law/policy
headings; financial services,
integration/single market;
harmonisation of laws (94–97 TEC);
harmonisation of laws (114–118

214

INDEX

United Kingdom
Constitutional Treaty (2004) (CT), opposition to 2
freedom, security and justice, Protocol 21 on the position of the United Kingdom and Ireland in relation to (LTFEU) 9
Fundamental Rights, European Charter of (2000), Application to Poland and the UK, Protocol on (LTFEU Protocol) 9–10, 18, 62, 69–70
preliminary reference procedure (35(1) TEU (PJCC)), opt-in Declaration and 76
variable geometry 17–18
à la carte geometry 18
Protocol on the Application of the Charter of Fundamental Rights to Poland and the UK and 18
eurozone membership 17–18
Schengen Conventions (1985 and 1990) 17
vertical mergers, definition, anti-competitive/foreclosure effect 186

veto, *see also* access to documents, right of (Regulation 1049/2001), Member State veto (Art. 4(2)); co-decision/ordinary legislative procedure, veto, right of; comitology, veto, right of; voting (Council)
visas: *see* asylum, immigration, visas and other policies related to the free movement of persons (61–69 TEC)
voting (Council)
LTEU provisions 10, 11, 27–8
qualified majority voting (QMV)
Declaration 7 on 16(4) TFEU and 205(2) TFEU 28
Nice Treaty and 28 n. 40
weighting: CT provisions 27–8; LTEU provisions (16(4) LTEU) 10, 11, 27–8
unanimity principle
European Council's right to authorize QMV (48(7) LTEU) 45
LTEU provisions 10
withdrawal from EU, right of, LTEU 50 6